Literature and Image in the Long Nineteenth Century

Literature and Image in the Long Nineteenth Century:

Speaking Picture and Silent Text

Edited by

Amina Alyal

Cambridge
Scholars
Publishing

Literature and Image in the Long Nineteenth Century:
Speaking Picture and Silent Text

Edited by Amina Alyal

This book first published 2023

Cambridge Scholars Publishing

Lady Stephenson Library, Newcastle upon Tyne, NE6 2PA, UK

British Library Cataloguing in Publication Data
A catalogue record for this book is available from the British Library

ISBN (10): 1-5275-1972-4
ISBN (13): 978-1-5275-1972-5

To the memory of

Rosemary Mitchell

Deacon, Poet, Professor Emeritus of Victorian Studies
at Leeds Trinity University and former Director of the
Leeds Centre for Victorian Studies (LCVS)

much missed by all who knew her

Poema pictura loquens, pictura poema silens

—Plutarch quoting Simonides of Keos

CONTENTS

LIST OF ILLUSTRATIONS

ACKNOWLEDGMENTS

I am grateful for the support of the Leeds Centre for Victorian Studies @LCVSLeeds in the writing of this book, including funding copyright image use, for the support of Leeds Trinity University (LTU), especially the Research Office, the Writing Group, the Library, and my colleagues, especially in the final stages, and especially in English @LTUEnglish. Images have been obtained with the support of the National Gallery, Birmingham Museum and Art Gallery, the Rossetti Archive, and the Maas Gallery. The British Library, the Wellcome Collection, Project Gutenberg, the Internet Archive, the Victorian Web, Google Books and Wikimedia Commons have been invaluable repositories of public domain material, both text and image. Last but not least I thank my family, who have supported me throughout the process.

A version of Chapter Nine originally appeared as a short blog: Stephen Basdeo, "Victor Hugo's Ninety-Three (1874)." *Reynolds's News and Miscellany*, 27 September 2021, https://reynolds-news.com.

INTRODUCTION

As Horace's famous dictum suggests, word and image can each do more than they are expected to do, and indeed trespass upon each other's territories.[1] The authors of this book explore some of the ways in which we can understand how word and image worked together in the nineteenth century, in terms of both picture and poetry/fiction. It is worth saying here that the term "poesis" has traditionally had a broader meaning than the one we currently give to poetry, and includes creative writing generally.[2] *Literature and Image in the Long Nineteenth Century* keeps in mind how word and image negotiate and compete for each other's spaces. It seeks to interrogate how image arises from absences in texts, and image gives rise to narrative or voice. Topics include ekphrasis, illustration, literary representations of artists, the visual in writing, the staging of images and the textualization of theatrical tableaux, and related cultural and ideological tropes. A more relevant Latin tag is therefore the one of which the title is a loose translation, the statement (originally in Greek) by Simonides of Keos, quoted by Plutarch: "poema pictura loquens, pictura poema silens (poetry is a speaking picture, painting a silent [mute] poetry)".[3] Hence a useful term for the endeavours of the scholars in this present volume is one discussed for example by Antonia Losano: "interart criticism". As Losano indicates,

> [i]nterart criticism is an enormous and varied field, including studies of the influence of painitngs on particular authors, […] broader studies that argue for similarities across art media in the same historical period, […] studies in the way narrative relies on or makes use of the more formal elements of painting (description, [perspective, fore- and background, etc) […] and theoretical or historical studies of "the visual" as such.[4]

---

[1] Ut pictura poesis in Alex Preminger, ed., *The Princeton Handbook of Poetic Terms* (Princeton New Jersey: Princeton University Press, 1965; reis. 1986), 288.
[2] See for example Barbara Herrnstein Smith, "Poetry as Fiction." *New Literary History* 2, no. 2 (1971): 259–81. https://doi.org/10.2307/468602.
[3] Preminger, *Princeton Handbook*, 288.
[4] Antonia Losano, *The Woman Painter in Victorian Literature* (Columbus: The Ohio State University, 2008), 5.

Broadly, there are three aspects of this field covered by this volume: ideological and philosophical resonances of image and text in fiction (the first four chapters); that peculiar fusion of text and image that was the bread and butter of the Pre-Raphaelites (the next two chapters); and book illustration, especially the tensions between writer and artist as *authors* of the text (the last four chapters).

The arrangement is thematic and conceptual rather than chronological. The first and last chapters (by Nathan Uglow and Françoise Baillet, respectively) effectively introduce and conclude the book with wide-ranging content and argument that pull together many of the topics covered by the chapters in between. And although chronology is not a formative principle, the period covered needs a note of explanation—the debate spills over into the eighteenth and twentieth centuries with two of the chapters (Zoe Copeman on early Gothic and Paul Hardwick on Edwardian children's books). Although the collection is very Victorian in the bulk of its preoccupations, the conceptualisation of the "long nineteenth century" is aptly illustrated in the way these two chapters usefully extend into what feeds into the Victorian age and what its legacies are at the other end.

"Is painting a language?" asks Roland Barthes, before characteristically shifting focus onto the (endlessly deferred) nature of how images exist in the language that describes them, principally by evoking the cinema theorist Jean-Louis Scheffer: "What is the connection between the picture and the language inevitably used in order to read it—i.e., in order (implicitly) to write it? Is not this connection the picture itself?"[5] The picture and the language used to describe it are necessarily the topic of the first four chapters, in terms of the ways in which elusive concepts are captured or made concrete, concepts such as aging, racialization, and the self—or indeed figures of speech. Murray Krieger opines that "[w]hat emerges, in the aesthetic from Kant through the New Critics, is the possibility of a rebirth of the notion of the verbal emblem,"[6] and the verbal emblem provides a succinct introduction to the dialogue between word and image in our first chapter. All four chapters are concerned with the representation of verbalised appearance of self in the text, as the performative self, as a portrait, as grotesque fragmentation, and all are at least partially examined in terms of the evoked responses, attendant on genre, such as horror, laughter, or disconcertion, or various combinations of the same. Anxiety is

---

[5] Roland Barthes, *The Responsibility of Forms*, translated by Richard Howard. (1985; reis., Oakland, California: U of California press 1991). 149, 150.
[6] Murray Krieger, *Ekphrasis: The Illusion of the Natural Sign* (Baltimore, Maryland: Johns Hopkins, 2019), 198.

a key to much of this discourse—whether in Pooter's worries over being taken for a ride or the Creature's sense of societal rejection, in Medardus's fears about bodily corruption or Dorian's concealment of his moral corruption. Anxiety is, of course, always already about influence, and Bloom's recursive understanding of textual and conceptual dialogue adds texture to some of the interconnections and mutual influences covered in these chapters: "[...] the poem is now *held* open to the precursor, where once it *was* open, and the uncanny effect is that the new poem's achievement makes it seem to us, not as though the precursor were writing it, but as though the later poet himself had written the precursor's characteristic work."[7] Similarly, it is sometimes hard to tell which came first, the image or the verbal apprehension of it.

In Chapter One, "Speaking Pictures", Nathan Uglow reflects on the classical context for the rivalry between the "sister arts" of text and image, and traces its historical development through the Enlightenment and Romantic eras, before examining sections of two novels (and one narrative poem) at the end of the nineteenth century, making an important point that "the triumph of image over text is best evoked in, and demonstrated through, writing". Uglow explores how the emblem, predominantly in words rather than visual image, is reformulated into quasi-dramatic episodes in *The Diary of a Nobody* by George and Weedon Grossmith and *Three Men in a Boat* by Jerome K. Jerome, and informs Robert Browning's poem "Development". Uglow explores how common sayings ("pride goes before a fall") or popular images (Janus, the two-headed god looking to past and future) can lead to comic treatment, the effects of which arise from their being taken literally or to their logical extreme. He covers the question of the tension between text and image in terms of whether the image merely illustrates the text or forms the basis of character and scene to which the text merely adds "narration". Indeed, he briefly discusses mid-century sensation plays before going on to discuss the comic effects of incident (akin to drama) in the two episodic novels.

Chapter Two, "Ma®king a Monster: The Afterlife of Frankenstein's Creation and the Racialization of Criminality", follows this philosophical treatment of image in language, and indeed the intersection with stage spectacle, with Zoe Copeman's analysis of the "monstrous" Creature in

---

[7] Harold Bloom, *The Anxiety of Influence* (1973; reiss., Oxford: Oxford University Press, 1997), 16.

Frankenstein. Copeman dissects the textual parallels between the Creature made of pieces and Frantz Fanon's fragmentation of Darwin

Black identity by a white gaze. Copeman considers contemporary stage spectacle, finding that the dark blue or black greasepaint used in stage productions of *Frankenstein* and of *Othello* connect the two. Copeman develops this specific application of appearance into an examination of physiognomy and "a larger system of appearance-based discrimination", demonstrating how images of a "criminal" physiognomy gave rise to a pseudo-science, reflecting a Europe-wide movement to identify the "'standard' or 'normal' subject" and to present visually a constructed deviant form that encompasses the inchoate fears of society at the time— the criminal, the racialised other, the non-European. The chapter explores how taking the body apart and categorising its constituent features leads to a (re)construction that provides a seemingly concrete justification for social oppression.

Chapter Three, "The Gothic Novel and Grotesque Art: E. T. A. Hoffmann's *The Devil's Elixir*" leads naturally on from the previous chapter, Hannah-Freya Blake exploring the genesis of "the doppelgänger and dual-personality tropes of the Gothic", arguing that "the [Gothic comic] novel mimics the confusion of the grotesque form". Blake sees in the Bakhtinian qualities of this genre a confusion of being, between animal and human, and between the self in its (delusory?) authentic embodiment vs. its performative imitator. The chapter examines the moment when the self sees the doppelgänger as a moment of uncanny self-violation, an externalised internal gaze. Blake hence sees the form as ultimately of the "in-between"— text and image, laughter and fear, the solid and the intangible. The uncanniness of the form, Blake contends, lies in these contradictions and escaping certainties, a response to the fragmentation of modernity, and the performativity of identity. This leads on to tangled, multiplying narratives (or anti-narratives), in which reproduction produces incongruity and horrified laughter, pleasure and disgust as evoked by the grotesque. Her final point about the ways in which parody by its very nature underscores the performativity of identity leads to a conclusion about the anxiety of influence that Harold Bloom might have appreciated.

Chapter Four, "Ekphrasis and the Illusion of Self in Oscar Wilde's *The Picture of Dorian Gray*" continues the theme of the Gothic, as broached by the previous two, and also considers the self in terms of a split or copy. Erkin Kiryaman discusses "notional ekphrasis" within *Dorian Gray*, since the painting does not have an existence independent of the text evoking it (as indeed Barthes would see it). Kiryaman develops an intricate argument that how the portrait and the character interact can be illuminated by an application of Lacanian theory of the mirror stage. The chapter raises the spectre of the illusory self and even the narcissistic self, since it is Dorian's desire for permanent youth and beauty that is the trigger for magical transformation. This chapter too discloses the effects of including the stasis of a visual image in direct conflict with the temporality of narrative——in the case of this novel there is an uncanny reversal of those properties. Kiryaman argues that that very reversal allows for insight into "Dorian's oscillating self", negotiating the fear and desire of subsumption with the other that is implicit in the ekphrastic encounter. These implications of linguistic psychoanalysis lead him to demonstrate that the ekphrastic enterprise is itself unstable, movable as words are, incapable of achieving the stasis promised by the image.

In this last chapter, the very idea of portraiture and the artist is explored. The visual representation of character, in a unique equalisation of text and image, is the subject of the next two chapters, both on the Pre-Raphaelites, their visual art and poetry. As Barbara Onslow argues, the idea of the portrait was employed for ideological and gender-political purposes, Onslow's focus being specifically on female novelists who explore visual representation as unreliable idealisation in their novels. According to George Eliot (complaining about portraits and photographs): "How can a thing which is always the same be an adequate representation of a living being who is always varying?"[8] Nowhere is this question more comprehensively and wittily explored, perhaps, than in *The Picture of Dorian Gray*.[9] Onslow suggests that George Eliot's view influenced other women writers in their complaints about false idealisation, and that this view was that "Art *should* celebrate beauty and avoid falsity" [my italics].[10]

   This rather implies that that the Romantic notion that "Beauty is truth, truth beauty,—that is all/ Ye know on earth, and all ye need to know"[11] continued to be felt in the bones of literary writers well into the Victorian period—Pre-Raphaelitism is perhaps the most fertile ground for that sentiment to flourish, for example in the declared intents of the Pre-Raphaelite Brotherhood (PRB) to be "direct and serious and heartfelt" and

---

[8] Quoted in Barbara Onslow, "Deceiving Images, Revealing Images: The Portrait in Victorian Women's Writing." *Victorian Poetry* 33, no. 3/4 (1995): 450–75. http://www.jstor.org/stable/40002332, 456.

[9] Oscar Wilde, *The Picture of Dorian Gray and Other Writings* (London: Ward, Locke & Co., 1891).

[10] Onslow, "Deceiving Images", 457.

[11] John Keats, "Ode on a Grecian Urn" in John Keats, *Lamia, Isabella, The Eve of St Agnes, and Other Poems* (London: Taylor and Hessey, 1820), lines 49-50.

"produce thoroughly good pictures and statues".[12] For the Pre-Raphaelites, in contrast, beauty and truth resonate together, in an aim possibly more Wordsworthian than Keatsian of "looking directly to nature".[13] John Ruskin asserted this (mysterious) apprehension of "loveliness" and "truth" first in 1865, although he endorsed it in 1893:

> Art is neither to be achieved by effort of thinking, nor explained by accuracy of speaking [...] the more beautiful the art, the more it is essentially the work of people who *feel themselves wrong*;—who are striving for the fulfilment of a law, and the grasp of a loveliness, which they have not yet attained, which they feel even farther and farther from attaining the more they strive for it. And yet, in still deeper sense, it is the work of people who know also that they are right. The very sense of inevitable error from their purpose marks the perfectness of that purpose, and the continued sense of failure arises from the continued opening of the eyes more clearly to all the sacredest laws of truth.[14]

This is a full statement of what Barthes would later call the "the old humanist superstition",[15] the notion, perhaps Platonic in origin, that the artist sees an abstract truth and beauty of which "nature" merely acts as a suggestion.[16] And hand-in-glove with this sentiment goes the belief that art should be useful as well as beautiful. "[I]f you only try to make showy drawings for praise," wrote Ruskin in 1893, "or pretty ones for amusement, your drawing will have little of real interest for you, and no educational power whatever."[17] It was not until the truly post-Romantic energy of the decadent movement that beauty superseded truth, the aesthetic predominated and the principle of l'art pour l'art took over, which Stefano Evangelista and Catherine Maxwell see as the legacy of "Pater's emphasis

---

[12] William Michael Rossetti, ed., *Dante Gabriel Rossetti: His Family-Letters, with a Memoir*, vol. 1 (London: Ellis and Elvey,1895),135.
[13] Quoted by Elizabeth Prettejohn, "Introduction" in Elizabeth Prettejohn, ed., *The Cambridge Companion to the Pre-Raphaelites* (Cambridge: Cambridge University Press, 2012), 4
[14] John Ruskin, "Lecture III. The Mystery of Life and its Arts." In Ruskin, *Sesame and Lilies* (1893; reis., London: George Allen, 1894), transcribed by David Price. www.gutenberg.org.
[15] Barthes, *Responsibility of Forms*, 149
[16] See for example Sir Philip Sidney, *The Defence of Poesie* (London: William Ponsonby, 1595).
[17] John Ruskin, "Preface to the Later Editions", in *Sesame and Lilies*

on pleasure rather than utility or didacticism".[18] (After all, "All art is quite useless").[19]

The Pre-Raphaelites' pre-eminent image as artists over writers belies their focus on the text, as Elizabeth Prettejohn articulates:

> How then should we interpret the relationship between the visual and the literary arts, between drawing and painting on the one hand and reading and writing on the other, in a movement that takes its name so obviously from the history of painting?[20]

The Pre-Raphaelites both painted and wrote: Dante Gabriel Rossetti is well known as a poet, for example, as is Elizabeth Siddal, his partner and model.[21]

> The enthusiasm for trying one's hand at any medium, already apparent in the first entry of the *P. R. B. Journal*, doubtless reflects the reckless confidence of youthful inexperience, but it is also closely related to a distinctive feature of Pre-Raphaelitism, [...] its readiness to transgress the conventional boundaries between art forms, and moreover between the creative arts ad those activities more usually considered scholarly, art-historical or critical. Thus we have not only "literary" painting and "pictorial" poetry, but also art criticism by poets, literary criticism by artists, and works in a variety of media that engage with the emerging scholarly discipline of art history, or that conduct criticism through creative means.[22]

---

[18] Stefano Evangelista and Catherine Maxwell, "The Arts in Victorian Literature: An Introduction." *The Yearbook of English Studies* 40, no. 1/2 (2010): 1–7, 2. http://www.jstor.org/stable/41059778. For Théophile Gautier's dictum "l'art pour l'art" and related views of Poe, see Preminger, *Princeton Handbook*, 210. For aestheticism and decadence, see Carolyn Burdett, "Aestheticism and Decadence", British Library, https://www.bl.uk/romantics-and-victorians/articles/aestheticism-and-decadence.

[19] Wilde, *Dorian Gray*, vii.

[20] Ibid., 2.

[21] Rossetti's principle poetic works are *Sir Hugh the Heron, A Legendary Tale, in Four Parts*. London: G. Polidori's Private Press (For Private Circulation Only), *1843*. 8vo (204 x 156 mm); and *Poems* (London: F. S. Ellis, 1870). The latter was reissued in various forms including as *Ballads and Narrative Poems* (Hammersmith: Kelmscott Press, 1893), with all the Kelmscott focus on the book as a work of visual art. Images may be viewed here: https://collections.library. yale.edu/catalog/11148897. Siddal's poems were published posthumously in *Poems and Drawings of Elizabeth Siddal* (Canada: Wombat Press, 1978).

[22] Prettejohn, "Introduction", 6.

So an exploration of the Pre-Raphaelites continues that focus on porous categorisation that the first chapters have begun, and in the person of the practitioners of both the sister arts. Apart from their own facility in the form, the artists' relationship to others' poetry, and Tennyson in particular, produced some of the most iconic paintings of the movement, which achieved a status that went far beyond illustration, and stood alone as coherent art in their own right. Poetry and pictorial art in the hands of the Pre-Raphaelites are scrutinised in the next two chapters.

Chapter Five, "The Sensuous Pastoral: Vision and Text in Pre-Raphaelite Art" examines the focus on detail and desire in the twin arts of Dante Gabriel Rossetti. Richard Leahy examines the method in the construction of what he terms "the sensuous pastoral" in PRB visual art, microscopic attention to a plethora of detail in the imagined or remembered "nature" that results in "hyper-realised minutiae of description [...] emphasising the sensuous desires in their works", noting that a similar effect is apparent in their poetry. Leahy argues that this heightening of observation connects to what we might call the PRB's mission statement, and its focus on a paradoxical intensity of feeling that is super-imposed onto the depiction of natural detail. "The simple face becomes significant when examined through the Pre-Raphaelite gaze", so that details such as hair or natural landscapes are both objectified and infused with subjectivity. Hence, the attempt of the artist to capture or control the muse or object of his desire is in part a demonstration of its elusiveness. Rossetti's poems are further amplified by a comparison with Elizabeth Siddal's, demonstrating both a closeness and a gendered difference in the two poets.

Chapter Six, "'Half-sick of Shadows': Imagining Women, Reverse Ekphrasis and the Lady of Shalott", is also concerned with women and desire, in Pre-Raphaelite depictions of the Lady of Shalott. Cassandra Atherton and Paul Hetherington evoke "a notional third space" arising from the confluence of word and image. This space is also usefully the no man's land between the private and public situation of the woman who, typified in the lady of Shalott, resembles "a revenant returned, via poetry, from the legends of a remote chivalric past." This interpretation is underpinned by reference to a range of contextual pictorial representations of which the Lady is an example, with a general gesture towards the deathlike stillness of a Sleeping Beauty, or even a female corpse—and including the statement of Poe, that master of the Gothic, that this last is the ultimate poetic theme. Elizabeth Siddal's anomalous position as both muse and artist produces a different take on the Lady. In their paintings based Shakespeare or Tennyson, amongst others, the artists are shown to be "in a close artistic dialogue" with the poetry, "thus actively contributing to and modifying understandings of these texts". Atherton and Hetherington term this process, the repositioning of the poem through visual depiction, "reverse ekphrasis", unearthing a disturbingly mortuary frame of reference for the Pre-Raphaelite muse.

William Morris, who might be called an honorary or tangential Pre-Raphaelite, an artist who wrote, a writer who painted, and founder of the Arts and Crafts Movement, believed that with "really beautiful ornament and pictures, printed books might once again illustrate to the full the position of our Society that a work of utility might be also a work of art, if we cared to make it so."[23] The final four chapters of this volume are principally concerned with illustration. Book illustration in this period—perhaps more generally—can range from amplification of a text, to effectively dramatizing the text, to critiquing or reinterpreting it, to dictating or preceding it. George du Maurier, of Svengali fame, and an illustrator as well as a writer, argued that images stay in the mind long after the text they illustrate has been forgotten, if it has been read at all; even though his article nominally maintains the position that the illustration serves the text, his comments suggest he elevates, above the mere narrative, "the little figures in the picture [...] the arrested gesture, the expression of face, the character and costume, [which] may be as true to nature and life as the best actor can make them." [24] He asks,

> what does not the great Dickens himself owe to Cruikshank and Hablôt Browne, those two delightful etchers who understood and interpreted him so well! [...] It would be interesting to know for certain what Charles Dickens thought of these illustrations—whether they quite realised for him the people he had in his mind, or bettered them, even—for such a thing is not impossible; indeed, it is the business of the true illustrator to do this if he can" (350).

Here du Maurier seems to be wavering on the brink of admitting the creative role the illustrator might have to play, especially since his article also discusses Pre-Raphaelite "illustrators". Precedence is hard to determine, in some cases. In Rosemary Mitchell's words, "[t]he relationship of text and image, and the interplay of meaning between them, is often very subtle, and

---

[23] William Morris, "Printing" in *Arts and Crafts Essays* by Members of the Arts and Crafts Exhibition Society, with a Preface by William Morris (London: Rivington, Percival, & Co., 1893), 134.

[24] George du Maurier, "The Illustration of Books from the Serious Artist's Point of View. — I", *Magazine of Art* (1890), London: Cassell and Company: 349-53, 350. Digitised by Google Books, www.books.google.co.uk.

thus the question of priority, in terms of ideological content and influence, is sometimes difficult to establish."[25]

Mitchell investigates the case of William Harrison Hainsworth, who is inspired to produce his narrative after seeing the pictures that would later become illustrations to his novel *Boscobel*:

> The illustrations of this work are particularly significant, as they were prior to the text and inspired Ainsworth to write the novel. […] In the Preface to *Boscobel*, he explained that he had long wished to write a tale on the subject of Charles III's wanderings after Worcester, but "I deferred my design, and possibly might never have executed it, had I not seen a series of views depicting most graphically the actual state of the different places visited by Charles […] (281)

Illustrations, then, clearly do more than simply reproduce in another medium the narrative or descriptions of a writer, and how they may operate is examined in different instances in the last four chapters of this book.

Chapter Seven, "*Oliver Twist* and the Transportability of the Image", explores Cruikshank's illustrations and their independence from the text, taking this even further than du Maurier does. Courtney Krolczyk argues that these illustrations are adaptations on a par with the stage adaptations that appeared almost in tandem with the serialised narrative. Krolczyk discusses "the image's inherent transportability", arguing that some texts are more image-based than others, and that these are the most adaptable, in illustration or on the stage. She examines dramatisations of the novel, which remove the spotlight from systemic problems, arguing that this is an effect of adaptation "through individualised bodies on a stage". She points out that the Cruikshank illustrates already have elements of the stage in terms of tableau, that can be easily transposed to the theatre. Further, she investigates Cruikshank's claim that Oliver Twist was born of his own idea for a Hogarthian progress narrative in pictures, and considers the illustrations "as a group", whereupon they do make up "something of a Hogarthian progress narrative (after all, the subtitle of the novel was 'The Parish Boy's Progress')", although by examining illustrations for different sections of the novel, Krolczyk is able to determine the extents and limitations of the influence of Cruikshank's "progress" on the novel.

Chapter Eight, "Visions of Long Will: Langland and *Piers Plowman* for Children at the End of the Long Nineteenth Century" is on the subject of Florence Converse and two very different approaches to medievalism in

---

[25] Rosemary Mitchell, *Picturing the Past: English History in Text and Image 1830-1870* (Oxford: Clarendon Press, 2000), 22.

children's book illustrations. Paul Hardwick frames his chapter with reference to Douce manuscript of Chaucer (1426), one of the contexts in which to read the interpretative effects of the illustrations he examines, and how these "creatively nuance our reading". Hardwick argues that there are opposing views of the medieval era in Converse's time, that of the sentimentalised courtly Chaucer, and that associated with Langland's "unsparing truth-telling". He examines W. Heath Robinson's idealised illustrations for *Stories from Chaucer told to the Children* (1906) in comparison with Garth Jones's illustrations for *Long Will* (1903). A fruitful exploration of an image by John R. Skelton indicates ways in which Langland's "message of social equality" is either brought out or obscured by the mode of representation. Hardwick shows how Florence Converse's sometimes inconvenient Christian Socialism directs her representation of the Peasants' Revolt, aided by the "harsh, very human, corporeal realism" of Garth Jones, not included in later publication of the text, suggesting there may be ideological reasons for how Langland is illustrated.

Chapter Nine, "'La Torgue was Monarchy; the guillotine was Revolution': Anti-Medievalism in Victor Hugo's *Ninety-Three* (*Quatrevingt-Treize*)", continues the focus on ideological representation in image and text. Stephen Basdeo's theme is the historical novel by Victor Hugo based on revolution in France, situating the text's overt topic, the French Revolution, within the troubled politics of Hugo's own days, to which Basdeo argues he is acutely responsive. He reads Hugo's approach as "Revolutionary Anti-Medievalism", which "[uses] the Middle Ages to deride the medieval past and foreground the progressive nature of the French Revolution". This reading of Hugo gives rise to the view that Hugo, like Scott, aimed for entertainment along with political influence—Basdeo explores Hugo's own involvement, through published writing, in opposing Napoleon III with satire. Closely analysing the images that illustrate Hugo's novel, Basdeo demonstrates how the aristocrat is represented as out of sync with the times, and the revolutionary soldier as a protective figure. But he unpicks the subtleties and ambiguities of Hugo's stance, as represented, for example, in the positioning of figures in the illustrations, so that heroism is ultimately a matter of qualities that can be demonstrated by those on either side.

Chapter Ten, "The Question of Authority in Nineteenth-Century Book Illustration", offers a broad and at the same time rigorous examination of the "unstable and wavering border between text and image within the illustrated book [...] through three distinct moments in the history of Victorian pictorial literature". Françoise Baillet traces the development, throughout these key points in the Victorian period, of illustration, from

Hablôt K. Browne's faithful renditions of Dickens's instructions in *Dombey and Son* (1848), sometimes relegated for mechanistic reasons as much as any, to the margins, to the rise of the Pre-Raphaelite movement. In the Moxon Tennyson (1857), painters and poet are of equal artistic status, and Rossetti's illustration, for example, is known to be at odds with Tennyson's preferences, coming across as a "critical interpretation of the text". Finally, Baillet proceeds to William Morris and the Arts and Crafts movement, examining the Kelmscott Chaucer (1896) and *The Story of the Glittering Plain* (1894), in which "the unity of the whole design" is paramount, decorative borders, designer fonts and illustrations all contributing to Morris's vison of "harmony between text and image, [and] between craftsmen and artists". This chapter thus provides a cohesive close to the collection, in its journey through the Victorian period, and its tracing of shifting relationships between image and text.

Some of George du Maurier's speculations are answered by these chapters, and the sister arts explored in terms of a close partnership and even exchanging of roles. Literature may not always "speak", and indeed its silences are filled with the clamour of the pictorial at times, so that the two voices, while they can be harmonious, are at their most energised, perhaps, when producing discordant sounds—suggesting alternatives, opening up dialogue, and increasing the dimensionality of the "beautiful book".

Bibliography

Barthes, Roland. *Critical Essays*, translated by Richard Howard. Oakland California: University of California Press, 1991. This translation originally published New York: Hill & Wang, 1985. Originally published in French as *L'Obvie et l'obtus*. Paris: Editions du Seuil, 1982.

Bloom, Harold. *The Anxiety of Influence*. Oxford: Oxford University Press, 1997. Originally published Oxford; Oxford University Press, 1973.

Burdett, Carolyn. "Aestheticism and Decadence". British Library. https://www.bl.uk/romantics-and-victorians/articles/aestheticism-and-decadence.

du Maurier, George. "The Illustration of Books from the Serious Artist's Point of View. — I". *Magazine of Art* (1890). London: Cassell and Company: 349-53. Digitised by Google Books, www.books.google.co.uk.

Evangelista, Stefano, and Catherine Maxwell. "The Arts in Victorian Literature: An Introduction." *The Yearbook of English Studies* 40, no. 1/2 (2010): 1–7. http://www.jstor.org/stable/41059778.

Keats, John. *Lamia, Isabella, The Eve of St Agnes, and Other Poems*. London: Taylor and Hessey, 1820.

Krieger, Murray. *Ekphrasis: The Illusion of the Natural Sign*. Baltimore, Maryland: Johns Hopkins, 2019.

Losano, Antonia. *The Woman Painter in Victorian Literature*. Columbus: The Ohio State University, 2008.

Mitchell, Rosemary. *Picturing the Past: English History in Text and Image 1830-1870*. Oxford: Clarendon Press, 2000.

Morris, William. "Printing" in *Arts and Crafts Essays* by Members of the Arts and Crafts Exhibition Society, with a Preface by William Morris. London: Rivington, Percival, & Co., 1893.

Onslow, Barbara. "Deceiving Images, Revealing Images: The Portrait in Victorian Women's Writing." *Victorian Poetry* 33, no. 3/4 (1995): 450–75. http://www.jstor.org/stable/40002332.

Preminger, Alex, ed. *The Princeton Handbook of Poetic Terms*. Princeton, New Jersey: Princeton University Press, 1986. Originally published Princeton New Jersey: Princeton University Press 1965.

Prettejohn, Elizabeth, ed. *The Cambridge Companion to the Pre-Raphaelites*. Cambridge: Cambridge University Press, 2012.

Rossetti, Dante Gabriel. *Sir Hugh the Heron, A Legendary Tale, in Four Parts*. London: G. Polidori's Private Press (For Private Circulation Only), 1843.

—. *Poems*. London: F. S. Ellis, 1870.

—. *Ballads and Narrative Poems*. Hammersmith: Kelmscott Press, 1893.

Rossetti, William Michael, ed. *Dante Gabriel Rossetti: His Family-Letters, with a Memoir*, vol. 1. London: Ellis and Elvey,1895.

Ruskin, John. *Sesame and Lilies*. London: George Allen, 1894. This edition originally published London: George Allen, 1894). First published in shorter form London: Smith, Elder & Co. 1865. Transcribed by David Price, www.gutenberg.org.

Siddal, Elizabeth. *Poems and Drawings of Elizabeth Siddal*. Canada: Wombat Press, 1978.

Sidney, Sir Philip. *The Defence of Poesie*. London: William Ponsonby, 1595.

Smith, Barbara Herrnstein. "Poetry as Fiction." *New Literary History* 2, no. 2 (1971): 259–81. https://doi.org/10.2307/468602.

Wilde, Oscar. *The Picture of Dorian Gray and Other Writings*. London: Ward, Locke & Co., 1891.

CHAPTER ONE

SPEAKING PICTURES

NATHAN UGLOW

Introduction

At first glance, words and images seem so clearly different that we could never really get them mixed up. But in any discussion of words and images confusion is never far away. In everyday usage there is acceptance of this confusion: we understand that words engage metaphoric imagery and evoke visual scenes without losing a sense that we remain focused on words. And when images constitute evidence, we can speak of what those images "tell" us (or point out the "tell-tale signs") without implying an inability to distinguish image from word. Furthermore, we are happy to believe that the distinction between word and image is self-evident even as we acknowledge that word and image are, in practice, tricky customers.

The title of this volume of collected essays, *Speaking Pictures and Silent Text*, acknowledges a level of complicity between word and image, while also preserving that common-sense distinction between them: it is pictures that are speaking and words doing the showing.[1]

In the following pages I will argue that there is a specific late-Victorian approach to the word-image relation. I will illustrate this through three texts that happen to have been published in the same year, 1889. What they share is a relaxed and accepting view of the confusion between words and images: they don't try to resolve that confusion so much as find ways of exploiting it. I will introduce each of the texts at a later stage in order to contextualise the key passages, but a few words of introduction seem appropriate here.

---

[1] The title reflects that of various intermedia studies, such as Michael Bath, *Speaking Pictures: English Emblem Books and Renaissance Culture* (London: Longman, 1994) and Leonard Barkan, *Mute Poetry, Speaking Pictures* (Princeton: Princeton University Press, 2012).

Firstly, George and Weedon Grossmith's *Diary of a Nobody* will provide some basic illustration of the extent to which late-Victorian culture could derive enjoyment from the confusion between word and image.[2] This is not a text that aims at subtlety or nuance and is a useful scene-setter for my argument precisely because it is so willfully superficial. Perhaps unsurprisingly for a comedy, it seeks to entertain its readers without any pretentions to depth and succeeds in both these aims. It is a remarkably depth-less book, having no beginning, middle or end (it is a diary after all) and no character growth or plot development. It is a series of amusing episodes that could really come in any particular order, except for a few running gags. It is this very flatness that will put the visual and the verbal on the same level.

In my analysis I will zero in on a single set-piece episode, which is particularly flat, being nothing more than the literalization of a visual emblem. It is part of the essence of humour to take things in a literal way through verbal puns or taking elaborate imagery at face value. Comedy had always drawn on these elements, but I suggest that late-Victorian moment was generally receptive to this willful catachresis of the visual and the verbal and enthusiastic in exploring its effects.

Second up is Jerome K. Jerome's *Three Men in a Boat*, which rehearses the same themes as are found in the *Diary of a Nobody*.[3] The story aspect is downplayed in order to foreground the banter, irony, corny gags, shaggy dog stories and slapstick humour. In my analysis I explore one of its comic anecdotes, which constitutes an extended slapstick riff, entirely elaborated out of verbal humour. The relation of visual slapstick to verbal puns is further evidence for the view that the confusion of word and image offered opportunities to create new effects.

Finally, I turn to Robert Browning's late poem "Development", from his final collection *Asolando*.[4] This also entertains (it is "much-loved"), but I will argue it has a more sophisticated structure that trades on the tricksiness of words and images to foster reflection rather than laughter. The early sections of the poem present an idyllic vision of childhood play and the wonder of stories. This is the "much-loved" bit and the only bit the poem's few critics have examined. The later sections make it clear that this vision is the product of a bitter and frustrated narrator and perhaps only exists to

---

[2] George and Weedon Grossmith, *The Diary of a Nobody* (London: Arrowsmith, 1892).

[3] Jerome K. Jerome, *Three Men in a Boat (To Say Nothing of the Dog)* (London: Arrowsmith, 1889).

[4] Robert Browning, *Asolando* (London: Smith & Elder, 1890), pp.123-30.

fuel and justify his bitterness to himself. This will turn out to involve more complex and intricate confusions between word and image.

By focusing on three texts, my account is obviously going to be one-sided. The Grossmiths did add images to the second edition of the novel, but I will not be considering these, as my focus will be on the visual aspects of writing. To consider the verbal aspects of images would not require new arguments, but the shift between textual and pictorial analysis would complicate and extend an already long and complex story.

My focus is on the way these texts take an almost theatrical approach to designing scenarios to illustrate or embody a simple confrontation, just as jokes often involve a contrived story whose only purpose is to cue up a specific punchline.

My commentary on the texts will be the same kind of commentary we use when spelling out a joke. This kind of commentary does not add depth, but rather emphasizes surface. It is a matter of clarifying how the punchline and the lead up present the *same* point but from different perspectives. The differences are forced onto the same level. Example:

Q: What is the difference between Noah's Ark and Joan of Arc?
A: One was made of wood and the other was Maid of Orleans.

Here, it is a matter of verbal play between the similarity of phrases that sound alike but have different values. The punchline shows them to be alike and yet clearly different. It is this insistence on the identity of word and image, even as they are obviously different, that I argue starts to appear in late-Victorian writing and, though I don't explore it here, in visual design. The following section aims at a broad explanation of, and justification for, a distinctive late-Victorian aesthetic amenable to the aesthetics of flatness.

Background

I started by saying that word and image are both obviously distinct and unsurprisingly entangled. There is always a specific cultural framing for this situation; in some cultural situations the distinction of word and image is insisted upon and at others the identity is prioritised. In order to cue up my point that my texts demonstrate a late-Victorian take on this issue, I will sketch in some of the key positions on this issue, leading up to the late-Victorian period.

In the Enlightenment classical aesthetics policed the boundary between word and image with care. Text was the medium for making clear statements and image was the medium for depicting beauty. They were "sister arts" and even when they became rivalrous, word and image remained distinct. Writers could deploy poetic imagery and depict scenes; artists could design images that had evidentiary status, asserting claims about characters and situations. But it always remained clear when words were *rhetorically* reconstructing visual effects and equally clear when images deployed *pictorial* techniques to establish precise statements.

With the Romantic era the relation between words and images became more confusing. It was no longer simply a matter of techniques and tropes (rhetoric), constructing something in words that was similar to what images achieved, or constructing images that rivalled effects that writing achieved. Under Romantism the rivalry became more existential: which of the two was the royal road to reality and which was a wrong turn? One, and only one of them, was more complete and ontologically vital than the other. Whichever had this status was the only one that mattered. It properly had all the attributes, previously distributed between both words and images. Here, images really could be speaking images or texts really could be silently pictorial.

To clarify this distinction between an Enlightenment and a Romantic model of how images and words relate, I will appeal to Martin Meisel's *Realizations*, which seeks to document the transition from classical to Romantic through the changing relation of word to image.[5] Meisel's analysis of the altercation between Cruickshank and Dickens about who was the true author of Dickens's novels is a good example of what I have called the Romantic confusion between word and image.[6] Dickens assumed that Cruickshank *illustrated* his text and thus that his images were subordinate to his words, which is probably how we would understand it. But Cruickshank argued that his pictures showed character, relations, and scenarios and that Dickens's text merely joined the dots between the images. The story is *all there* in the images and Dickens was articulating the logic and managing simple transitions between scenes. It was as if Dickens merely added laborious subtitles or audio narration.

Cruickshank was not arguing that his images were making a fair imitation of textual effects, but that the storytelling power was *all* in the images and that the text was a mere supplement, an inessential aspect. The images spoke and the text really was silent. Cruickshank was claiming to *be* the author in a very real sense.

Well, Cruickshank lost that particular argument, but Meisel goes on to show how his viewpoint did have a future, becoming a common view of

---

[5] Martin Meisel, *Realizations: Narrative, Pictorial, and Theatrical Arts in Nineteenth-Century England* (Princeton: Princeton University Press, 1984).
[6] Meisel, *Realizations*, ch.2.

sensation theatre, where the script was likely to become just this means of navigating the audience from one elaborate visual set piece to the next. The term he used for this kind of drama is "speaking pictures".[7]

As a bit of a coda, it is worth flagging up that Meisel's acknowledgement singles out the intellectual contribution of two colleagues who helped shape his argument. Stephen Orgel and Michael Fried would both subsequently write studies about the confused status of image and text in the second half of the Victorian period. Orgel's *Imagining Shakespeare* explores the impact of historicism on the mid-Victorian staging of Shakespeare plays. Scenes became cluttered with bits of archaic material culture and actors were swathed in historical costume, visually signifying olden times. Fried's *Manet's Modernism* outlines a series of innovative painterly strategies that Manet deployed to give his images a stronger impression of actuality and testimony. In both cases, it is visual artefacts that seek not just to rival verbal statements, but to render them redundant or otiose.[8]

The Late-Victorian Situation

Having sketched in the way word and image were related in the Enlightenment and Romantic eras, I want to explore this idea that words and images were involved in an ontological struggle in the second half of the Victorian era. The populist humour of both the Grossmith brothers and Jerome K. Jerome and the late poetry of Robert Browning all seem to resurrect Cruickshank's idea that images are the essence of story, but in an additional twist they adopt this position *as writers*. In this they represent an additional phase to Meisel's story, which closes around the 1860s with the advent of plays constructed around spectacular moments. I suggest that in the 1880s there was an extra step to the paradoxical point that the triumph of image over text is best evoked in, and demonstrated through, writing.

These three texts will serve to represent a broader trend in storytelling particular to the late-Victorian period. That trend was for the flattening out of story structures such that even the idea of the beginning, middle and end could become attenuated. What survives is episodes, scenes, and situations. It was now possible for writing to become a series of scenes, each of which was akin to an emblem. The scenes dominate the content and little significance is given to the precise sequence of these scenes.

---

[7] Meisel, *Realizations*, ch.3

[8] Stephen Orgel, *Imagining Shakespeare: A History of Texts and Visions* (London: Palgrave Macmillan, 2003), and Michael Fried, *Manet's Modernism or the Face of Painting in the 1860s* (Chicago: University of Chicago Press, 1999).

I suggest that this reflects a change from a strongly linear understanding of story about growth and development that had become popular in mid-century storytelling, to a more jumbled, digressive and anachronic understanding of story. The jumbled or digressive version of story is not worse than the linear, but rather provides opportunities for different kinds of stories, messages and reflections.

My texts show some of that range of possibility. *The Diary of a Nobody* is iterative partly because it is in a diary format and partly because it is a comedy, a mode that relies upon inconsequential iteration. In comedies there tends to be zero character growth for any of the characters, each of whom simply is destined to repeat their characteristic stupidity each and every day. Browning's poem is non-linear in a different way: it is titled "Development", but any suggestion of directional progress is deliberately undermined as its narrator reflects on his own life with regret, fixating on an early scene that represents his own lost happiness and his bitterness at an education that doomed him to an inappropriate future. The poem reflects the truth that lives are experienced in the present, but also in prospect and retrospect. In some instances the past or the future exert such gravity that we can never achieve smoothly linear progression.

I am not suggesting that the flattened-narrative or the emblem series was the *only* way of telling stories during the 1880s. That would be obviously untrue. But it did become a possible mode of storytelling and it is distinctive and worthy of note because of its twin assumptions that linear and progressive structures distorted reality (which was more prone to regression, reversion, and other forms of anachronic interruption) and that the verbal depiction of scenes of poetic evocation of imagism better captured our temporal and psychological experience.

A good example of the refusal of traditional narrative structures is found in the very structure of Jerome K. Jerome's *Three Men in a Boat*. Here the story of the boat trip from London to Oxford sets up a traditional narrative (a journey or quest), but then does everything it can to subvert our expectations. The journey turns out to be a mere excuse for a sequence of comic routines, jokes and scenarios. The pseudo-quest narrative is even subverted when the three men get *close* to Oxford but then give up on a whim and go home before they get there. This is less of a high-theoretical rejection of narrative patterns, than an understanding that a strong quest-narrative structure would get in the way of the irony, play and gags that are the real point.

It would be possible to multiply other examples of flattened and anachronic narrative from the late-Victorian period, such as the imagism of the Decadent poets and the general vogue for stories based on primitivism, regression, and various other forms of nostalgic revivalism. These all develop new insights, ideas and perspectives from the rejection of linearity, and this is what made the late-Victorian period so interestingly different from previous decades. But there is not time to cover them here.

The Diary of a Nobody

The Diary of a Nobody was not the work of high literary inspiration in the Romantic inspiration mode. It was much closer to commercial hack work, and the cobbled together series of skits and gags that the authors, along with Jerome K. Jerome, helped popularize. It was originally serialized in *Punch* (1888-89) as a set of ephemeral riffs, based on the stick-in-the-mud attitudes of a middle-class clerk, Mr. Pooter, both at home and at work. The episodes are gathered together from passing bits of popular culture: anecdotes, jokes, corny puns, visual gags and mannered variations on a single theme. The Grossmith brothers were both music hall comedians and knew that the very milking of a joke, beyond reasonable limits, was a bravura performance in itself.

The diary was written and published in real time: at one point the diary drops out because George Grossmith was taking his own one-man show on tour. When it resumes, they excuse this gap when the protagonist, Mr. Pooter , notes that some pages from his diary went missing when the maid used them to light the fire (Chapter Seven). Comedy delights in its lack of structure and its improvised adoption of ephemeral themes. Every interruption was grist to its mill. The (ir)regular column was immediately successful and was gathered and published as a book (1892) and then republished with illustrations (1894).

The authors were involved in theatre (as actors, playwrights and producers), music, comedy, literature and art. Weedon Grossmith, in particular, had trained as a painter but then went on to become a star of the stage, working with Henry Irving as well as the D'Oyly Carte Opera Company. It was George who sang Gilbert and Sullivan's famous patter songs. The Grossmiths cared about words and images and had a keen dramatic sense. But, unlike the writers Martin Meisel studied in *Realizations*, they were interested in deploying a combination of arts not out of Wagnerian earnestness, but to create an amplified sense of fun.

Considering their comic novel will serve mainly to establish some basic ideas about the relation of words, images and ideas and about the depiction of aging. Their novel will help us get that story straight, but in doing so it will only be preparatory work for the subsequent analysis of Browning's poem, which will be more creative with that relation, getting the story crooked again.

I am using *The Diary of a Nobody* as a kind of warm-up act for Browning's poem "Development" because it is concerned to construct a clear division between the old and the young as part of the comic situation. Most of the humour draws upon this neat contrast. It is worth pausing here to note how distinctive was the way they drew the contrast between young and old.

The ancient world had plenty of comic dramas about youth and old age and these set the pattern of dramatic comedy into the nineteenth century. A typical plot would feature a Roman patriarch and his son and it was a story of possession versus ambition. Roman patriarchs owned everything and had supreme authority. Until the patriarch died the sons had far fewer rights. So, in the comedies the sons want the money and usually the young wife that the patriarch has, and they scheme with a crafty slave to enjoy the use of what they could not possess. Here, the structure is that the son is impatient to have the paternal authority; he wants to *be* the father figure.[9]

This is *not at all* the set up that the Grossmiths offer. The son, Lupin, has no desire or intention to *be* like his father. He shows no interest in having what his father *has*. His idea of work, conduct, value, and propriety are also at odds with his father's; Lupin's idea of fun is more immediate and short-term. The father and son have incompatible understandings about what constitutes the good life. Lupin is impatient because he wants something different and he is ready to just take what he wants. When Pooter tells his son that he has been a loyal company employee for years and has risen slowly and improved his salary (slowly) as a result, the son replies that through shady insider trading he has made twice as much money in a mere fraction of the time.

It is not just that they have different values; the tendency of the book is to suggest that the son's short-termism is more in line with the values of the age. Pooter's steady, precise and convention-minded approach is the source of most of his problems. He is the fish out of water.

What makes *The Diary of a Nobody* different from the Roman/classical model is the experience of industrial society in which social transformation was becoming more regular and more thorough. Each generation in the nineteenth century entered a very different type of world to that of their parents. The expected life course for each generation could be very different and the cultural values would also be subject to change. It's the type of

---

[9] For more information, see Martin T. Dinter, "Fathers and Sons," in Martin T. Dinter, ed., *The Cambridge Companion to Roman Comedy* (Cambridge: Cambridge University Press, 2019), 173–87.

situation depicted in Alvin Toffler's *Future Shock*.[10] Mr. Pooter's values are those of the *previous* generation. By dint of comic exaggeration, his values are depicted as fossils, relics of a lost age incomprehensible to almost all the other characters. Mr. Pooter has no future; he has been left behind by the march of progress. He continually fails to adapt to the modern world and nobody he meets ever shows any recognition of his alternative values. That would spoil the comedy.

With those comments in mind, we can examine an episode within *The Diary* that demonstrates how word and image could be interwoven in the design of the scene (what Meisel called the 'situation').

In the fifteenth chapter of the book Lupin takes his parents out for a ride in his new cab. This is a sporty new contraption in which he faces forward as driver, sitting next to his mother, but as there is only room facing forward, his father has to sit behind facing backward. Unsurprisingly, Lupin drives too fast and is heedless of the pedestrians and traffic around him. He causes mayhem, but he is looking forward and the mayhem is left in his wake. It is Mr. Pooter, facing backwards and already out of his comfort zone because of the speed, who has to face the fallout from the people Lupin has annoyed. As they bowl down Holloway Hill the son sees opportunity and fun, while the father sees only angry faces and hears only insults. The crowd hurl orange peel at him. Then we are on to the next diary entry, and we hear no more of this.[11]

This episode is actually a narrative version of the traditional allegorical emblem of youth and old age. Youth faces one way and old age the other. Titian depicted this motif in his *Allegory of Prudence*, after reading about it in it Macrobius's *Saturnalia*.[12] See fig. 1.1. The same allegorical image is literalized in the closing lines of Louis de Bernieres's *Captain Corelli's Mandolin*, where the driver of the motor*cycle* faces forward, and his passenger faces backward. In all these cases, the image symbolizes the generational cycle. I like how de Bernieres's version literalises that cycle as an actual motorcycle.

---

[10] Alvin Toffler, *Future Shock* (London: Random House, 1970).

[11] Actually, the cab is mentioned again later, but only to note that it had been sold and Lupin has moved onto some other new fad.

[12] Erwin Panofsky suggested both literary and visual sources for this emblem image in "Titian's Allegory of Prudence: A Postscript," in Erwin Panofsky, *Meaning in the Visual Arts* (London: Penguin Press, 1993), 181-204.

Figure 1.1. Titian, *Allegory of Prudence* (1550–1565). Oil on canvas, 76.2 × 68.6 cm (30.0 × 27.0 in). National Gallery, London.

Weedon Grossmith was likely to have known Titian's painting at first hand as it was in the collection of Alfred de Rothschild, in London, at the time. But the passage does not depend upon awareness of the painting for its effect, no more than it does at the end of *Captain Corelli's Mandolin*. In this episode of the *Diary* the entire narrative scene is elaborated out of a strong visual motif, representing an absolute difference between youth and old age. It has been placed in a narrative scenario that adds humorous context, but that only elaborates on the central motif (or situation).

This is essentially the same use of visual iconography that Meisel noted as common in stage productions of the 1860s. Freezing the action momentarily into recognizable iconographic groupings was a way of producing emphasis, a kind of dramatic punctuation. The specifically late-Victorian twist on this is that the emblem-narration is managed in and through text.

Three Men in a Boat

Secondly, we can turn to a parallel instance in the 3rd chapter of Jerome K. Jerome's *Three Men in a Boat*. Coming this early we are still at the establishing section of the plot and the narrator is introducing Harris, one of his two comrades. Perhaps in imitation of epic similes, or more likely as an excuse to exploit a good routine, the narrator decides that Harris reminds him of Uncle Podger, and then dives into an elaborate scene in which Uncle Podger tries to re-hang a picture.

This comic story is entirely gratuitous, but thematically consistent with the idea of paternal authority and its subversion, here self-subversion. The nub of the joke is that the father of the house claims to be practical and efficient in getting things done, even as he proceeds to bring everyone else into the chaotic operation that invariably goes wrong. It is played as pure slapstick and its stepwise catastrophising is a way of milking the joke while incrementally raising the stakes. It would play well as a music hall slapstick routine, which is probably where it actually came from.

This story presents a literal take on someone getting above himself (he steps on some tables to rehang the picture. See fig. 1.2. After creating chaos he is taken down a peg or two (he crashes to the ground). The most relevant saying is 'Pride goes before a fall' and its variants, biblical in origin (Proverbs 16.18). This is an intensely visual gag and the idea of rising up and falling down would become a staple of silent comedy films.

The gag works because what is shown is the literal version of the visual metaphorics inherent in common sayings. Social climbing and being high and mighty are part of a general pattern of speech in which power and importance are signaled in a spatial way. To be low is to be vulgar, part of the inferior masses. To be raised up is to be superior. In promoting himself above his abilities the father of the house is "setting himself up for a fall". The entire episode is grounded in and highlights a secret spatial aspect of words and ideas. There is a willingness to harvest comic potential from this confusion, rather than the attempt to reduce or control the play.[13]

Where the Grossmith brothers developed narrative potential out of a visual emblem of youth and age, itself drawn from a mix of textual and visual instances, such as Titian's *Allegory of Prudence*, Jerome K. Jerome draws comic potential from the spatial and directional bias to our thinking, as reflected in many of our sayings. But whether it is a story drawn from a visual emblem or from the spatial/visual basis for our own thinking and

---

[13] Bakhtin argued that the essence of comedy was *bathos*, bringing the high down low. Slapstick literalises this essence of comedy. Mikhail Bakhtin, *Rabelais and His World*, trans. Hélène Iswolsky (London: John Wiley & Sons, 1984).

speaking, the late-Victorian aspect of this scene is the fact that both the Grossmiths and Jerome K. Jerome elaborate this confusion in a single medium.

The Theme of Intergenerational Strife

Both scenarios discussed above have revolved around a contrast between maturity and youth, though that theme is sustained and developed more richly in *The Diary of a Nobody*. Robert Browning's poem "Development" will also be about that same theme of inter-generational contrast, playing on the contrast between innocent youth and regretful old age. By contrast, the Grossmiths were not really interested in this idea of social change beyond the fact that it offers them a chance to pit a ponderous older father figure, a stickler always wanting to do things by the book, against a young buck out to have fun and acquire social or financial advantage without much heed for work, loyalty or duty. It is the contrast that offers comic potential and there is no proto-sociological desire to reflect or comment on social trends.

Figure 1.2. "Uncle Podger hangs a picture." Jerome K. Jerome, *Three Men in a Boat*, Chapter 3. Illustr. A. Frederics (Bristol: J. W. Arrowsmith; London: Simpkin, Marshall, Hamilton, Kent & Co. Ltd., 1889). Project Gutenberg. Public domain.

But the theme of inter-generational difference was an area of social and medical innovation in the 1880s when the category of senility was being proposed, defined and tested.[14] And it was being defined using precisely the same set of ideas and concepts that the Grossmiths were exploiting for comic effect and that Browning, as we will soon see, was inspecting out of intellectual curiosity.

The experience and even description of senility was not new. It had long been understood in terms of the ossification of the mind, a weakening of our physical and spiritual elasticity, and a kind of regression to a second childhood. The description wasn't new, but the scientific definition and classification of it as a biological and natural fact was. Rather than just something that befell some individuals, it was now presented as a natural tendency inherent in all of us. The scientific aspect put additional stress on definitions, the meanings of visual signs and the narrative construction of an aging process.

Senility thus came to mean mental debility with a particular focus on having fallen out of step with surroundings. What is now called Dementia or Alzheimer's were medically defined through these tropes. The research that generated and justified these new diagnostic categories claimed to be empirical, but was actually guided and shaped by the tropes that the Grossmiths had deployed. Increasingly doctors are recognizing that our ability to understand and palliate the actual experience of conditions like Dementia and Alzheimers is hampered by these Victorian concepts.

So, there *is* a proto-sociological aspect to *The Diary of a Nobody* precisely because of its direct approach to comic contrasts between heedless youth and cautious old age. Despite the vast gap between comedy and medical diagnostics there is an exact connection between their core ideas. The old are shown to be living beyond and outside their own native era; they don't understand the contemporary world, which is being shaped in the image of the young, the generation coming up behind them. Their values, conduct and attitudes now jar with their environment. They are relics, left behind by the tide of progress. The young are the opposite, heedless of the values, conduct and attitudes of the older generation and, as the world seems set up in their image, they tend to benefit from doing so.

The Grossmiths define aging through the differences between generations, assuming that each generation will have adapted to a distinct

---

[14] For an excellent demonstration of this point, see Teresa Mangum, "Growing Old: Age" in Herbert F. Tucker, ed., *A New Companion to Victorian Literature and Culture* (Oxford: John Wiley & Sons, 2014), 97–109.

social, cultural and technological environment. The comic value of the book draws entirely on how they exploit those contrasts.

The Grossmiths were not the first to make such claims; many of Walter Scott's novels, for example, draw on the contrast between an outdated heroic attitude and a more in-date commercial attitude. But where Scott is interested in social and historical culture shifts between lowland and highland Scots (for example), the Grossmith brothers are much closer to the biological and medical version of generational difference.

Robert Browning's late poem "Development", published in 1889, also focuses on images of youth and signs of old age. The poem also relates aging to distinct life stages, but it is more questioning about that process, prompting us to see the signs of aging in relation to other stories that are much less linear. In a typically Browning way, he provides opportunities to question and explore the motivations of those who exploit the discourse of aging. If we proceed through different phases in our life, what is our responsibility to the "us" in those other phases? Who should be responsible for the way our life turns out? I will argue that Browning's poem stages a narrator who makes casuistical arguments about his life. In other words, he uses weasel words, misinterprets the evidence, and generally works to position himself as the very emblem of virtue betrayed. A lot of this is down to how he depicts the process of aging.

"Development"

Browning's "Development" complicates the relation of words and images. It is a poem that starts out by presenting a strong visual image of a child acting out scenes from Homer's *Iliad*, improvising the setting with his toys and employing a cast that includes his pet dog. It is charming and has earned the poem a growing online presence.

But the poem has a harder edge than its charming opening suggests. As the poem progresses we get a stronger sense of a narrator looking back on his own childhood development. He glories in his earlier sense of wonder and imagination as a period of lost innocence but does so in order to establish a strong contrast with his subsequent development. As he grew older, he was taught to read Homer in Greek and then to read the German Higher Criticism of the *Iliad*. In other words, he was shown how the poem was bodged together from diverse and disparate stories and that the seams and fractures were evident. In this process the sense of wonder and charm was eradicated, and the poem was left a tattered wreck.

For the narrator education is depicted as something that was done to him; he did not grow out of his childhood stage so much as have it torn from him. It is not an inward flowering or a natural outgrowth from curiosity to true knowledge and understanding, but a bewildering forced march that took him away from his true self into habits and thought patterns he finds alienating and discomforting.

The narrator clearly feels that his education evicted him from a childhood phase of life too soon and his "development" since then is charted as a progress destruction of what he held dear. The child he describes is presented as the real him. But that child is lost and the him-that-he-is-now seems ill at ease, conflicted, and dominated by bitterness and regret. The poem is an exercise in blaming someone else for the person he has become, as if he had no active part in that development. He wants to persuade himself that he is not at all responsible for who he is now. It is a strange situation, but perhaps not uncommon and all the more interesting for all that.

It is a poem that is grounded in three fundamental elements. First, there is the charming scene of wonder, joy, and innocence. This is a strong piece of verbal image-making. Second, there is the accompanying narrative in which that scene is depicted as a lost golden age, obscured by a series of educational phases that replace the experience of wonder with technical understanding. And thirdly, there is the guiding concept of development that structures (or de-structures) the poem. On the one hand, this is the idea of Victorian progress as a linear path from simplicity to complexity and from innocence to experience. But on the other hand, it is Victorian hindsight, nostalgic, but also recriminatory, forensic, and self-justifying.

There is a description of a stepwise development, but also an evaluation grounded in a stark contrast drawn between the initial state and the mature state. The narrator is both the object of the narration and the speaking subject, but he wants to imply the self that is depicted is more truly him than the self that is doing the depicting. The poem is complex and intricate, but it relies on our ability to juxtapose the image of the child and the jarring tone of the old man, and to appreciate that contrast. Let's follow the progression of the poem to catch the stress being made on development.

My father was a scholar and knew Greek.
When I was five years old, I asked him once
"What do you read about?"
                                        "The siege of Troy."
"What is a siege, and what is Troy?"
                        Whereat
He piled up chairs and tables for a town,
Set me a-top for Priam, called our cat

> —Helen, enticed away from home (he said)
> By wicked Paris, who couched somewhere close
> Under the footstool, being cowardly [...] (1-9).

We segue to the next step of development being dangled before the boy, reading Pope's translation of Homer's Greek:

> It happened, two or three years afterward
> That—I and playmates playing at Troy' Siege—
> My Father came upon our make-believe.
> "How would you like to read yourself the tale
> Properly told, of which I gave you first
> Merely such notion as a boy could bear?
> Pope, now, would give you the precise account
> Of what, some day, by dint of scholarship
> You'll hear—who knows?—from Homer's very mouth (24-32).

Soon, we turn to the study of Greek to read Homer in the original. This is where study starts to edge out the fun, but the boy still manages to enjoy his Greek reading:

> Time passed, I ripened somewhat: one fine day,
> "Quite ready for the Iliad, nothing less?
> There's Heine, where the big books block the shelf:
> Don't skip a word, thumb well the Lexicon!" (44-47).

But having read the Greek the boy is now steered toward German Higher Criticism and F.A. Wolf's famous *Prolegomena*, which exposes Homer as a fictitious entity and his poem as no more than a compilation of pre-existing stories and fragments.[15] This is less fun, but more accurate:

> Thus did youth spend a comfortable time;
> Until—"What's this the Germans say in fact
> That Wolf found out first? It's unpleasant work
> Their chop and change, unsettling one's belief:
> All the same, where we live, we learn, that's sure."
> So, I bent brow o'er *Prolegomena*.
> And after Wolf, a dozen of his like
> Proved there was never any Troy at all,
> Neither Besiegers nor Besieged, nay, worse,—
> No actual Homer, no authentic text,

---

[15] Antony Grafton, Glenn W. Most, and James E.G. Zetzel, eds., *F.A. Wolf: Prolegomena to Homer, 1795* (Princeton: Princeton University Press, 1985).

No warrant for the fiction I, as fact,
Had treasured in my heart and soul so long […] (62-73).

The poem then descends into the second half, the half that is decidedly less charming and more ambiguous. This takes the form of a complaint about his father's education plan. The poet rejects the view that his father was easing him from the world of poetry to the world of scholarship and on to the world of science. He reads his own education as the pleasant immersion in story and fantasy followed by its gradual but disastrous replacement with clear moral discernment. As he now sees it, his father would have been better to drop the distracting storytelling aspect and teach clear thinking and moral behaviour directly.

His father's plan has worked only too well. The poem ends with his explaining that he now reads Aristotle's *Ethics*, in the original Greek he adds, and we assume he reads Aristotle ("the Stagirite") rather than poetry or fiction. The poem ends with some summary reflections that are very ambiguous:

Now, growing double o'er the Stagirite,
At least I soil no page with bread and milk,
Nor crumple, dogs-ear and deface—boys' way (113-115).

He has been formed into this figure, "growing double", and without any trace of childish behaviour, behaviour he can now only see in terms of irritating defacement. There is no mention of a child of his own, but we can certainly imagine the education plan he might come up with would lack those charming scenes that so appeal to modern readers.

The poem's literary context

As previously mentioned, the poem "Development" comes from Browning's final volume of poems, *Asolando*, published a matter of weeks before his own death. It was a collection that was squarely in Browning's trademark style: the poems were at once simple and accessible even as they also indulged in abstruse historical allusion and complex narrative structure.[16] Many had the structure of a joke with the early sections functioning like a set-up and the ending coming as a punchline that shifts our perception of what happened. Already famed for his dramatic monologues, it was no surprise that Browning presented clear images and

---

[16] The best guide what dramatic monologues are and what they can do remains Alan Sinfield, *Dramatic Monologue* (London: Methuen & Co., 1977).

narratives in many of these, recounted by narrators whose motives and intentions were both intricate and suspect.[17]

The joke-type poems are easier to deal with as the punchline wraps things up. In one poem, "The Pope and the Net", we learn the story of a priest who rises through the Church hierarchy with a fishing net as his personal emblem. This seems to present him as a fisher of men, preaching the Gospels among the humble labourers. Such humble spiritual ambitions see him become pope, whereupon he removes the emblem from his audience chamber. When the cardinals question him about it, he tells them the net has caught its fish. The punchline is delivered in the final half of the final line of the poem and flips our perspective on the story so far narrated. Its impact hangs on the ambivalence of the emblem and the secret insight that humility and riches were two sides of the same coin in the medieval Church.

Our poem, "Development", isn't *quite* like that; it is not wrapped up at the end. If anything, it has a maze-like structure that is designed to complicate, not simplify. It is designed to sum up a cultural trope and sharpen its confusions and dead ends (its aporiae). It is designed to be a summation of cultural knowledge on the topic of development, which has often been taken to be the representative theme of the Victorian era.

The idea of such a cultural gathering is supported by the literal descriptions in many of the poems of the act of gathering, harvesting, and collecting in order to distil a pure essence. The pope's fishing net is one example; the image of a bee gathering pollen in its "bag" is presented as "All the breath and bloom of the year in the bag of one bee" (the opening line of "Summum Bonum"). This is itself a poetic topos—the idea that poems are culture harvested and then distilled can be found in classical times and was popular in the Renaissance. Poetry is flowers and garlands. Through selection the poet can achieve true representation—that idea of the whole world in a grain of sand.[18]

Richard S. Kennedy is one of few academics to reflect on Browning's final collection. He takes "Development" as its *representative* poem precisely because it focuses on development as a kind of journey through life. He sees the volume's "Epilogue" as emphasising that forward momentum: "One who never turned his back but marched breast forward. /

---

[17] A helpful modern edition with introduction and commentary is available in Richard S. Kennedy, *Robert Browning's "Asolando": The Indian Summer of a Poet* (Columbia: University of Missouri Press, 1993). There is almost no additional academic scholarship to this volume.

[18] Macrobius (again) makes this point in the preface to his *Saturnalia*, himself distilling an entire classical heritage of this topos.

Never doubted clouds would break" (11-12).[19] This looks like a Victorian idea of linear progress but walking forward need not imply linearity; it is also what we do when we double back on ourselves in a maze.

The poem

We have already seen how "Development" starts with an image of a child imaginatively recreating Homer's *Iliad* with his toys and his pet dog. Having learned Greek so he can read the poem for himself, he then learns to read German Higher Criticism and his days of visual enactment are over. Images are broken into words.

In this context German Higher Criticism means F. A. Wolf's famous argument that the *Iliad* was not so much of a single coherent poem "written" by a single author, as an act of cultural editorship: various existing poems and stories were cut-and-pasted together with the cracks and joins more-or-less smoothed over.[20] What had been the singular poem of a singular author is now disaggregated. Homer didn't write the poem; an editor created both poem and author. The narrator feels that in this process he has been subject to the same process. In the encounter with Higher Criticism his self-image has crumbed into word fragments.

Biographers have sought to align this poem with Browning's own educational development. Browning had long loved ancient epic and he had been reading and commenting on Higher Criticism for most of his career. He could parody the German professors as being dry as dust, myopically focusing on verbal intricacies in texts that were widely deemed to be about the fate of humanity and life itself. But we should not forget that he was himself addicted to intricate detail and abstruse scholarship. That was very much his wheelhouse.

Browning never seemed to regret the kind of analytical operations that Higher Criticism taught. If anything, he found in them a source of wonder of their own: he clearly delighted in the academic habit of discerning difference, identifying problems, and proposing highly speculative answers. He used this to generate wonder, humour, and curiosity, not to eradicate them. Browning had a Romantic sense of joy but it was not the product of

---

[19] See Richard S. Kennedy and Donald S. Hair, *The Dramatic Imagination of Robert Browning: A Literary Life* (Columbia: University of Missouri Press, 2007), 413.

[20] Antony Grafton provides an excellent introduction to the modern English translation: Grafton, Most, Zetzel, *Prolegomena*.

Romantic innocence and simplicity.[21] He will have traced his development very differently to the narrator of "Development".

What attracted Browning was the issue of beginnings: how ideas or behaviours got started. In his poetry beginnings are rarely presented as coming out of nowhere; they are always shown as being created through misunderstanding and reverse-engineering: bringing the cultural resources of one culture together to make sense of ideas, experiences and dogma from another culture. A neat example is "An Epistle Concerning the Strange Medical Experience of Karshish, the Arab Physician" (from *Men and Women*, 1855) in which the eponymous Arab physician is totally bamboozled by the idea that Jesus could be God incarnate.[22] He has no concept that can make sense of a greater being having been incorporated in a lesser being. After hearing about Jesus from Lazarus, whom he attended as a doctor, he starts to explore the kinds of concept that could accommodate this experience. He is divided between his proto-Higher-Critical understanding and his emotional conviction—that sense of wonder that he can't shake off. In a sense he "gets" the mystery of the Trinity better than the rationalists and dogmatists.

That was a special case, but Browning's poems often trade on the gap between a problem and the suggested answer, or an object and its description by a viewer. The suggested answers often miss their mark, the verbal descriptions prove partial or distorted. What these poems are about is troubling ambiguities. Browning reserves room for wonder, error, and wrong-headedness and what seems like innovation is always just a composite of those mistakes and misunderstandings.

As the title of the poem "Development" suggests, the issue that this kind of doubling of vision and understanding is applied to is the idea of development itself.

The idea of development

The concept of development implies movement across two or more states. Tracing paths of development is a matter of identifying a beginning and an end and drawing a line through various points between them. On the one hand it unifies those phases, but on the other hand it divides the object into

---

[21] A case clearly set out in Suzanne Bailey, "'Decomposing' Texts: Browning's Poetics and Higher-Critical Parody" in Jude V. Nixon, ed., *Victorian Religious Discourse: New Directions in Criticism* (London: Palgrave Macmillan, 2004), 117-29.
[22] Robert Browning, *Men and Women* (London: Chapman and Hall, 1855).

those phases. This idea that life was the prime example of development was new in the nineteenth century.[23]

Development became a technical term for the life-cycle as traced in the life cycle of the organism: the phases of youth, maturity and old age. It was also understood to be the pattern of underlying history, as societies progressed through primitive/mythic states and onto progressively more organised phases: pastoral, warrior and industrial. Herbert Spencer made a reputation with his ambitious generalization of this concept: everything moves from undifferentiated simplicity to functional complexity and elaborated articulation. This was a kind of law for nature and culture alike.[24]

The bildungsroman novels presented a character experiencing life and learning from that experience, developing a coherent outlook, adapting to a changing social world. The hero or heroine has to be flexible and tactful, rather than a zealot, but invariably comes to a position of influence.[25] There were few novels like this in the 1840s and 1850s (though these tend to be the ones studied at university). Statistically, the bildungsroman was only ever a drop in the ocean of Victorian publishing. The majority of novels published in the Victorian era was what we would recognise as genre fiction, specifically not about "self culture". The religious/moral novels of the type that Dinah Craik and Geraldine Jewsbury (for example) wrote were less concerned with development and more concerned with our ability to identify and choose the path of moral duty over the path of temptation. This creates a much simpler and often more powerful message and in terms of volume and public success certainly outweigh the bildungsroman. The novels of adventure written by men like Harrison Ainsworth, Frederick Marryat, G.H. Henty and H. Rider Haggard are more like picaresque novels in which the hero's virtues are ingenuity, endurance and, usually, moral honour. The hero tends to learn new skills rather than more encompassing moral outlooks. There were new genres, like comedy, but also sensation fiction, detective fiction, and supernatural fiction that sold heavily because of their power to affect the reader. There was even a trend for stories that specifically satirised the moral boosterism of the bildungsroman—and I would certainly place *Jude the Obscure* in *this* category. The majority of the novels in those decades did *not* concern themselves with development. Instead, they were defined by genre rules. Their heroes or heroines faced

---

[23] A helpful resource is Mark Bevired., *Historicism and the Human Sciences in Victorian Britain* (Cambridge: Cambridge *University Press*, 2017).

[24] See Michael Taylor, *The Philosophy of Herbert Spencer* (London: Bloomsbury Academic, 2007).

[25] Franco Moretti, *The Way of the World: The Bildungsroman in European Culture*, trans. Alberto Sbragia (London: Verso, 1987).

stark choices between morality and happiness, typically sacrificing their happiness for moral principles, or perhaps they failed to make the choice and then they were punished by the plot. They did not have to develop an individualised or context-specific way of being moral, so much as live up to existing moral and social ideals.

We can align Browning's "Development" with both types of development, the genetic version in which everything grows according to a pre-set pattern, and the more voluntaristic version in which a degree of agency is available to us, through our own initiative or through educational support, as we develop. The bildungsroman is there in the description of the stages of education, leading from childhood to maturity. But the ambiguity lies in how we manage that process. The narrator describes an education that tactfully and sensitively guided him through the stages of growth from childlike wonder, access to the skills needed to be an autonomous learner and then experience in higher order critical thinking. But his own view seems to be that the first stage of wonder and play were cruelly unpicked by the later stage of criticism and he questions why he was exposed to the golden joy of youth, if its cancellation was always destined to happen. If the end point was moral seriousness, why not go straight to that (removing any individual agency) and dispensing with detour that was cruelly deceptive and an unnecessary delay. As such, the narrator's stern judgement on that education process reflects the moralizing rival account.

Why did Browning produce such a complicated poem about "Development"?

Rival models of development

The concept of development became ever more widespread and by the 1880s the concept had developed into a series of rival accounts or theories. Mostly, the differences clustered around whether development is an internal law for each thing, or whether it is something imposed by the environment or historical context. The simple concept of development of incremental or linear growth was no longer the main model and was challenged by various non-linear theories of growth through phases, life-cycles of growth and decline, degeneration, atavistic returns or "survivals", and such like.[26]

When Browning wrote his poem, most of the tropes about development were well-known, but his interest in Higher Criticism and its debates will

---

[26] There is a helpful discussion of these broader biological and historical narratives in their 1880s context in Peter Bowler, *The Non-Darwinian Revolution: Reinterpreting a Historical Myth* (Baltimore: Johns Hopkins University Press, 1992).

have made him long familiar with the main ideas. Browning's poem relies on our ability to recognize in the idea of growth both a positive enhancement or a negative departure and loss.

Browning's poem is a story of personal and individual development, but the concept of development shuttled seamlessly between the personal and historical levels. The development of the individual was bound up with the development of its larger units: tribe, culture, or race. In the decades after linear progress had lost its sheen, these debates were increasingly lively.

It is worth taking a quick survey of the rival options, as these constitute the horizon of meaning for the poem. Let's start with a simple contrast about ages of humanity and the aging of a human.

- **Model 1: linear growth**. Many saw development as a kind of internal law: acorns always grow into oak trees. The programme for that growth is given at the start, even though the unfolding happens over time. This model minimises the role of context and the whole live-and-learn aspect that was important to the *bildungsroman*.
- **Model 2: epochal growth**. A more historicist model would carve out distinct epochs in the development of cultures (and individuals). Each epoch has its own mentality. Giambattista Vico was the first to outline such a scheme. At the dawn of man people understood the world poetically, then either reality knocks us into more realistic shape or some natural process occurs through which we develop more sophisticated outlooks—either way we end up seeing the world very differently. What was poetry is now a structured chain of principles and causes. Hegel was another exponent of this kind of structuring and many of the German Higher Critics drew, directly or indirectly, from his version of it. The thing about Hegel's system was that once you had left a stage there was no going back. If you accidentally pour milk into a coffee you can't really get it back out again. It is a system built on forward-momentum.
- **Model 3: life cycles**. A graph of dynamic vitality can be drawn according to which we start off young but weak, then rise to our peak of strength and vitality before declining to a kind of second childhood. This model applied interchangeably between individuals and collectives, something that Greek thinkers already understood. This came to have intuitive validity and was very popular in Victorian medicine and even popular culture through the theory of decline or degeneration. The pessimism of the late-Victorian era was grounded in this nagging sense that degeneration had set in and the effects were just now beginning to start piling up.

- **Model 4: atavism**. We might be modern, but under conditions of stress we can regress, often quite sharply and suddenly. The pressure of modern life effectively primes us for such regression (*Dr Jekyll and Mr Hyde*) or drives it out of hiding (*Dracula*). Gustave Le Bon would produce an entire psychology based upon the regressive traits of the crowd. Here, the fate of a life is not *purely* internal, but the role of the culture and society is blunted to simple triggers.

- **Model 5: decline**. A more old-fashioned view of progress was that after a moment of perfect creation there was a progressive falling away from that perfect initial state. Movement is always a loss. Victorian sentimentality was keen on this story. Matthew Arnold's poem "The Scholar Gypsy" is about the way intellectual purity is pushed to the margins in a complex, busy modern society. In our highly organised society, we can only hope to glimpse truth and beauty out of the corner of our eye.

The narrator of the poem follows the fifth model: development as departure and loss. He regrets the loss of his childhood innocence and blames the education that gave him logic and critical skills. He wants to participate in beauty not analyse it. He laments his development. The basis of this lament is that his development was not a natural growth of his soul, but the result of an imposed structure. Education was something done to him, not by or with him.

This is a familiar kind of claim and as we read the poem it should be recognisable from Victorian novels about the education process. In George Eliot's *The Mill on the Floss* Tom Tulliver is a bright boy on whom education is imposed.[27] He is an active and curious boy, but classroom lessons are the path offered, and he finds this constraining and frustrating. He does less well than he might and it plays with his sense of self-worth and status. Tom resembles the mythic heroes, strong and brave and so on, but he is cramped in a rationalised system that allocates value based upon intellectual ability, not physical and moral ability.[28] Many of Walter Scott's novels explore just this theme, as does Dickens's memorable treatment of it in *Hard Times*.

But, as already noted, Browning didn't advocate that position. If there was ever someone who could find joy and beauty in scholarly detail it was

---

[27] George Eliot, *The Mill on the Floss* (Edinburgh and London: William Blackwood and Sons, 1860).

[28] On the Victorian awareness of education's over-intellectual approach, see Dinah Birch, *Our Victorian Education* (Oxford: Blackwells, 2007).

Browning. Intellectual development was not the enemy of humanity, but the gateway to it. He seems more interested in the bitterness of the narrator and his claim that development was done to him. There is casuistical reasoning in this wish to distance himself from responsibility for himself.

In other words, the narrator shows us more about his development through his equivocation, than he does by telling us about it in direct statements. This is a true dramatic monologue, in which the manner of presentation contradicts the content that is presented. The image of the idyllic childhood is a product of this casuistical reasoning. It may or may not be true, but it is an image with suspect motivation: it is an over-determined scene (or "situation"), constructed equally out of words and images.

Browning's second childhood

Browning was seventy-seven when he wrote this poem. It is a tricksy poem nestling in a collection that does seem to be modelled on the idea of the joke: misdirection, perspective shifts, and punchline endings. This play-like structure takes him close to the idea of life-cycles (as Model 3, above). The vitality of middle-age has fallen off and there is a reduction to the childlike levels of weakness and pleasure in simple things.

This does match his declining physical state when he wrote these poems, but not his mental state, which still seems ebullient. This is more like a second childhood as an achieved state—the classical trope of the puer senex (a return to a joyous liberty).

Perhaps, Browning was thinking of Bacon's essay "Of Youth and Old Age", which is the classic statement of the virtues of the second childhood.[29] Bacon outlines a stadial theory of life with youth marked out as unduly rash and maturity being more timid and reflective. Young men see visions, but old men dream dreams. Senility comes last and is a phase marked less by mental sclerosis and physical ossification than by that return to childhood wonder.

Henri Bergson would develop this theme in his study of comedy.[30] We are creatures prone to develop habits and these become more rigid and inflexible over time. The function of comedy is to loosen us up and to restore some of that elastic energy that so marked our childhoods. This account,

---

[29] Francis Bacon, *The Major Works*, edited by Brian Vickers (Oxford: Oxford World's Classics, 2008), 424-25. In his introduction Vickers notes Bacon's use of "syntactical parallelism in order to characterise the two opposed stages of life" (xxxi).

[30] Henri Bergson, *Le Rire* (Paris: Ancienne Librairie Germer Baillière & Co., 1900).

partly cultural and partly biological, allows space for the kind of second childhood that Browning seemed to make his own. It is an age when word and image are productively and creatively confused.

Conclusion

In this chapter I have discussed three texts that show a marked propensity to use visual emblems as the basis of their narrative construction. The visual emblems often circle around a situation of conflict and the text is entirely absorbed in developing narratives and images that elaborate this confrontation, testing out its potential meanings, implications, and effects. In this structural design there is a rejection of text as a linear medium, constructing stories that have a clear linear progression from start to end.

Martin Meisel outlined the basis for this type of storytelling in the early and mid-nineteenth century. He charted the entanglement of word and image in the nineteenth century, identifying a series of phases and strategies, but made only stray comments on the story beyond the 1860s. I have tried to continue his account with a suggestion of how this developed in the late-Victorian period.

I have suggested that there was a flattening out of story and history. Narrative movement could be presented as a series of static images or of set-piece scenes. The experience of atavism, anachronism, and cultural survivals becomes more prominent; the experience of movement, linear development and transitions becomes less prominent and more obscure. Think of images of evolution that focus on a line-up of different images and the vain search for missing links.

This was the same move that American art historian George Kubler made in his 1962 *The Shape of Time*.[31] He rejected the attempt to line up ancient American artefacts in ways that emphasized the linear development of form in order to attend more closely to the meanings that the diverse forms could impart or acquire, irrespective of sequence. Kubler's text had a strong impact on visual artists in the 1960s and 1970s, emphasizing flatness and contrast as a way of communicating meaning.[32]

Kubler's approach presumed visual forms had a grammar and its visual aspects were best treated as semantic aspects. Visual material remained visual, but it gained a semantic basis that was modeled on verbal forms of

---

[31] George A. Kubler, *The Shape of Time: Remarks on the History of Things* (Yale: Yale University, 2008) and Briony Fer, *The Infinite Line: Re-Making Art after Modernism* (Yale: Yale University Press, 2004), ch.4.

[32] See Pamela Lee, *Chronophobia: On Time in the Art of the 1960s* (Cambridge: MIT Press, 2006), ch.4.

meaning.[33] This is similar to the late-Victorian approach I have sought to articulate. The late-Victorian period was emerging from a mid-Victorian period that was geared toward humanist depth and linear progress. Its willful confusion between word and image was not theoretically motivated, but driven by curiosity, experiment, commercial opportunity, and cross-cultural exchange. It was rougher, more chaotic, and a whole lot less predictable than its modern equivalents but all the more interesting for that.

Bibliography

Bacon, Francis. *The Major Works*, ed. Brian Vickers. Oxford: Oxford World's Classics, 2008.

Bailey, Suzanne. "'Decomposing' Texts: Browning's Poetics and Higher-Critical Parody" in Jude V. Nixon, ed. *Victorian Religious Discourse: New Directions in Criticism*. London: Palgrave Macmillan, 2004.

Bakhtin, Mikhail. *Rabelais and His World*. Translated by Hélène Iswolsky. London: John Wiley & Sons, 1984.

Barkan, Leonard. *Mute Poetry, Speaking Pictures*. Princeton: Princeton University Press, 2012.

Bath, Michael. *Speaking Pictures: English Emblem Books and Renaissance Culture*. London: Longman, 1994.

Bergson, Henri. *Le Rire*. Paris: Ancienne Librairie Germer Baillière & Co., 1900.

Bernieres, Louis de. *Captain Corelli's Mandolin*. London: Secker & Warburg, 1994.

Bevir, Mark, ed. *Historicism and the Human Sciences in Victorian Britain*. Cambridge: Cambridge University Press, 2017.

Birch, Dinah. *Our Victorian Education*. Oxford: Blackwells, 2007.

Bowler, Peter, *The Non-Darwinian Revolution: Reinterpreting a Historical Myth*. Baltimore: Johns Hopkins University Press, 1992.

Browning, Robert. *Asolando*. London: Smith & Elder, 1890.

—. *Men and Women*. London: Chapman and Hall, 1855.

Dickens, Charles. *Hard Times*. London: Bradbury & Evans, 1854.

Dinter, Martin T., ed. *The Cambridge Companion to Roman Comedy*. Cambridge: Cambridge University Press, 2019.

---

[33] We can see how Martin Meisel's arguments might have been extended into the late-Victorian period in Michael Fried, *Manet's Modernism: The Face of Painting in the 1860s* (Chicago: University of Chicago Press, 1999). Despite the title this book covers the final third of the century, and takes as its central theme "aesthetic of flatness".

Eliot, George. *The Mill on the Floss*. Edinburgh and London: William Blackwood and Sons, 1860.

Fer, Briony, *The Infinite Line: Re-Making Art after Modernism*. Yale: Yale University Press, 2004.

Fried, Michael. *Manet's Modernism or the Face of Painting in the 1860s*. Chicago: University of Chicago Press, 1999.

Grafton, Athony, Glenn W. Most, and James E.G. Zetzel. *F.A. Wolf: Prolegomena to Homer, 1795*. Princeton: Princeton University Press, 1985.

Grossmith, George and Weedon. *The Diary of a Nobody*. London: Arrowsmith, 1892.

Jerome, Jerome K. *Three Men in a Boat (To Say Nothing of the Dog)*. London: Arrowsmith, 1889.

Kennedy, Richard S. *Robert Browning's "Asolando": The Indian Summer of a Poet*. Columbia: University of Missouri Press, 1993.

Kennedy, Richard S. and Donald S. Hair. *The Dramatic Imagination of Robert Browning: A Literary Life*. Columbia: University of Missouri Press, 2007.

Kubler, George A. *The Shape of Time: Remarks on the History of Things*. Yale: Yale University, 2008.

Lee, Pamela. *Chronophobia: On Time in the Art of the 1960s*. Cambridge: MIT Press, 2006.

Mangum, Teresa. "Growing Old: Age" in Herbert F. Tucker, ed. *A New Companion to Victorian Literature and Culture*. Oxford: John Wiley & Sons, 2014.

Meisel, Martin. *Realizations: Narrative, Pictorial, and Theatrical Arts in Nineteenth-Century England*. Princeton: Princeton University Press, 1984.

Moretti, Franco. *The Way of the World: The Bildungsroman in European Culture*. Translated by Alberto Sbragia. London: Verso, 1987.

Nixon, Jude V. E d. *Victorian Religious Discourse: New Directions in Criticism*. London: Palgrave Macmillan, 2004.

Orgel, Stephen, *Imagining Shakespeare: A History of Texts and Visions*. London: Palgrave Macmillan, 2003.

Panofsky, Erwin, *Meaning in the Visual Arts*. London: Penguin Press, 1993.

Sinfield, Alan, *Dramatic Monologue*. London: Methuen & Co., 1977.

Taylor, Michael, *The Philosophy of Herbert Spencer*. London: Bloomsbury Academic, 2007.

Toffler, Alvin, *Future Shock*. London: Random House, 1970.

Tucker, Herbert F., ed. *A New Companion to Victorian Literature and Culture*. Oxford: John Wiley & Sons, 2014.

CHAPTER TWO

MA®KING A MONSTER:
THE AFTERLIFE OF
FRANKENSTEIN'S CREATION
AND THE RACIALIZATION
OF CRIMINALITY

ZOE COPEMAN

" 'Let me go,' he cried; 'monster! Ugly wretch! You wish to eat me and tear me to pieces. You are an ogre. Let me go, or I will tell my papa."[1]

"'Mama, see the Negro! I'm frightened!' [...] the little white boy throws himself into his mother's arms: "Mama the ——'s going to eat me up."[2]

Upon a chance encounter with a young child, the Creature of Mary Shelley's *Frankenstein* (1818) fleetingly believes that he may gain acceptance into human society through the eyes of an "unprejudiced" youth. Having already been spurned by the first humans he has encountered—a fallen-from-grace family known as the De Laceys—a need for kinship overtakes him. He forcibly seizes the boy. Frightened, the boy screams, "Hideous monster! Let me go. My papa is a syndic—he is M. Frankenstein—he will punish you" (104). Anger overcomes the Creature as he fulfils the boy's prophecy: "You wish to [...] tear me to pieces" (144). With murder on his hands, there is no longer any dispute. The Creature is re-modelled from an innocent being into the most loathsome monster of all: a murderer.

---

[1] Mary Shelley, *Frankenstein or the Modern Prometheus*, ed. by Maurice Hindle (1818; reis., London: Penguin Books, 2003), 144.
[2] Frantz Fanon, *Black Skin, White Masks*, Get Political Series (1952; trans. 1967, 1986; reis., London: Pluto Press, 2008), 84; I have purposefully retracted a word from Fanon's initial statements so as not to re-appropriate its associated violence, dash lines appear where words have been retracted.

This episode of becoming criminal is eerily replicated over a century later in Frantz Fanon's account of an encounter with a young white boy. It is at this moment, after another child yells, "Look, a Negro!" that Fanon realizes that he has been made into an object.[3] His self is fragmented, fractured into different purported subjectivities before being pieced together again by a white gaze. That self, perceived through a white boy, proclaims him as not just a reconstituted object, but a monster capable of murder and cannibalism. This projection is what scholars following Fanon have dubbed "the Fact of Blackness."[4] Though the process of Fanon becoming Other mimics the Creature's own trial, there is no death at Fanon's hand. And yet, that does not preclude the white gaze from ma®king Fanon as criminal. Under white eyes, Fanon is "fixed." He is "laid bare" and sees "in those white faces that it [he] is not a new man who has come in, but a new kind of man, a new genus."[5] My use of the ® in the term "ma®king" throughout this chapter refers to the phenomenon of first marking someone as different before making them into someone (or something) new that Fanon describes in his own theoretical work and is frequently employed throughout the text of *Frankenstein* through its most famous creation, the Creature.

It is not new to interpret the creation made by the "mad scientist" Victor Frankenstein as Black. Many contemporaries of Mary Shelley made the cognitive leap to read the "monster" as an escaped enslaved man, liberally employing this narrative to suit both anti- and pro-slavery agendas.[6] Comparisons abound, as H. L. Malchow's first text to critically analyse Blackness in *Frankenstein* attests. Malchow demonstrates how *Frankenstein* and its Victorian adaptations drew on stereotyped images to reimagine the Creature as a romanticized Other. These visualizations "stirred deep popular anxieties" over non-white populations abroad that would in turn affirm for the English that the top of their racialized hierarchy

---

[3] Fanon, *Black Skin, White Masks,* 84.

[4] This English translation of the fifth chapter within Fanon's *Black Skin, White Masks* was originally titled "L'expérience vécue du Noir" and may be translated conversely as "The Lived Experience of the Black"; for a discussion on the differences between these translations and the implications for reading Fanon, see Simone Browne, *Dark Matters: On the Surveillance of Blackness* (Durham, NC: Duke University Press, 2015), 6-8.

[5] Fanon, *Black Skin, White Masks*, 87.

[6] Rei Terada, "Blackness and Anthropogenesis in *Frankenstein*," in Orrin Wang, ed., *Frankenstein in Theory: A Critical Anatomy* (New York: Bloomsbury Academic, 2021), 131; for an overview of the complexities of how race was defined during the time *Frankenstein* was written, see Roxann Wheeler, *Complexion of Race: Categories of Difference in Eighteenth-Century British Culture* (Philadelphia: University of Pennsylvania Press, 2000).

was male, upper-class and white.[7] While commentaries on colonialism and various other hegemonies have been traced within *Frankenstein*, as Rei Terada points out in her most recent contribution to this field, these arguments struggle to find the final linchpin that concretely fixes the Creature as Black. And perhaps, that is the point. The youngest Frankenstein does not cry out for the reader, "Look, a Negro!" as the white boy does to Fanon. Instead, the Creature is simultaneously given form and rendered amorphous. A gigantic human-like shape and a small blot on the landscape, he is caught between existing and not-existing. Despite being re-constituted into a new frame or self, that self is consistently denied to the reader. And yet, Frankenstein's creation is later categorized and subsequently identified by the other characters in the novel through *his* very denied appearance.[8] It is the goal of this text to analyse the afterlives and repercussions of this phenomenon of ma®king the Creature as Other.

What this present chapter on the intersection of word and image in *Frankenstein* proposes is that the similar visceral responses made towards Fanon and Frankenstein's Creature are linked not through Blackness in the novel, but through a larger system of appearance-based discrimination. As this study will show, this system—known as physiognomy—has frequently been employed to transform the amorphous cultural otherness of the Creature into a concrete visual Other. Physiognomy, known throughout eighteenth- and nineteenth-century England and Europe as the study of the internal through the external, enabled the classification of individuals into discrete categories of sameness and difference. Physiognomy became the main support for many pseudo-scientific theories of the age. Within his *Inquiries into Human Faculty* (1883), published nearly seventy years after the first edition of *Frankenstein*, Francis Galton produced what is largely credited as the first "composite portrait". Superimposing the photographed visages—or physiognomies—of multiple men and women atop one another, Galton sought to create a condensed visual representation of a criminal type. Galton's composite portraits expedited physiognomic processes of identification by combining a multitude of features into a single, ghostly frame. Reading the Creature's physiognomy similarly, as a body re-ordered through the hybridization of fragmented features, this interdisciplinary

---

[7] H. L. Malchow, "Frankenstein's Monster and Images of Race in Nineteenth-Century Britain," *Past & Present*, no. 139, 127-130.
[8] References to the "Monster" or "Creature" as "it" versus "he" (and even "she") abound. For the purposes of this discussion, the Creature will be referred to by the pronoun "he" as he is referred to throughout the novel. Exceptions to this pronoun are when the Creature is rendered amorphous and/or when he is purposefully Otherized by other characters within the novel.

study aims to elucidate the various systems through which the public imaginary of nineteenth-century Britain applied Blackness to Frankenstein's Creature by ma®king certain bodies as benign and others as criminal.[9]

The Physiognomic Frame

Any summary of physiognomy and its reconstitution within the eighteenth century is necessarily reductive. Yet, a gross characterization is imperative to understand the extent to which the exterior body and the interior self became intertwined in nineteenth-century artistic, literary and scientific circles. Physiognomy had long been a paradigm in the West for reading "the nature of man" through the face. Throughout the early modern period, European portraitists largely drew on various physiognomic theories to impart their sitters' likenesses.[10] In 1775, with his *Physiognomische Fragmente, zur Bedförderung der Menschenkenntniss und Menschenliebe*, the Swiss theologian Johann Kaspar Lavater recapitulated once disparate and outdated treatises on physiognomic thought to create a manual for distinguishing character through facial features alone. His work was both lauded and deeply criticized throughout all of Europe. Nevertheless, his initial treatise and its subsequent editions were quickly translated into all major European languages.[11] The first English edition, translated as *Essays on Physiognomy, Designed to Promote the Knowledge and the Love of Mankind*, appeared in 1789 with illustrations by the Royal Academic painter and Lavater's childhood friend Henry Fuseli. The aim was that—now

---

[9] I wish to extend my gratitude to Tita Chico for her advice on this paper for a seminar re-examining texts from the "Long Enlightenment," as well as the coordinators for the Northeast Modern Languages Association (NeMLA) 2022 panel discussion "Queering Dark Academia," Corina Wieser-Cox and Nina Voigt, who allowed me to apply these principles of Otherization in *Frankenstein* through physiognomy to a contemporary social media phenomenon known as "dark academia." Dark academia as a subculture romanticizes the Gothic in popular culture today in an often light-hearted manner on Instagram and other social media sites. Its use of physiognomy and other modes of outward identification (as well as tropes from Victorian literature), however, re-instill negative stereotypes.

[10] Hans Belting, *Face and Mask: A Double History* (Princeton: Princeton University Press, 2017), 106-112.

[11] Melissa Percival, *The Appearance of Character: Physiognomy and Facial Expression in Eighteenth-Century France* (Leeds: W.S. Many for the Modern Humanities Research Association, 1999), 161.

complete with lavishly illustrated pocketbooks in hand—just about anyone could ascertain the character of his fellow man.[12]

Just how Lavater re-defined physiognomy reveals the implications of such a paradigm. A deeply religious man, Lavater believed that the first portrait had been Christ's face miraculously appearing on Saint Veronica's veil. Despite lacking knowledge of Christ's true physiognomy, Lavater thought that morality lay in not just acting like the son of God but looking like Him as well. As a result, within his *Essays on Physiognomy*, Lavater created a system through which morality could be determined by the degree to which someone's face deviated from Christ's.[13] The standard from which these principles derive came not from a veritable depiction of a real man, but from a European icon. Conceived by Lavater as male and white, Christ's face as standard served as justification for excluding other genders and not-white individuals from this abstract system of morality. Yet, over the course of the nineteenth-century, anyone not-male and not-white would be forcibly entered into this "abstract machine," establishing a gendered and racialized hierarchy that affirmed the wealthy, white and abled cis-male as the definitive *head* of society.[14]

There is something to be said of Mary Shelley's own relationship to Lavater's *Essays on Physiognomy* through its illustrator Henry Fuseli, a known friend of her mother Mary Wollstonecraft. Mary Shelley and the painter also knew each other personally, Fuseli having supped at her father William Godwin's house during her youth. Fuseli's notorious painting *The Nightmare*, first exhibited at the Royal Academy of London in 1782 to much buzz and acclaim, was noted to have left such an impression of violence on the writer that she may have used it as inspiration for the scene in *Frankenstein* in which the protagonist Victor finds his betrothed Elizabeth Lavenza cast as a distorted image atop their marriage bed. See fig.2.1. "She [Elizabeth] was there, lifeless and inanimate, thrown across the bed, her

---

[12] It is also clear from the text that *Essays on Physiognomy*, within the "Author's Preface" in particular, is meant for a male readership, J.C. Lavater, *Essays on Physiognomy Designed to Promote the Knowledge and the Love of Mankind*, trans. Thomas Holloway (London: G. G. J. & J. Robinson, 1800).

[13] Percival, *Appearance of Character*, 173-174.

[14] Physiognomy is equated to this "abstract machine of faciality" in Gilles Deleuze and Félix Guattari, *A Thousand Plateaus: Capitalism and Schizophrenia* (London: Athlone Press, 1988).

head hanging down, and her pale and distorted features half covered by her hair."[15] Potential influences of *Frankenstein* aside, physiognomy is a

Figure 2.1. Henry Fuseli, *The Nightmare* (1781) oil on canvas. Detroit Institute of Arts, Founders Society Purchase with funds from Mr. and Mrs. Bert L. Smokler and Mr. and Mrs. Lawrence A. Fleischman, 55.5.A. Wikimedia Commons. Public domain.

key component of the text for reading who is a trustworthy character and who is not. In Victor's formative first year at the University of Ingolstadt, he is taught by two opposing professors, the "little squat" M. Krempe with his "repulsive countenance"and the "mildblackface and attractive" M. Waldman with his "aspect expressive of the greatest benevolence."[16] It is the latter who inspires Victor to continue to pursue his childhood interest in ancient Greco-Roman natural philosophy, and it is through this

---

[15] Quoted in Sophia Andres, "Narrative Challenges to Visual, Gendered Boundaries: Mary Shelley and Henry Fuseli," *Journal of Narrative Theory* 31, no. 3, 259-262; originally from Shelley, *Frankenstein*, 199.
[16] Shelley, *Frankenstein*, 47-48.

encouragement that Victor's passion for finding the spark of immortality is re-ignited. Through M. Waldman's guidance, the plot is pushed from a speculative mode of wonder into an experimental mode of creation.

Denied the Creature's countenance and thus his full physiognomy, nineteenth-century readers lacked such a signifier for determining the creation's true character. The overall lack of engagement with physiognomy and even clear bodily description of the Creature, as opposed to Victor's professors and Elizabeth, is telling for its very absence. Before Elizabeth's features became distorted in death, she is described in the first edition of the text as a "being heaven-sent" with blonde hair and blue eyes.[17] Despite her heavenly status, the third edition of *Frankenstein* (1831) reveals her parentage—or stock—as German and Maltese. And through her, a general physiognomy of those nations emerges as a "charming countenance."[18] It is interesting to note here the increasing importance placed in a nation's shared physiognomy in the predetermination of a person's moral aptitude that occurs between the publishing of these two versions of *Frankenstein*. Conversely, the Creature has no national heritage to piece together his features—or any that are clearly defined for the reader. The process of identifying his un-readable body throws into distortion his actions. Without the exterior to classify the soul, the reader becomes reliant on character witnesses to determine his true motive. Yet, throughout the novel these witnesses prove all too biased in their own abilities to interpret their fellow man.

What these last few sentences impart is the degree to which the entire narrative of *Frankenstein* plays out as a trial with multiple first- and second-hand accounts recounted by a single in-person witness (the narrator Robert Walton) to his remote judge and sister Margaret Saville. Without Margaret's input, however, the judge effectively becomes the reader. Using physiognomy as a framing device for this trial reveals how the Creature's exterior comes into being through the witnessing of him as criminal. For though the Creature lacks a national heritage, aspects of his creation emerge to proclaim a replacement lineage. One that would fix him in the public imaginary as forever monstrous.

The Physiognomy of Monstrosity

Though this examination will address the creation of a "monster" through nineteenth-century adaptations of Frankenstein, it is the gradual erasure of the

---

[17] For this 1818 description, see Mary Shelley, *Frankenstein* (Berkeley, 1968), 31.
[18] Shelley, 36.

grotesque in Mary Shelley's original novel that enabled the Creature and his story to perform this role and countless others. Besides being equated to a recently freed slave, the Creature has also been conceived of as a colonized subject, a femininized Other or an amalgamation of the "unruly lower classes."[19] Interpretations proliferate. As such, a complete study of all versions would be, as William Christie cautions, "literally incomprehensible."[20] Rather, understanding the Creature's and the novel's metamorphoses into a monster and monstrously generative text respectively requires first addressing what is present and absent in its first three editions published between 1818 to 1831.

The most in-depth description provided of the Creature proceeds from his creator Victor and his account of his awakening:

> His limbs were in proportion, and I had selected his features as beautiful.
> Beautiful!—Great God! His yellow skin scarcely covered the work of
> muscles and arteries beneath; his hair was of a lustrous black, and flowing;
> his teeth of pearly whiteness; but these luxuriances only formed a more
> horrid contrast with his watery eyes, that seemed almost of the same colour
> as the dun-white sockets in which they were set, his shrivelled complexion
> and straight black lips [...][21]

Thereafter, the various witnesses to the Creature's deformity define him by single words or phrases at a time. He is "wretched", "vile", "miserable" and, of course, a "monster" (102). His first description reveals, however, that what is "wretched" about the Creature is not necessarily his physiognomic traits, but the signs of death adorning his features. The reader is briefly given an assessment of the white watery eyes, black putrid lips and yellow lurid skin akin to a reanimated mummy, yet also the peculiarities of a corpse as a thirteenth-century English verse illustrates: "When my eyes mist, / And my hearing hisses, / And my nose gets cold, / And my tongue

---

[19] For the Creature as a "feminized Other", see Sandra A. Gilbert and Susan Gubar, *The Madwoman in the Attic: The Woman Writer and the Nineteenth-Century Literary Imagination* (New Haven and London: Yale University Press, 1979), 221-22; Meena Alexander, *Women in Romanticism* (Basingstoke and London: Macmillan, 1989), 129; William St Clair, *The Godwins and the Shelleys: The Biography of a Family* (London: Faber and Faber, 1989), 437. For the Creature as the "unruly lower classes," see Paul O'Flynn, "Production and Reproduction: The Case of Frankenstein," *Literature and History*, ix (1983), 194-213. An investigation of these sources in relation to Frankenstein can be found in William Christie, "The Critical Metamorphoses of Mary Shelley's *Frankenstein*," *Sydney Studies in English* 25 no. 1991 (1991). For a compilation of those that read the Creature as an "enslaved man now freed", see Malchow, "Frankenstein's Monster," 90-93.

[20] Christie, "The Critical Metamorphoses of Mary Shelley's *Frankenstein*," 47.

[21] Shelley, *Frankenstein*, 58.

folds, / And my face slackens, / And my lips blacken […] / All too late!"[22] Established in the Creature's first description is an uncanny expression of human physiognomy. His limbs are proportionate and his features beautiful, but the familiarity of these human traits alongside the peculiarity of death establishes the Creature as a monstrous nightmare in the most Gothic sense of the term.

In her investigation of abhuman bodies in Gothic novels, Kelly Hurley maintains that the horror these monsters generate results from their ability to render categories of selfhood obsolete. Essentially, a monster with an uncanny resemblance to the human frame engenders anxiety over humanity's own frames of existence.[23] In their first encounter nearly two years after his "birth," the Creature admonishes his creator Victor, "God in pity made man beautiful and alluring, after his own image; but my form is a filthy type of yours, more horrid from its very resemblance."[24] Not only does death plague the Creature, so too does the Icon that defied death before him: Christ. After his resurrection, Christ became the most moral creature to walk the Earth. The Creature's own resurrection proves a defamation of this divine act. Accordingly, the Creature exists simultaneously within and without Lavater's conceived system of physiognomic analysis with which Mary Shelley was well familiar. Unlike mankind, the Creature does not derive from Christ's benevolence, but from Man's folly. Lavater, like many eighteenth-century natural philosophers, believed in the ultimate degeneration of the human species. As mankind—in those natural philosophers' eyes—had declined since the time of the Greeks, no person living in the eighteenth century could possess the ideal physiognomy that was Christ's and thus could never be a truly "moral creature".[25] The Creature, thus, exists outside the traditional physiognomic paradigm. Entering into a new system entirely, Victor's creation becomes a filthy form able to approach categories of humanity yet never able to fully identify with any one of them. This liminality is conveyed in later descriptions, where alongside general descriptors like "tremendous and abhorred" little else describes him but a "figure of a man."[26] Rei Terada proposes that this

---

[22] Quoted in Sarah Tarlow and Emma Battell Lowman, *Harnessing the Power of the Criminal Corpse* (London: Palgrave Macmillan, 2018), 39; originally compiled in R.T. Davies, *Medieval English Lyrics: A Critical Anthology* (London: Northwestern University Press, 1964), 74.

[23] Kelly Hurley, *The Gothic Body: Sexuality, Materialism, and Degeneration at the Fin de Siècle* (Cambridge, Cambridge University Press, 1996), 5.

[24] Shelley, *Frankenstein*, 133.

[25] Lavater, *Essays on Physiognomy*, 118.

[26] Terada, "Blackness and Anthropogenesis in Frankenstein," 138.

framing of the monster as mere figure reveals the uncertainty over his true nature. For Victor this uncertainty quickly crystallizes into a concluding verdict. As light illuminates the "deformity of its aspect, more hideous than belongs to humanity," Victor proceeds to claim—before even hearing the Creature's testimony—that "it" was the murderer of his younger brother William (77-78).

It is worth returning here to the framing of these multiple narratives as a series of testimonial accounts. Before Victor begins his narration, Robert describes him in detail as simultaneously a wild and benevolent man made credible by his "celestial spirit" (30). This perceived infallible character is supported by Victor's own framing of himself through the honour and reputation of his father. At length, Victor explains that his family was "one of the most distinguished" of Geneva (33). In accordance with natural philosophy tracts of the eighteenth century that used the rank of their authors to justify their observations and results, Victor establishes himself as a credible witness.[27] In contrast, the Creature's story—told by Victor—is framed through lack. Victor's first description of his creation renders the latter's testimony to Robert invalid. At the end of the novel, as the Creature attempts to justify his actions in his own words, Robert is reminded of Victor's initial framing of him: "when I called to mind what Frankenstein had said of his powers of eloquence and persuasion, and when I again cast my eyes on the lifeless form of my friend [Victor], indignation was rekindled within me. 'Wretch!' I said" (223). Even Justine, the servant accused of young William's death and sentenced to hang for it, is first presented through one of Elizabeth's letters as a kind soul with a becoming countenance (66-68). Her introduction as a guiltless character verifies Victor's resolution over the Creature's own guilt. Robert knows this testimony as well. Through Victor's initial authority, the Creature is proclaimed a criminal.

The Physiognomy of Criminality

Remarkable to this process of condemnation is the frequent use of imagination to justify the Creature as monstrous. It is because of imagination that the Creature may be rendered flesh in the first place. In contrast, Victor's imagining of a female creation inevitably stops him from realizing the Creature's request for a mate. Over months with the Creature's threat hanging over his head, Victor laments and conjectures over the

---

[27] Tita Chico, *The Experimental Imagination: Literary Knowledge and Science in the British Enlightenment* (Stanford, Stanford University Press, 2018), 36.

abhorrence of a female creation before asserting in the absolute that—were he to complete his task—"one of the first results of those sympathies for which the daemon thirsted would be children, and a race of devils would be propagated upon the earth, who might make the very existence of the species of man a condition precarious and full of terror" (170-71). Although Victor's conclusion suggests that this new race would supplant humankind, he is unclear through what means. Equally probable to the destruction of the human race through violence is its eradication through miscegenation. This fear is evident in Victor's subsequent response—notably to himself—that a female creation "might turn with disgust from him [the Creature] to the superior beauty of man […]" (170). Horror is once more incited through the creation's imagined ability to eradicate the boundary between that which is human and not-human.

This anxiety over miscegenation and its results is replicated in the eugenicist Francis Galton's later justification for marking a criminal type from the rest of the British population. Known for his contributions to the study of heredity, Galton transformed into the father of eugenics by systematically attempting to categorize humankind. For readers of *Inquiries into Human Faculty*, he states plainly,

> My general object has been to take note of the varied hereditary faculties of different men, and of the great differences in different families and races, to learn how far history may have shown the practicability of supplanting inefficient human stock by better strains, and to consider whether it might not be our duty to do so by such efforts as may be reasonable, thus exerting ourselves to further the ends of evolution more rapidly and with less distress than if events were left to their own course.[28]

As is evident from this excerpt, Galton was indebted to his cousin Charles Darwin's works *The Descent of Man* (1871) and *Expressions of Emotions in Man and Animals* (1872).[29] Using these texts along with evolutionary theory more broadly, Galton believed that interbreeding with "inefficient human stock" created criminal behaviours within more "civilized" races of humankind.[30] To find what he believed to be sources of regression, Galton created a systematic procedure for reading criminal physiognomies: the composite photographic portrait (6-7).

---

[28] Francis Galton, *Inquiries into Human Faculty* (J.M. Dent & Co., 1907), 1.

[29] Charles Darwin, *The Descent of Man* (London: John Murray, 1871). Charles Darwin, *Expressions of Emotions in Man and Animals* (London: John Murray, 1872).

[30] Galton, *Inquiries into Human Faculty*, 42-47.

Galton's contrived photographs were by no means singular. Despite claiming objectivity through mechanical reproduction, scientific photographs of the age were highly manipulated illustrations. In *Expressions in Man and Animals*, for example, Charles Darwin found that no single photograph could encapsulate what he concluded to be the animal expressions of fright and rage apparent in humans. To portray his theory that these expressions were animal by nature, Darwin commissioned composite images from the artist Oscar Gustave Rejlander.[31] A disciple of his cousin Darwin and of his process, Galton made his own composites by carefully choosing a set number of subjects from his archive of photographs taken of convicted criminals. Fixing them one on top of another based on a calculated middle line, he gradually exposed a single plate to each image for a predetermined amount of time until he reached results to his satisfaction. To test the efficacy of his experiment, Galton reordered the photographs and exposed a new plate to the same sample until the second product resembled the first. The similarity between the two plates proved for Galton that the resulting image was that of the shared features of these men and not a result of the procedure itself.[32]

Paradoxically, these composites also appeared more "human" to Galton than their individual portraits. Within *Inquiries into Human Faculty*, Galton confessed, "They produce faces of a mean description, with no villainy written on them. The individual faces are villainous enough, but they are villainous in different ways, and when they are combined, the individual peculiarities disappear, and the common humanity of a low type is all that is left" (11). Those peculiarities do not disappear entirely, however, but remain fixed to the surface of the plate as ghostly traces to haunt the general type that they produce. See fig. 2.2. Like Frankenstein's Creature, Galton's portraits appear like a man but one unable—by their very nature—to fully approach anything other than a ghostly description of one. Their viewers are given the impression of eyes, nose, mouth and shape of the head, but require an explanatory text to determine the type of being into which these beings converge. Because of the simultaneous presence and absence of the sources of its production, the composite portrait remains a figure on which the viewer imagines a criminal body based on the authority of that text's author. Galton's work was highly regarded during his lifetime, even earning him a

---

[31] Peter Hamilton and Roger Hargreaves, *The Beautiful and the Damned: The Creation of Identity in Nineteenth-Century Photography* (London: National Portrait Gallery, 2001), 76-77.

[32] Galton, *Inquiries into Human Faculty*, 6.

knighthood in 1909.[33] In *Frankenstein*, that authority lies with the academically trained titular character. Yet unlike Galton, Victor curiously leaves out the method by which his creation is produced. Pieced together from various sections of the novel, the Creature is revealed to also be a composite of different materials stolen from the "dissecting room and the slaughter-house", that is sculpted as clay into a human being of "gigantic stature."[34] If gathered from the dissecting table, however, the Creature is framed as a composite of criminals, and—like Galton's photographs—predetermined from the start as criminal.

The ascribing of the Creature as criminal would not have been lost on nineteenth-century readers. Throughout the early modern period in Europe, dissection was viewed as a desecration to the human frame. For centuries, only criminals were allowed to be publicly dissected. The passing of the Murder Act into British law in 1752 institutionalized this already well-established practice by decreeing that anyone convicted of murder would be sentenced to hang until dead in highly public displays that, indeed, ended with the desecration of the criminal's corpse. The act came out of a period in British history where increased urbanization led to a growing anxiety over murderers lying in wait in those very streets. In its official capacity, the Murder Act directly claimed to quell the rise in murder cases by adding a "further Terror and peculiar Mark of Infamy" to the punishment of murderous crimes.[35] Not only were murderers hanged in public execution events that drew out the whole of the community, but their corpses were also forbidden to be buried and put to rest. Criminal corpses either were given to medical societies to be dissected or were gibbeted. Also known as hanging in chains, gibbeting involved the stringing up of murderers post-execution in iron cages by the roadside. Though gibbeting had largely fallen out of favour by Mary Shelley's time for the ghoulishness of such events, between 1814 and 1816 six men were hung in chains along the Thames. Their bodies—as was the custom—remained for years and even prompted a Mr. Dykes in 1824 to complain to the Home Secretary about the "revolting, disgusting, pitiable" sight.[36] The initial death of criminals was no less gruesome.

---

[33] James R. Newman, "Francis Galton," *Scientific American* 190, no. 1 (January 1954): 72-77.

[34] Shelley, *Frankenstein*, 54-56.

[35] The full Murder Act's decree quoted in Tarlow and Lowman, *Harnessing the Power of the Criminal Corpse*, 86.

[36] Sarah Tarlow and Zoe Dyndor, "The Landscape of the Gibbet," *Landscape History* 36, no. 1 (2015): 80.

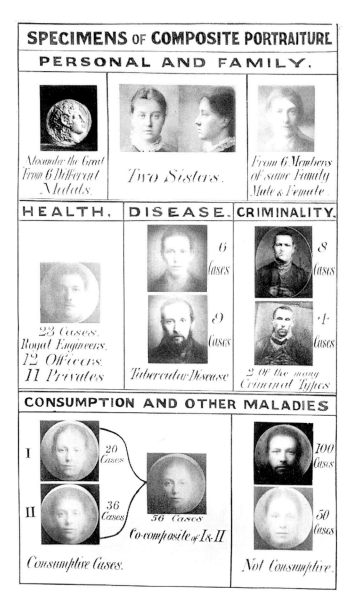

Figure 2.2 Frontispiece for *Inquiries into Human Faculty, and its Development* (London: Macmillan, 1883), Credit: *Inquiries into human faculty and its development* / by Francis Galton. Wellcome Collection. Public domain.

Hangings were known as messy affairs that ended with the body evacuating itself of all bodily fluids whilst still on the scaffold.[37] Later anatomization, or the opening of the corpse, was also highly visible as it occurred right after death at a local anatomy theatre so that the public could watch. The overt spectacle of such events transformed how the public perceived anatomizations and subsequent dissections. To see or read of a dissected body was to know that it had been a murderer.

Whether the Creature was intended to be a composite of dead criminals or an automaton as has recently been suggested,[38] adaptations recreated Victor's description of this "demoniacal corpse" into a brutish figure unable to be divorced from the deeds he is predetermined to enact.[39] The more streamlined versions of the second and third edition not only took advantage of the novel's instant success, but also made the text more adaptable to the stage.[40] The caricaturing of Victor as "mad scientist" and the Creature as "Frankenstein the monster" occurred in these stage productions. First to portray a physical representation of the Creature in 1823, Thomas Cooke famously reduced the figure into a muted beast that James Whale's film adaptation would render iconic a century later.[41] With the making of the Creature as visible, the Creature's ability to give his own testimony was literally erased, and paradoxically—with the visualization of his features— any sense of his humanity debated throughout the novel also effaced.

Made as criminal and marked as monstrous, the once amorphous Creature within the novel was necessarily transformed on the stage into a figure with an unambiguous physiognomy. What these adaptations forced readers and subsequent viewers to confront is what did that physiognomy look like? In his original representation, Cooke used a dark blue greasepaint to enhance the Creature's corpse-like body. Other actors performing as the monster followed suit. Yet in so doing, that very visual language would link Frankenstein's creation and all his perceived criminality to another stage performance operating at the same time—Shakespeare's *Othello*—and to the actors that would don blackface to portray its titular character.[42]

---

[37] A Samuel Hey of Leeds wrote in a private correspondence in 1831, "I rather expect a post-mortem tomorrow, which I understand is the most horrible thing possible, on account of the intolerable stench." Quoted in Elizabeth T. Hurren, *Dissecting the Criminal Corpse: Staging Post-Execution Punishment in Early Modern England* (New York: Palgrave Macmillan, 2016), 37.

[38] Tarlow and Lowman, *Harnessing the Power of the Criminal Corpse*, 119.

[39] Shelley, *Frankenstein*, 59.

[40] Malchow, *Frankenstein's Monster*, 120-21.

[41] Ibid., 120-22.

[42] Ibid., 122.

The Physiognomy of Blackness

The lack of descriptive information about the Creature requires the reader's imagination to "fill in the figure".[43] What unites Frankenstein with the criminal composite portraits of the late nineteenth century is the perceived cleanliness of this procedure. Mary Shelley imagines a landscape divorced from the very putrefaction that frames the novel's narrative. Stripped down to a basic physiognomy—with no indication of the extent of decay associated with its creation—the Creature is rendered an abstraction. This is evident in the gradual displacement of its form. Descriptions of the Creature become more vague, repetitive and hackneyed until he is conceived of as merely a black speck on the horizon.[44] Though initially given a body, this physicality is effectively removed from its context to be placed into another schema entirely. The composite portraits of known criminals created by Galton similarly remove the horror that made these individuals "villainous" in the first place.[45] Galton's photographs take the unruly—those who threaten society by their very existence—and re-order them into discrete categories. They too would make up a new schema. A full face may emerge in each composite, but the body remains isolated, disjointed and fragmented to allow singly unifying features like a nose, mouth or browbone to become the identifying factor of their common humanity (or lack thereof). Yet the removal of the grotesque from the surface does not prevent anyone from reading into these images and text the threat that they engender to the human frame, or rather the white human frame. Important to this identification procedure is the extent to which its very mechanisms are obscured, lending the impression of scientific objectivity to a highly subjective and discriminatory process.

Galton's pursuit of an average Briton and the subsequent subduing of any prescribed deviations from this average was not singular by any means. It was a collaborative effort across the European continent to stratify nations and their classes through the burgeoning notion of race as somehow a now biologically fixed trait. The Belgian statistician Adolphe Quetelet was just one influence for Galton and other criminal anthropologists of the latter half of the nineteenth century. Quetelet observed in 1842 that "The greater the number of individuals observed, the more do individual peculiarities, whether physical or moral, become effaced, and leave in a prominent point of view the general facts, by virtue of which society exists and is

---

[43] Terada, "Blackness and Anthropogenesis in Frankenstein," 140.
[44] Ibid., 138-139.
[45] Galton, *Inquiries into Human Faculty*, 11.

preserved."[46] One such "general fact" became the criminal body's Otherness. Quetelet had used his research on biosocial data in the 1840s to set up a hierarchy of physiognomic types based on their deviation from a prescribed "normal" or "standard" subject that would include a representation of a contemporary African at one end and a bust of an ancient Greek on the other. Quetelet's system was instrumental for Galton's own to affirm that the common Brit was closer to the Greco-Roman of the past than the African of the present.[47] Moreover, on this constructed hierarchy, Galton equated the supposedly "regressive" physiognomic traits of criminals to the features of non-Europeans.[48] This attempt to fix the criminal body as ultimately a non-European body comes at a time when the enslaved/enslaver dialectic was increasingly disintegrating. The British abolitionist movements of the late eighteenth to early nineteenth century and the American Civil War in the mid-nineteenth manifested a deeply held anxiety throughout Britain and other major European empires.[49] Without the categories of "slave" and "master", various scientific fields manifested a new racial framing device in order to maintain white privilege. Or rather, they resumed an already existing dialectic, just now through racialized means: the criminal Other and the innocent citizen.

Whilst Galton, and even more prominently Cesare Lombroso in Italy, were classifying the human race(s) in the latter half of the century, *Frankenstein* remained a popular text with a new edition published almost every decade. By the publishing of *Inquiries into Human Faculty*, the term "Frankenstein" had already transformed into a general term to describe a useless, brutish or misunderstood being—interchangeably, or more often all at the same time. A lithograph published the same year as the third edition of *Frankenstein* even depicts a "Frankenstein Physiognomist" using his own body to judge the characteristics of others. See fig. 2.3. In the years leading up to the American Civil War, Frankenstein's creation would appear in American political cartoons as a metaphor for slavery on that continent.[50] As a being initially without a discrete form, the Creature for many nineteenth-century readers became more specifically Black. These visual representations from stage productions to caricatures recreated the once ill-

---

[46] Quoted in, Allan Sekula, "The Body and the Archive," *The MIT Press* 39, no. October (Winter 1986): 11-13, originally in Adolphe Quetelet, *A Treatise on Man and the Development of His Faculties*, trans. R. Knox (Edinburgh, Chambers, 1842), 6.

[47] Sekula, "The Body and the Archive," 22-23.

[48] Galton, *Inquiries into Human Faculty*, 47.

[49] Malchow, *Frankenstein's Monster*, 116.

[50] Patricia A. Matthew, "'A daemon whom I had myself created': Race, Frankenstein and Monstering," in Wang, *Frankenstein in Theory*, 178-179.

defined Creature into a metaphor of Blackness. What is at stake in this recreation is the very criminal constitution inherent to the Creature's body in the novel *Frankenstein* that inevitably carries into his various public re-imaginings—for this procedure problematically reifies in the public imagination a link between metaphorical criminality and very real, living individuals.

Figure 2.3. Published the same year as *Frankenstein*'s third edition. A physiognomist whose body is entirely made up of faces, sitting at a table diagnosing people's physiognomic characteristics with the help of a book. Coloured lithograph by G.E. Madeley after G. Spratt, 1831. Wellcome Collection. Public domain.

Galton's work in the field of criminal anthropology proved foundational to establishing a surveillance practice still employed by European and American judicial systems today: racial profiling.[51] Patricia A. Matthew concludes from the Creature's encounter with the young William Frankenstein that "The creature's threat and subsequent fulfilling of it feed into the monstering metaphor that continues to haunt Black people, especially in encounters with the police."[52] In her recent study addressing the repercussions of Blackness in *Frankenstein*, Matthew focuses specifically on the murder of Michael Brown and the ways in which the media monsterized Brown only to humanize his murderer Darren Wilson.[53] Matthew's research enables yet another contemporary connection to this discussion.

In his *Jerome Project* series that he began in 2014, the artist Titus Kaphar created his own composite portraits from the mugshots of imprisoned men of the same name as his father, effectively re-establishing them as simultaneously named and unnamed individuals (as these criminological profiling systems had come to define these men).[54] Re-scribing three portraits over one another in chalk atop a black asphalt ground makes these forcibly reconstituted faces emerge awkwardly and out of sync to lend an even more haunting appearance to the final product than Galton's photographic productions. The composites undoubtedly hark back to Galton's work in eugenics and the erasure of the individual to produce a general criminal corpus that would claim criminality a part of the body rather than a product of society. Kaphar's contemporary work reveals how that corpus in the twenty-first-century United States is ultimately figured as Black.

With the rise in mass media coverage of police brutality in the early 2010s, Kaphar switched gears to create composites of black men unjustly murdered by the police. In one such image entitled *Brown, Bell, Garner*—named after their individual portraits of Michael Brown, Sean Bell and Eric Garner—these men's features are simultaneously thrown into relief and distortion. Michael Brown's most visible traits are the ghostly traces of his graduation cap and gown, which Kaphar took from his high school graduation picture to now become a part of Bell and Garner as well. These signs of Brown's past and potential future disrupt the process of profiling

---

[51] For an in-depth review of this history, see, Browne, *Dark Matters* (2015).

[52] Matthew, "Race, Frankenstein and Monstering," 181.

[53] Ibid., 174.

[54] Laura C. Mallonee, "Portraits of Prisoners in Gold Leaf and Tar," *Hyperallergic*, March 2nd, 2015, https://hyperallergic.com/183665/portraits-of-prisoners-in-gold-leaf-and-tar/.

based on physiognomy and reveal the injustices of the physiognomic profiling procedure. Currently housed at the STAMP Gallery at the University of Maryland College Park, the work is presented to a student body at a similar formative stage in their lives. By resituating these men outside of physiognomy's discriminatory schema, Brown—and in effect Bell and Garner—are reframed as graduating seniors about to start college in the prime of their life. Such a breakdown of the abstract machine that once defined criminality in the body reveals that the abstract criminal corpus and an individual human body are nowhere near the same. A comparison between Galton's composites and Frankenstein's Creature tells us nothing about criminality nor Blackness especially, but it does expose the reality that systemic procedures like racial profiling continue to govern individuals in regressive, highly racialized and fatal terms.

A Conclusion

My goal throughout this examination of the physiognomic abstraction processes present in *Frankenstein* is not to make a one-to-one equation between the landscape that Frankenstein's Creature traverses and the one Black individuals were forced to navigate in nineteenth-century Britain—let alone the twenty-first-century United States—but rather to expose the mechanisms by which criminality was embodied and racialized through both pseudo-scientific initiatives and public entertainment. Both *Frankenstein* and Galton's composite portraits sanitize criminality. Effectively, the tidying up of the "untameable" nature of crime removes it from a single body and displaces it into a general category of beinghood that would be defined by Galton and his successors in the field of criminology as not-white.

Before ever committing a crime, the Creature is fixed as Other and marked as criminal. It is well within the purview of this study to argue that Shelley's creation of an abstract monster in her debut novel *Frankenstein* contributed to its transformation into a monstrously generative text and Shelley herself as the "mother of science fiction."[55] Since its first publication in 1818, *Frankenstein* has been re-imagined countless times. Nearly every year, a new scholarly analysis of the novel is published. As these studies frequently attest, Mary Shelley's influential text emerged out

---

[55] Megen de Bruin-Molé, "'Hail, Mary, the Mother of Science Fiction' Popular Fictionalisations of Mary Wollstonecraft Shelley in film and television, 1935–2018," *Science Fiction Film and Television* 11, no. 2 (2018): 233.

of parallel discussions over galvanism and criminality.[56] The pursuit of the secrets of life in the medical sciences mirrored the search for the origins of difference in natural history. Fundamental to criminology in particular was the debate whether criminals were "born" or created through their environments.[57] Whether or not Shelley intended to remark on these debates, the criminal body as somehow contaminated or physically inferior has lived on in the public imagination surrounding her tale in part because of the author's employment of physiognomy, a visual system that would transform the text into a "speaking picture" of general Otherness.

While Frankenstein's creation may have started out as an abstraction on which to project societal fears, people are not. The nineteenth century's inscribing of Blackness onto the Creature cannot be divorced from the real-world injustices of ma®king an innocent as criminal. Like the Creature, those who are subjected to this physiognomic profiling are often subsequently denied the ability to testify—and at the very least speak—for themselves to a neutral audience. As inevitably more narratives, scholarships and even aesthetics emerge from the prolific text that is *Frankenstein*, it is important to consider the frameworks from which such a story was produced not only for how it produces entertainment but for how it may re-produce stereotypes. With this chapter, I hope to encourage a crucial conversation on the ways in which novels, film productions and other sources of entertainment continue to use physiognomy as a discriminatory visualization device that often speaks in favour of racist ideologies.

Bibliography

Alexander, Meena. *Women in Romanticism*. Basingstoke and London: Macmillan, 1989.

Andres, Sophia. "Narrative Challenges to Visual, Gendered Boundaries: Mary Shelley and Henry Fuseli." *Journal of Narrative Theory* 31, 3 (Fall 2001): 257-82.

Belting, Hans. *Face and Mask: A Double History*. Princeton: Princeton University Press, 2017.

Browne, Simone. *Dark Matters: On the Surveillance of Blackness*. Durham: Duke University Press, 2015.

---

[56] For just a few of the most recent, see Yvette Koepke, "Lessons from Frankenstein: Narrative Myth as Ethical Model," *Medical Humanities* 45 (2019): 27-36; Wang, *Frankenstein in Theory*; Sharon Ruston, *The Science of Life and Death in Frankenstein* (Oxford, UK: Bodleian Library Publishing, 2021).

[57] Tarlow and Lowman, *Harnessing the Power of the Criminal Corpse*, 18.

Chico, Tita. *The Experimental Imagination: Literary Knowledge and Science in the British Enlightenment.* Stanford: Stanford University Press, 2018.

Christie, William. "The Critical Metamorphoses of Mary Shelley's Frankenstein." *Sydney Studies in English* 25 no. 1991 (1991): 1-34.

de Bruin-Molé, Megen. "'Hail, Mary, the Mother of Science Fiction' Popular Fictionalisations of Mary Wollstonecraft Shelley in Film and Television, 1935–2018." *Science Fiction Film and Television* 11, no. 2 (2018): 233–55.

Darwin, Charles. *The Descent of Man.* London: John Murray, 1871.

—. *Expressions of Emotions in Man and Animals.* London: John Murray, 1872.

Deleuze, Gilles and Félix Guattari. *A Thousand Plateaus: Capitalism and Schizophrenia.* London: Athlone Press, 1988.

Fanon, Frantz. *The Wretched of the Earth.* Translated by Richard Philcox. New York: Grove Press, 2004.

—. *Black Skin, White Masks.* Translated by Charles Lam Markmann. London: Pluto Press, 2008. Originally published in French, Paris: Editions du Seuil, 1952. First published in English translation by Charles Lam Markmann, New York: Grove Press, 1967; this translation originally published in England, London: Pluto Press, 1986.

Foucault, Michel. *Discipline and Punish: The Birth of the Prison.* Translated by Alan Sheridan. New York: Vintage Books, 1995.

Galton, Francis. *Inquiries into Human Faculty and its Development.* Edited by Gavan Tredoux. J.M. Dent & Co, 1907.

Gilbert, Sandra A., and Susan Gubar. *The Madwoman in the Attic: The Woman Writer and the Nineteenth-Century Literary Imagination.* New Haven and London: Yale University Press, 1979.

Hamilton, Peter, and Roger Hargreaves. *The Beautiful and the Damned: The Creation of Identity in Nineteenth-Century Photography.* London: National Portrait Gallery, 2001.

Hurley, Kelly. *The Gothic Body: Sexuality, Materialism, and Degeneration at the Fin De Siècle.* Cambridge: Cambridge University Press, 1996.

Hurren, Elizabeth T. *Dissecting the Criminal Corpse: Staging Post-Execution Punishment in Early Modern England.* New York: Palgrave Macmillan, 2016.

Koepke, Yvette. "Lessons from Frankenstein: Narrative Myth as Ethical Model." *Medical Humanities* 45 (2019): 27-36.

Labriola, Patrick. "Edgar Allan Poe and E. T. A. Hoffmann: The Double in "William Wilson" and *The Devil's Elixirs*," *The International Fiction Review* 29 (2002).

Lavater, Johann Caspar. *Essays on Physiognomy Designed to Promote the Knowledge and the Love of Mankind.* John Murray, H. Hunter, and T. Holloway, 1792.

Malchow, H. L. "Frankenstein's Monster and Images of Race in Nineteenth-Century Britain." *Past & Present*, 139 (May 1993): 90-130.

Mallonee, Laura C. "Portraits of Prisoners in Gold Leaf and Tar." *Hyperallergic*, March 2nd, 2015. https://hyperallergic.com/183665/portraits-of-prisoners-in-gold-leaf-and-tar/.

Matthew Patricia A." 'A daemon whom I had myself created': Race, Frankenstein and Monstering," in Wang, *Frankenstein in Theory A Critical Anatomy.* New York: Bloomsbury Academic, 2021.

McKittrick, Katherine. "(Zong) Bad Made Measure." In *Dear Science and Other Stories*. Durham: Duke University Press, 2021.

Newman, James R. "Francis Galton." *Scientific American* 190, no. 1 (1954): 72–77.

O'Flynn, Paul. "Production and Reproduction: The Case of Frankenstein." *Literature and History*, ix (1983), 194-213.

Percival, Melissa. *The Appearance of Character: Physiognomy and Facial Expression Eighteenth-Century France.* Leeds: W.S. Many for the Modern Humanities Research Association, 1999.

Percival, Melissa, and Graeme Tyler. *Physiognomy in Profile: Lavater's Impact on European Culture.* Newark: University of Delaware Press, 2005.

Ruston, Sharon. *The Science of Life and Death in Frankenstein.* Oxford, UK: Bodleian Library Publishing, 2021.

Sekula, Allan. "The Body and the Archive." *The MIT Press* 39, no. October (Winter 1986): 3-64.

Shelley, Mary. *Frankenstein or the Modern Prometheus.* Edited by Maurice Hindle. London: Penguin Books, 2003. Originally published London: Lackington, Hughes, Harding, Mayor and Jones, 1818.

St Clair, William. *The Godwins and the Shelleys: The Biography of a Family*. London: Faber and Faber, 1989.

Tarlow, Sarah and Emma Battell Lowman. *Harnessing the Power of the Criminal Corpse.* New York: Palgrave Macmillan, 2018.

—. "The Landscape of the Gibbet." *Landscape History* 36, no. 1 (2015): 71-88

Rei Terada, "Blackness and Anthropogenesis in *Frankenstein*," in *Frankenstein in Theory: A Critical Anatomy.* Edited by Orrin Wang (New York: Bloomsbury Academic, 2021)

Wang, Orrin N.C. *Frankenstein in Theory: A Critical Anatomy.* New York: Bloomsbury Academic, 2021.

Wheeler, Roxann. *The Complexion of Race: Categories of Difference in Eighteenth-Century British Culture.* Philadelphia: University of Pennsylvania Press, 2000.

CHAPTER THREE

THE GOTHIC NOVEL AND GROTESQUE ART: E. T. A. HOFFMANN'S *THE DEVIL'S ELIXIR*

HANNAH-FREYA BLAKE

In the nineteenth century, the doppelgänger and dual self takes a psychological turn in which the identification of the narrator/protagonist as the "original" version of the double (or, in some cases, multiple avatars) becomes an arbitrary assignment. Thanks to James Hogg's *The Private Confessions and Memoirs of a Justified Sinner* (1824), Edgar Allan Poe's short story "William Wilson" (1839), and Robert Louis Stevenson's *Strange Case of Dr Jekyll and Mr Hyde* (1886), the doppelgänger and dual-personality tropes of the Gothic are now a staple of uncanny Gothic horror, coercing characters and readers alike to confront the instabilities of reality and the fragmentation of selfhood in the modern world.[1] The power of horror in these texts moves from supernatural spectacle to confrontation with the uncanny spectre-self, a mirror-maze confusion divested of the absolute supernatural and replaced by unsettling ambiguity. Hoffmann's *The Devil's Elixir*, initially published in 1815 and later translated into English in 1824, is one of the first to explore this effect.[2] Hoffmann achieves this principally by combining the doppelgänger with the grotesque.

This chapter explores the relationship between the Gothic and the grotesque, demonstrated through a close analysis of E. T. A. Hoffmann's *The Devil's Elixir* (1815). From the frescos unearthed in fifteenth-century Rome, the paintings of the temptations of St Anthony, to the Theatre of the Grotesque in the early twentieth century, the grotesque has principally been

---

[1] James Hogg, *The Private Memoirs and Confessions of a Justified Sinner* (1824; reis. Oxford: Oxford World Classics, 2010). Edgar Allan Poe, "William Wilson" in *The Fall of the House of Usher and Other Writings* (1839; reis., Oxford: Penguin Classics, 2003. Robert Louis Stevenson, *The Strange Case of Dr Jekyll and Mr Hyde.* (1886; reis., London: Penguin Classics, 2003).

[2] E. T. A. Hoffmann, *The Devil's Elixir (*London: Blackwood, 1824). https://openlibrary.org/books/OL6980951M/The_devil's_elixir.

a visual art form. As such, attention is given to the ways in which Hoffmann applies the principles of the grotesque image to Gothic narrative, and the results of this aesthetic interchange.

Mikhail Bakhtin's concept of the carnivalesque will be used to assess the ways in which *The Devil's Elixir* can be regarded a grotesque novel, alongside Maximillian Novak's view that the plot of the Gothic novel, if it is to be recognised as grotesque, should be "a series of intertwined stories held together by some loose unifying pattern".[3] It will be argued that the multiple layers of narrative and doppelgängers contribute to the grotesque effect, transforming the "loose unifying pattern" of grotesque art into Gothic text.

Both the Gothic and the grotesque, as will be shown, have a peculiar propensity to eschew clear definition or categorisation, exploring and exposing the flux of the in-between. Through the exploration of the intersections between narrative and image, it becomes apparent that the affinity between the Gothic and grotesque is multifaceted. Their incongruous parts not only evoke fright and disgust, but also inspire laughter and humour, which is considered the most significant aspect of the affinity between the grotesque and Gothic that this chapter explores. In addressing the role of humour in Hoffmann's novel, this chapter endorses, and advances, Avril Horner and Sue Zlosnik's proposition that the Gothic has a "comic turn".[4] In the example of *The Devil's Elixir*, this comic turn is principally the result of the grotesque.

Mikhail Bakhtin's understanding of the grotesque develops from his discussion of carnival, which suspends hierarchy and all its attendant privileges and prohibitions, enabling the breakdown of boundaries to celebrate the material body; every member of society is brought to the same level. In what he calls "grotesque realism", Bakhtin suggests that the essential principle is "degradation [...] the lowering of all that is high, spiritual, ideal, abstract; it is a transfer to the material level, to the sphere of earth and body".[5] Justin Edwards and Rune Grauland further suppose that "the grotesque offers a creative force for conceptualizing the indeterminate", generating "discombobulating juxtapositions" and

---

[3] Maximillian E. Novak, "Gothic Fiction and the Grotesque," *Novel: A Forum on Fiction* 13 (1979): 54.

[4] Avril Horner and Sue Zlosnik, *Gothic and the Comic Turn* (Hampshire: Palgrave Macmillan UK, 2005).

[5] Mikhail Baktin, *Rabelais and His World*, trans. Hélène Iswolsky (Bloomington and Indianapolis: Indiana University Press, 1984), 9.

"conflicting possibilities, images and figures".[6] Grotesque art is particularly concerned with the abnormal body, made up of exaggerated and deformed features, sometimes mixed with non-human body parts—a body that is incoherent as a whole, confusing the human with the bestial, positioning the body in flux between states. The grotesque body, incomplete and deformed, ultimately "forces us to question what it means to be human".[7]

The grotesque, then, exposes the falsity, and even the absurdity, of boundaries, binaries, and hierarchies. Philip Thomson describes the grotesque as "the unresolved clash of incompatibles", while Geoffrey Harpham explains that the grotesque does not necessarily emerge from the components of an image, but rather because "it refuses to be taken in whole because it embodies a confusion of type".[8] Similarly, the Gothic notoriously eschews boundaries and defies generic classification; it toys with uncertainty, with collisions between binary opposites—between life and death, reality and fantasy, sanity and insanity. David Punter, in a monograph collating his body of work on the Gothic over a sixteen-year period, suggests that the genre is "above all a literature of transgression", an "adolescent literature, the literature of the 'in-between'" in which "there is always a concomitant move to uncover what may be repressed, subdued, cast into the shadows".[9] Both the Gothic and grotesque, therefore, have a peculiar propensity to eschew clear definition or categorisation, exploring and exposing the flux of the in-between.

Such similarities lead Maxmillian Novak to propose that the Gothic and the grotesque are synonymous in nature, suggesting that "[t]he skeleton with its combination of deathly terror and horrible grin is the essence of the grotesque and the essence of the Gothic".[10] Victor Sage echoes this image of the "horrible grin" in his discussion of the role of comedy and farce in the Gothic, in which he unmasks the "grin of the skull beneath the skin" (a phrase borrowed from T. S. Eliot's 1918 poem, "Whispers of Immortality").[11] Sage in particular analyses Bram Stoker's *Dracula* (1897)

---

[6] Justin D. Edwards and Rune Graulund, *Grotesque* (Oxford: Routledge, 2013), 3.

[7] Edwards and Graulund, *Grotesque*, 3.

[8] Philip Thomson, *The Grotesque* (London: Methuen & Co Ltd, 1972), 27. Geoffrey Harpham, *On the Grotesque: Strategies of Contradiction in Art and Literature* (New Jersey: Princeton University Press, 1982), 6.

[9] David Punter, *The Gothic Condition: Terror, History and the Psyche* (Cardiff: University of Wales Press, 2016), 2-3.

[10] Novak, "Gothic Fiction and the Grotesque," 51.

[11] Victor Sage, "Gothic Laughter: Farce and Horror in Five Texts," in Allan Lloyd Smith and Victor Sage, eds., *Gothick Origins and Innovations* (Amsterdam: Rodophi, 1994), 198.

which, for Sage, best demonstrates "the peculiarly self-conscious complexities of humour which attach themselves to the gothic tradition" (197). Sage focuses on Van Helsing's philosophical musings on "King Laugh", who makes everyone "dance to the tune he play", regardless of the circumstance; "[b]leeding hearts", the German Doctor continues, "and dry bones of the churchyard, and tears that burn as they fall—all dance together to the music that he make with that smileless mouth of him".[12] This scene presents gallows humour, imagining death as a merry dancer and recalling the medieval *danse macabre*. See fig. 3.1. Sage, however, further equates "King Laugh" with "King Death", a memento mori, whereby "true laughter [...] is an enactment of true death".[13] The Gothic, like the grotesque, brings opposing sentiments like laughter and death in a disturbing mix.

For modern humour theorist Paul Lewis, incongruity is at the heart of both horror and humour. In another early discussion of the Gothic and comic not dedicated solely to Gothic parodies, Lewis argues that "the very incongruities that can shock or frighten us can also, seen from a slightly different vantage point, or after a moment's consideration, make us laugh".[14] If laughter can be a response to what is amusing as well as to what is unsettling, the unifying element is incongruity. James Beattie, in his essay "On Laughter and Ludicrous Composition" (1776), proposed that laughter

arises from the view of two or more inconsistent, unsuitable, or incongruous parts or circumstances, considered as united in one complex object or assemblage, as acquiring a sort of mutual relation from the peculiar manner in which the mind takes notice of them.[15]

---

[12] Bram Stoker, *Dracula* (Oxford: Oxford University Press, 2008), 175.

[13] Sage, "Gothic Laughter," 198.

[14] Paul Lewis, *Comic Effects: Interdisciplinary Approaches to Humor in Literature* (New York: State University of New York Press, 1989), 113.

[15] James Beattie, "On Laughter, and Ludicrous Composition," in James Beattie, *Essays* (Edinburgh: 1777), 347.
https://www.google.co.uk/books/edition/Essays_On_Poetry_and_Music_as_They_Affec/q_heAAAAcAAJ?hl=en&gbpv=0

Figure 3.1. Michael Wolgemut, from *The Dance of Death* (1493). Folio CCLXI recto from Hartman Schedel, *Chronicle of the World* (Nuremberg, 1493). Wikimedia Commons. Public domain.

Beattie recognises that the "inconsistent, unsuitable, or incongruous parts" which inspire laughter are culturally variable, and further appreciates that "unsuitable" subjects, including subjects of which society morally disapproves, can also be amusing. This idea of incongruous clashes is taken up by Horner and Zlosnik in *Gothic and the Comic Turn*, the sole extended monograph on the Gothic and the comic. Their argument is that the Gothic's "tendency to hybridity" creates "incongruity [that] opens up the possibility of a comic turn in the presence of horror or terror".[16] Further, they propose that humour in the Gothic should be seen to function on a spectrum:

> it is perhaps best to think of Gothic writing as a spectrum that, at one end, produces horror-writing containing moments of comic hysteria or relief and, at the other, works in which there are clear signals that nothing is to be taken seriously (15).

---

[16] Horner and Zlosnik, *Gothic and the Comic Turn*, 17.

In their view, there are distinctions between moments of "comic hysteria or relief" from the onslaught of terror and other instances in which the intention to be comical is made clear. For Horner and Zlosnik, the hybrid roots of the Gothic in both the comic and the tragic opens up the possibility for Gothic characteristics to be turned to comic effect. Understanding the Gothic to be part of a "complex and popular cultural response to modernity", both the horror and humour of the mode gesture toward "the fragmented condition of the modern subject", in which the comic turn offers a "position of detachment and scepticism towards such cultural nostalgia" (3). The mode's mixed nature, wavering between extremes and shirking the confinement of generic boundaries, is part of this uncertainty of facing the modern world. The sinister elements of the Gothic, therefore, "is easily converted to the comic flamboyance of the grotesque as excess, particularly during periods of rapid change resulting in a sense of instability and flux" (17).

The incongruous effects of the Gothic which inspire conflicting responses of fright and humour is comparable to the equally conflicting effects of the grotesque. "The classic reaction to the grotesque", Thomson explains, is "the experience of amusement and disgust, laughter and horror, mirth and revulsion, simultaneously".[17] Reviewers of *The Devil's Elixir* in 1824 commented similarly on this mixture of responses, highlighting both its horror and humour. The reviewer for *Blackwood's Edinburgh Magazine* highly favoured the horrific and comic aspects of *The Devil's Elixir*, admiring Hoffmann's blend of the "exquisitely ludicrous" with the "haunted hero [...] without in the smallest degree weakening the horrors".[18] *The Literary Chronicle* also suggests that "some of his horrors are relieved by an occasionally comic scene or character", having rendered horror which, in their view, was no longer as popular as it was, "subservient to a more serious purpose".[19] Hoffmann's novel, on the other hand, has such absurd scenes of madness that the comic, which is tied to the affect of the grotesque, is irrefutable.

The Devil's Elixir is linked with the grotesque from the outset through the elixir itself. The translator's preface from Blackwood's 1824 edition associates *The Devil's Elixir* with "a grotesque and half-ironical, half-serious sketch", and compares the irregular mix of the novel to the works of Jacques Callot, a seventeenth-century French printmaker who dabbled in

---

[17] Thomson, *The Grotesque*, 24.
[18] "The Devil's Elixir", *Blackwood's Edinburgh Magazine*, July 1824, 57.
[19] "Review of New Books," *Literary Chronicle and Weekly Review*, September 1824, 561.

caricature and the grotesque—including a depiction of the temptations of St Anthony. See fig. 3.2. The story of St Anthony is popular among many artists of the grotesque in the late Middle Ages, including in works by Martin Schöngauer (c. 1470), Hieronymus Bosch (c. 1505), and Mathias Grünewald (1512-16). Callot's influence on Hoffmann's writing is further evident in his first collection of tales, *Fantasiestücke in Callots Manier* (1814), the first two volumes of which were prefaced by German Romantic Jean Paul.[20]

The plot is tricky to follow, with a dizzying number of doppelgängers described by an unreliable narrator uncertain of his own sanity as he reflects on his life and its incredible events. This difficulty was observed by critics at the time; a writer for *The Literary Chronicle* and *Weekly Review*, for example, complained that "the story is as incoherent as it is extraordinary [...] we almost despair of making anything like a story out of the work".[21] A review in *The Monthly Miscellany* similarly labels the novel "a wild, aimless, bewildering romance, abounding with all that is extravagant, absurd, and impossible".[22] This confusion is, arguably, a result of Hoffmann's dedication to the grotesque. There are numerous digressive episodes, interactions with madmen, and near misses before the plot repeats, as if compulsively, scenes of temptation overlooked by the frightening figure of the painter who haunts him throughout the novel. The doubles themselves are part of this "loose unifying pattern", as there are more doppelgängers than Medardus and his brother.

---

[20] E. T. A. Hoffman, *Fantasiestücke in Callots Manier* [Fantasy pieces in Callot's Manner] (Bamberg: Kunz, 1814).

[21] "Review of New Books," 563.

[22] "Review of New Publications", *Monthly Miscellany*, August 1824, 79.

Figure 3.2. Jacques Callot, *Temptation of St. Anthony*, first version, ca. 1616-1617. Etching sheet trimmed to plate: 37 x 49.3 cm. (14 9/16 x 19 7/16 in.) Bequest of Junius S. Morgan, Class of 1888. Wikimedia Commons. Public domain.

This "confusion of type" and "loose unifying pattern" is part of what constitutes the novel as the grotesque, and the doppelgänger plays a key part. It was translated and published the same year as James Hogg's *The Private Confessions and Memoirs of a Justified Sinner* (1824), and *The Monthly Miscellany* compares the two with some confusion, recognising that in both "the hero has his double or demon" but, "whether the numerous crimes that are perpetrated by the hero, or the demon", the author "does not appear to know".[23] The reviewer considers the ambiguity to be an error of Hogg's (and Hoffmann's) clarity, rather than the uncanny indistinctness of the doppelgänger effect. Which is the doppelgänger, and whether or not they are even real, is merely a matter of perspective, as *The Devil's Elixir* demonstrates. Medardus wavers between certainty of his own status as "host" and being driven to madness by the thought that he might be his own double, a doubt that seemingly begins at the first sight of the other.

---

[23] "Review of New Publications," 82.

Yet, in the scheme of the plot, the first person to assume the identity of the other is Medardus himself. After a young man (Victorin) falls over the edge of a cliff—which may or may not have been the fault of the monk—Medardus takes up the man's sword and hat, leading his servant to mistake him for Victorin in disguise. Rather than correcting the servant's mistake, Medardus is overtaken by "[a]n inward irresistible impulse to act the part of the deceased Count".[24] Effectively, while in the castle, Medardus peforms a double bluff, playing the part of a man who pretends to be Medardus himself. The repeated appearance of Victorin in the garb of a monk and his ludicrously insane behaviour points to the effect that Medardus as Victorin's double has had upon him, much in the way that Medardus's own madness reflects the effect of viewing himself in other doppelgängers.

The so-called original, or "host" in Andrew Webber's terms, converges with the double in doppelgänger narratives, blurring the boundaries between objective and subjective selfhood. The doppelgänger, Webber explains, is primarily visual in nature, whereby the "host" comes to see its "other self as another, as visual object [...] the subject may not so much have as actually be the Doppelgänger by seeing itself".[25] For example, while Medardus sleeps at the hunter's house to shelter from a storm, he dreams that he is disturbed by a "dark form" in whom he claims to have "recognised myself in the capuchin habit, with the beard and tonsure!".[26] Upon waking, "the abominable dream" becomes reality, as he "actually be[holds] at the table, with his back turned [...] a figure dressed in the capuchin habit!" (263).

The horror of the double is further demonstrated by their auditory effect, as Webber explains that the doppelgänger's speech "echoes, reiterates, distorts, parodies, dictates, impedes, and dumbfounds the subjective faculty of free speech".[27] This is best demonstrated by a scene in volume two when, held prisoner for murder, Medardus is once again haunted by his double in the habit of a monk. The sound of the double's voice, like his appearance, confuses Medardus's own surety that he is himself:

> Now, methought I recognised the voice as one that I had known before, but it was not then so broken and so stammering. Nay, with a chill shivering of horror, I almost began to think there was something in the accents that I now heard, resembling the tones of my own voice, and involuntarily, as if I

[24] Hoffmann, *Devil's Elixir*, 106.
[25] Andrew Webber, *The Doppelgänger: Double Visions in German Literature* (Oxford: Oxford University Press, 1996), 3.
[26] Hoffmann, *Devil's Elixir*, 261.
[27] Webber, *Doppelgänger*, 3.

wished to try whether this were really so, I stammered, in imitation, "Me-dar-dus!—Me-dar-dus!"[28]

These qualities of confusion and hallucination typically invite a psychological reading of the double, particularly regarding the uncanny. Of course, Freud used Hoffmann's tale "The Sandman" to explore his theories of the unheimlich, establishing an association between Hoffmann's works and psychoanalysis. Doppelgänger narratives, for both Patrick Labriola and Amit Marcus, explore confrontations with the uncanny as projections of repressed anxieties; the double is the result of fragmented selfhood, the consequence of social restrictions made upon natural impulses. In Romantic literature, according to Marcus, the doubles are analogous with contrary impulses to destroy and to create. In *The Devil's Elixir*, the double is both internal, "a dissociative projection of psychic contents", and also external, "a separate and autonomous person"—it is both "a sign of self-fragmentation and its cause".[29] To be rid of the sign that ironically causes duality can only therefore be achieved by suicide, as in Edgar Allan Poe's "William Wilson" and Robert Louis Stevenson's later *Dr Jekyll and Mr Hyde*. However, as Labriola shows, Hoffmann's tale is unusual in that Medardus's encounters with his double enable him to undergo development and "to create a conscience and to reflect upon his actions by the end of the novel".[30]

While it might be tempting to draw on psychoanalysis to discuss the double figure manifestations of repressed anxieties and desires—as Labriola does—Bakhtin's principle of the grotesque body also gives insight into how the double may emerge and why it enables Medardus to repent. Bakhtin understands the grotesque as a material body that is "ever unfinished, ever creating", revealing its growth and excess during "copulation, pregnancy, childbirth, the throes of death, eating, drinking, or defecation".[31] It is at these moments that the "chain of genetic development", the principle of the grotesque body, becomes evident—what Bakhtin describes as "two links shown at the point where they enter into each other" (26). One of the points at which "the chain of genetic development" becomes evident includes

---

[28] Hoffmann, *Devil's Elixir*, 36.
[29] Marcus Amit, "Recycling of Doubles in Narrative Fiction of the Twentieth and Early Twenty-First Centuries," *Partial Answers: Journal of Literature and the History of Ideas* 11, no. 2 (2013): 194.
[30] Patrick Labriola, "Edgar Allan Poe and E. T. A. Hoffmann: The Double in 'William Wilson' and *The Devil's Elixirs*," *The International Fiction Review* 29 (2002):115.
[31] Bakhtin, *Rabelais*, 26.

drinking, where "two links" of the grotesque body "enter into each other" (26). In drinking the elixir, Medardus reveals the "two links" of his selfhood, conjuring the double—his brother—whose identity merges with own.

Primarily visual in nature, the likeness between Medardus and Victorin, his double, emphasises the physical, material characteristics of his body—the grotesque realism of his existence. Though he appears at times to be spectral in nature, that the double is his half-brother points to simultaneous states of spectrality and solidity, somewhere between being distinct from Medardus and being reliant on his existence. This blend of states is evident when Victorin emerges, as if from the dead, to confront Medardus at his castle:

> But, oh horrible sight! at that moment arose, and stood bodily before me, the hideous blood-stained and distorted figure of Victorin! Methought it was not I, but he, that had spoken the words in which I thought to triumph! At the first glance of this apparition, (whether real or imaginary,) my hair stood on end with horror (176).

Readers, especially English readers, may well have expected the return of Victorin's vengeful spirit at this point, as is typical of Gothic ghost stories in the era. However, Victorin "stood bodily"—solidly—before Medardus, "blood-stained and distorted" from his fall. Yet Medardus still refers to him as an "apparition", uncertain whether he is "real or imaginary", positioning Victorin between dead and undead, material and immaterial, a ghastly reminder of his own mortality. Further, as this quotation demonstrates, the sight of the double always has a physical effect on Medardus, again emphasising the grotesque relationship between the two. Here, his "hair stood on end with horror", whereas in other instances he collapses or, with repeated exposure, becomes increasingly gaunt and dishevelled in appearance.

The emphasis on visual horror is also mirrored by sexual and pictorial spectacle. As Webber explains, the narrative is one of "double vision", where Medardus's gaze is both "violating" and "violated" (191). Medardus's desire is bound to both being the observer and being observed; he experiences other instances of sexual pleasure when looking at objects while becoming an object under observation himself. Taken through an exhibition of paintings at a club he frequents, he is only temporarily inspired to repent by the portrait of the Abbess he so reveres, as he then sees the exact likeness of Aurelia. Gazing upon the picture, he "devoured the charms" of Aurelia's likeness from the "enchanted canvass [sic]" which "gleamed out in full splendour" and, though pondering whether her "childlike pious looks" accuse him of murdering her brother, is inspired only with a "malicious spirit of scorn and irony" (223). He only regrets that he had not made Aurelia his own the same night he had stabbed her brother, and so begins to formulate "a thousand plans" to obtain the object of his desire. No sooner does he make the resolution to pursue her, than he again encounters the painter—or so he believes.

Entering the club room, he "perceived at once [...] the stranger", yet "his countenance was not turned towards me" (227). Following this, "[a] conviction of the truth immediately flashed on [his] mind" that this was the same "horrible Unknown" who had stared at him in the church and followed his every step since (227). Not having seen the man's face, his own "conviction of truth" determines that the stranger is the same man; readers are, once more, left to doubt Medardus's reliability. This unreliability, however, also shows that Medardus's voyeurism turns to exhibitionism, returning to the "double vision" in which pleasure and anxiety simultaneously involve "violating" and being "violated".

If the double emerges from the grotesque when Medardus drinks from the elixir, it is not so much the revelation of Medardus's repressed anxieties and desires that causes horror, as Labriola would have it, but the recognition of himself as grotesque. The carnival, home of the grotesque, once "celebrated temporary liberation from [...] the established order" and "marked the suspension of hierarchical rank, privileges, norms, and prohibitions".[32] The festivities this engenders are, however, horrifying to Medardus's sense of pride: his hubris cannot tolerate the suspension of hierarchy, not while he seeks to be at the pinnacle of society. Although he initially drinks the elixir to restore his strength, having been struck down in fright by the appearance of the painter at the church, the effect is so exhilarating that he hopes also to "have once more the power of obtaining that noblest of earthly supremacies, an empire over the minds of others!" (75). This ambition is promptly achieved as, like Lewis's Ambrosio, he speaks so "ardently" and "impressively" that his audience "were confounded" (78). However, this is not enough to satisfy his inexhaustible desire, and he ventures out into the world where his pursuits become increasingly depraved. In seeking to aggrandize himself by taking the elixir, ironically the opposite takes effect, as he becomes increasingly debased, brought low, dragged down into the material and carnal world.

It is as a result of this debasement that his sense of self fractures, and with it his perception of reality. Hoffmann's novel has such absurd scenes of madness that the comic, which is tied to the effect of the grotesque, is irrefutable. Bakhtin recognised Hoffmann's works, among other German

---

[32] Bakhtin, *Rabelais*, 9.

Romanticists and Sturm und Drang tales, as "perhaps the most powerful and original development" in what he terms the "new Grotesque" (37). Bakhtin identifies a shift in the madness of the folk carnival by the Romantic era; madness in the new grotesque "acquires a somber, tragic aspect of individual isolation", losing the "festive" madness that was once "a gay parody of official reason, of the narrow seriousness of official 'truth' " (39).

Instead, in *The Devil's Elixir*, madness falters in the attempt to parody the truth by ironically and impulsively revealing the truth. For example, Pietro Belcampo, possibly the most absurd madman in the narrative, is nevertheless astute in his estimations that Medardus is a monk. Following the murder of Hermogen, Aurelia's brother, Medardus needs to disguise himself and, fortunately, finds himself in the company of the eccentric hairdresser. Belcampo is expertly able to parody Medardus when he compares his movements to that of a monk, ironically stumbling on the truth. Complaining that Medardus has "not resigned himself to his natural character", Belcampo struggles to "amalgamate together all the contradictions and conflicts in [Medardus's] character and gestures" and identifies "something that directly points at monachism" (201). Belcampo goes on to mockingly recite "[e]x profundis clamavi ad te, Domine. Oremus. Et in omnia secula seculorum!" with expert mimicry, "imitating, at the same time, to the very life, the postures and gesture of a monk" (202). Yet no sooner has Belcampo mockingly recited the prayer than he changes posture, assuming "a proud look of defiance", and declaring, "I am more wealthy, more wise, prudent, and intelligent, than all of ye, ye blind moles!" (202). This humorous hubris parodies Medardus's own triumphant pride when he took to the altar to preach.

Belcampo is not merely a parody of Medardus in these performances; he is another avatar of Medardus himself. The doppelgänger, Webber argues, is "an inveterate performer of identity" and "could be said to represent the performative character of the subject".[33] In mimicking Medardus's monkish movements, Belcampo demonstrates the performativity of his rituals and habits, illustrating the falsity of his holy devotions. Even Medardus admits that "[i]mperfect and ridiculous as the man's *expressions* were, yet there was so much home truth in his remarks" (201, original italics).

His appearance is ridiculous too, making the comic component of the grotesque evident. Belcampo is described in terms reminiscent of the harlequinade character of commedia dell'arte, complete with a "pointed red nose—a pair of glistening eyes—lips drawn upwards into an exquisite grin

---

[33] Webber, *The Doppelgänger*, 3.

[...] and, above all this, a high powdered toupee" (95). He wears "a large ostentatious frill, a fiery-red waistcoat [and] a frock-coat, which in some places was too narrow, in others too wide; of course [it] did not fit anywhere!" (95). Belcampo also behaves as bizarrely as he looks, cutting the monk's hair with "the most absurd writhing, twisting, grimaces, and extravagant discourse", alternately appearing angered and happy, as at one moment "he looked cross and gloomy—now smiled—anon stamped and clenched his fist—then smiled again" until Medardus cannot keep himself from laughing (202).

As another version of Medardus in all but appearance, Belcampo is the only character to witness the painter and share Medardus's belief that he is both real and of supernatural origin. In fact, it is Belcampo who plants the seed that he is "Ahasuerus, the Wandering Jew, or Bertram de Bornis, or Mephistopheles, or Benvenuto Cellini, or Judas Iscariot; in short, a wicked revenant" (239). The possibilities of what the painter might be, the repetitive "or", reflects Medardus's own numerous identities. At this point in the novel, Medardus himself has adopted several names; born Franciscus, he took the name Medardus when he became officiated, and later declared himself to be St Anthony in a moment of delusional grandeur; following this, when he ventures out into the world, he takes on the identity of Victorin; with Belcampo, he assumes the name Leonard, recalling his former abbot's name, Leonardus.

As if this were not confusing enough, Belcampo is, in fact, another double; he commonly speaks in third person, referring to himself as Belcampo, but also relates conversations with himself under the name Peter Fairfield. He explains to Medardus that "there is an infamous wicked fellow that lurks concealed within me, and says, 'Peter Fairfield, be no longer an ass, and believe that thou existest; for I am properly thou'" (242).

Belcampo is an example of what Novak considers the "comic grotesque", such as the harlequin figure, involving the "clowning of the servants and the disturbing psychological involvement of their masters", which is more likely to arouse laughter than disgust, the latter, in his view, being the grotesque in its "proper sense".[34] Though other theorists of the grotesque do not propose such a distinction, the difference between "comic" and "proper" grotesque—between laughter and disgust—could easily be understood on a spectrum, in much the same way Horner and Zlosnik regard the comic and the Gothic.

Hoffmann not only achieves this through the complexity of his own narrative structure, but also by establishing a textual dialogue between *The*

---

[34] Novak, "Gothic Fiction and the Grotesque," 58.

Devil's Elixir and Matthew Lewis's *The Monk* (1796).[35] Though critics have long remarked that *The Monk* is one of the sources for Hoffmann's novel, discussions of the novels are generally focussed on textual comparisons. For example, Patrick Labriola suggests that Hoffmann's monk Medardus produces his own double in order "to live out the sexual fantasies and need for authority that he has repressed as a monk", suggesting that this need for power is first expressed by preaching to an awe-struck crowd, much like Lewis's own monk Ambrosio.[36] William Crisman further argues that Hoffmann "works to translate and make patent the narrative that he sees latent in *The Monk*" in *The Devil's Elixir* and the short story "Councilor Krespel"; this latent content, according to Crisman, is the implicit father-daughter attraction between Ambrosio (as Holy Father) and Antonia, which is again repeated in the attraction between Medardus and Aurelia.[37]

Aurelia even compares herself to Antonia when reading *The Monk* among her brother's romances. Though Hoffmann does not name the novel directly, the description of the tale is unmistakeable, as Aurelia summarises it as "the history of a monk, who, being overcome by temptations of the devil, renounced his vows, and fell in love with a young lady, who in consequence perished miserably" (122). She admits to reading the romance "with avidity", confessing that "though the lessons that it contained might have expected to open [her] eyes to the dangers which [she] was drawing on [herself]", she could not stop her own compulsive interest in Medardus (122). This is to be her downfall, as Medardus comes to kill her in a moment of madness, in a similar state of "reckless cruelty" as Ambrosio when he kills Antonia, both monks suddenly being "repulsed" by the object of their desires upon finally obtaining them (284). By making such clear intertextual references, Hoffmann arguably positions *The Devil's Elixir* as a doppelgänger narrative—or perhaps it is the other way round.

Conclusion

E. T. A. Hoffmann's *The Devil's Elixir* is a complex novel of grotesque proportions. Novak's argument that there ought to be "a series of intertwined stories held together by some loose unifying pattern" for a Gothic novel to be considered grotesque is achieved by the multiple layers of plot, intertwining stories, and a dizzying number of doppelgängers to add

---

[35] Matthew Lewis, *The Monk* (1796; reis. Oxford: Oxford University Press, 2008).
[36] Labriola, "Edgar Allan Poe and E. T. A. Hoffmann": 72.
[37] William Crisman, "Romanticism Repays Gothicism: E.T.A. Hoffmann's 'Councilor Krespel' as a Recovery of Matthew G. Lewis's *The Monk*," *Comparative Literature Studies* 40, no. 3 (2003): 315.

to the confusion; the novel textually mimics the confusion of the grotesque form. With the abundance of doppelgängers in *The Devil's Elixir*, it might even be said that Hoffmann's allusions to *The Monk* position his text not as a parodic response, but rather as a double.

Through the numerous identities and disguises Medardus assumes, the confusion of doppelgängers and madmen, Hoffmann expertly blends horror with the comic. Both the Gothic and grotesque share an ambivalence and resistance to clear boundaries, exploring instead the liminal spaces of the in-between, the "discombobulating juxtapositions", and the incongruous. This aspect of incongruity lends itself to theories of laughter, which views laughter as a result of the recognition that disparate parts have been mutually related. Harpham's description of the grotesque as a "confusion of type", incongruity is linked to theories of the grotesque as much as it is to the Gothic.

Hoffmann used the comic potential of the grotesque to question the very nature of selfhood. His use of the grotesque and the double advances the comic potential of the Gothic into the realm of the absurd with characters like Belcampo, whose harlequinade characteristics parody Medardus and draw attention to the performativity of his own nature. Other avatars of Medardus are less comical, destabilising both his sense of selfhood and the narrative itself. Just as Horner and Zlosnik suggest of the Gothic and comic, I would argue that the grotesque also functions on a spectrum, moving between moments of repulsion and horror, and of disgust and humour.

Applying Bakhtin's understanding that the essential characteristic of the grotesque is "degradation [...] the lowering of all that is high, spiritual, ideal, abstract; it is a transfer to the material level, to the sphere of earth and body", Hoffmann uses the grotesque in less celebratory terms than the carnival once had. Rather, with the use of the double and the comic both, an opportunity for sombre reflection presents itself. Unlike other doppelgänger narratives which typically end in suicide, Medardus lives on to repent his sins. Hoffmann demonstrates that the grotesque and its comic potential have a role to play in reminding us of our place in the world, and leads me to a final, fitting thought upon the role of comedy made by Howard Jacobson:

> If comedy, in all its changing shapes, has one overriding preoccupation, it is this: that we resemble beasts more closely than we resemble gods, and that we make fools of ourselves the moment we forget it.[38]

---

[38] Howard Jacobson, *Seriously Funny: From the Ridiculous to the Sublime* (London: Penguin Group, 1997), 2.

Bibliography

Anon. "The Devil's Elixir", *Blackwood's Edinburgh Magazine*, July 1824.
—. "Review of New Books", *Literary Chronicle and Weekly Review*, September 1824.
—. "Review of New Publications", *Monthly Miscellany*, August 1824.
Bakhtin, Mikhail. *Rabelais and His World*. Translated by Hélène Iswolsky. Bloomington and Indianapolis: Indiana University Press, 1984.
Beattie, James. "On Laughter, and Ludicrous Composition." In James Beattie, *Essays*, 319-486. Edinburgh: William Creech, and London: E. & C. Dilly, 1777.
https://www.google.co.uk/books/edition/Essays_On_Poetry_and_Musi c_as_They_Affec/q_heAAAAcAAJ?hl=en&gbpv=0
—. *Essays*, 319-486. Edinburgh: William Creech, and London: E. & C. Dilly, 1777.
https://www.google.co.uk/books/edition/Essays_On_Poetry_and_Musi c_as_They_Affec/q_heAAAAcAAJ?hl=en&gbpv=0
Crisman, William. "Romanticism Repays Gothicism: E.T.A. Hoffmann's 'Councilor Krespel' as a Recovery of Matthew G. Lewis's The Monk." *Comparative Literature Studies* 40, no. 3 (2003): 311-328.
Edwards, Justin D., and Rune Graulund. *Grotesque*. Oxford: Routledge, 2013.
Harpham, Geoffrey Galt. *On the Grotesque: Strategies of Contradiction in Art and Literature*. New Jersey: Princeton University Press, 1982.
Hoffmann, E. T. A. *Fantasiestücke in Callots Manier* [Fantasy Pieces in Callot's Manner]. Bamberg: Kunz, 1814.
—. *The Devil's Elixir*. London: Blackwood, 1824.
https://openlibrary.org/books/OL6980951M/The_devil's_elixir.
Hogg, James. *The Private Memoirs and Confessions of a Justified Sinner*. Oxford: Oxford World Classics, 2010. Originally published London: Longman, Hurst, Rees, Orme, Brown, and Green, 1824.
Horner, Avril, and Sue Zlosnik. *Gothic and the Comic Turn*. Hampshire: Palgrave Macmillan UK, 2005).
Jacobson, Howard, *Seriously Funny: From the Ridiculous to the Sublime*. London: Penguin Group, 1997.
Labriola, Patrick. "Edgar Allan Poe and E. T. A. Hoffmann: The Double in "William Wilson" and *The Devil's Elixirs*." *The International Fiction Review* 29 (2002): 69-77.
Lewis, Matthew. *The Monk*. Oxford: Oxford University Press, 2008. Originally published Waterford: J. Saunders, 1796.

Lewis, Paul. *Comic Effects: Interdisciplinary Approaches to Humor in Literature.* New York: State University of New York Press, 1989.

Marcus, Amit. "Recycling of Doubles in Narrative Fiction of the Twentieth and Early Twenty-First Centuries." *Partial Answers: Journal of Literature and the History of Ideas* 11, no. 2 (2013): 187-217.

Novak, Maximillian E. "Gothic Fiction and the Grotesque." *Novel: A Forum on Fiction* 13 (1979): 50-67.

Poe, Edgar Allan. "William Wilson" in *The Fall of the House of Usher and Other Writings.* Oxford: Penguin Classics, 2003. Originally published in *Burton's Gentleman's Magazine*, October 1839, 205-2012.

Punter, David. *The Gothic Condition: Terror, History and the Psyche.* Cardiff: University of Wales Press, 2016.

Sage, Victor. "Gothic Laughter: Farce and Horror in Five Texts." In *Gothick Origins and Innovations*, edited by Allan Lloyd Smith and Victor Sage, 90-203. Amsterdam: Rodophi, 1994.

Stevenson, Robert Louis. *The Strange Case of Dr Jekyll and Mr Hyde and Other Tales of Terror.* London: Penguin Classics, 2003. First published as *Strange Case of Dr Jekyll and Mr Hyde* by Longman, Green & Co., 1886.

Stoker, Bram. *Dracula.* Oxford: Oxford University Press, 2008.

Thomson, Philip. *The Grotesque.* London: Methuen & Co Ltd, 1972.

Webber, Andrew J. *The Doppelgänger: Double Visions in German Literature.* Oxford: Oxford University Press, 1996.

CHAPTER FOUR

EKPHRASIS AND THE ILLUSION OF SELF IN OSCAR WILDE'S *THE PICTURE OF DORIAN GRAY*

ERKIN KIRYAMAN

Oscar Wilde's *The Picture of Dorian Gray*, which was published in *Lippincott's Monthly Magazine* in 1890 and published as a novel in 1891, narrates the story of Dorian Gray who falls in love with his own portrait painted by Basil Hallward, the artist-character in the novel.[1] See fig. 4.1. The story of the novel revolves around Dorian Gray's narcissistic desire to remain young and beautiful forever, and his wish is conveyed to the solid painting that takes on both his old age and his mortal being. The novel negotiates the concepts of art and of the artist, and is therefore exclusively acknowledged as a significant example of ekphrasis in the novel form.[2] Because of its representation of Dorian's painting and its effect on Dorian and the artist, the novel is categorised as ekphrastic. Ekphrasis, which is defined as "the verbal representation of visual representation,"[3] is at the centre of the novel since the novel is devoted to the story of a portrait painted by Basil and it also pins down the themes of art, artistic and aesthetic creation, and beauty. The representation of the painting holds a significance in the novel as it also represents Dorian's exploration of self. When Dorian falls in love with his painting as Narcissus does with his reflection in water, the painting is posited as a character, and therefore becomes a key to

---

[1] Oscar Wilde, *The Picture of Dorian Gray and Other Writings* (1891; reis., New York: Pocket Books, 2005).

[2] Özlem Uzundemir, in *İmgeyi Konuşturmak*, suggests that Wilde's novel can be regarded as the first notional ekphrastic example in the novel form because it represents a fictional work of art and constructs a fictional artist (93). Özlem Uzundemir. *İmgeyi Konuşturmak* (İstanbul: Boğaziçi Üniversitesi Yayınevi, 2010).

[3] James A. W. Heffernan, *Museum of Words: The Poetics of Ekphrasis from Homer to Ashbery* (London: The University of Chicago Press, 1993), 3.

discovering Dorian's changing self in the novel. The painting complicates Dorian's identity, and produces an illusion and a fantasy of his self-identity. This study argues that the portrait of Dorian functions as an illusionary version of his actual identity, and will analyse the ways in which text and image intersect in order to navigate Dorian's oscillating self.

Ekphrasis in *The Picture of Dorian Gray* stems from the idea of illusion since one of the characteristics of ekphrasis is that it stands for the actual image, and therefore, acts as an illusion. Murray Krieger, in *Ekphrasis: The Illusion of the Natural Sign* argues that "to look into ekphrasis is to look into the illusionary representation of the unrepresentable [...] representation is allowed to masquerade as a natural sign."[4] Krieger's point underlines that ekphrasis is also a "mirage" (xvi), as the words can suggest "the illusion of [...] an impossible picture" (xvi-xvii). The nature of ekphrasis is dependent on an image that is translated into a verbal form. Since painting is also a representation, and since ekphrasis recreates a represented form in a painting, this becomes a multi-layered representation. In *The Picture of Dorian Gray*, the artistic exchange between the character and the work of art is in fact an exchange of their own idiosyncratic characteristics. The mutual exchange positions the painting as subject and Dorian as object. At the very beginning of the novel, Basil represents Dorian's present form and sees him as a motive for his own art as he states that "He is all my art to me now."[5] The novel, with its verbal properties, mirrors the painting of Dorian, who experiences a kind of joy, and this moment reflects that "[t]he sense of his own beauty came on him like a revelation" (29). At this point, the novel is an example of "notional ekphrasis"[6] as it represents a fictional work of art rather than a genuine one created by an actual artist. The representations of Dorian in a painting, the painting in the novel, and the exchange between the painting and Dorian constitute a multidimensional model of representation. The exchange between Dorian and his represented image ends in the illusionary self as "[b]y exposing the artifice inherent in characterization even as it thematizes the exchange of influence between portrait and subject, [...] *The Picture of Dorian Gray* makes explicit the characterization inherent in constructions of identity."[7] That is why the

---

[4] Murray Krieger, *Ekphrasis: The Illusion of the Natural Sign* (London: The John Hopkins University Press, 1992), xv.

[5] Wilde, *Dorian Gray,* 14.

[6] John Hollander, "The Poetics of Ekphrasis," *Word & Image*, No. 4.1 (1988): 209. http://dx.doi.org/10.1080/02666286.1988.10436238.

[7] Kathryn Humphreys, "The Artistic Exchange: *Dorian Gray* at the *Sacred Fount*," *Texas Studies in Literature and Language*, No. 32.4 (Winter 1990): 527. https://www.jstor.org/stable/40754949.

painting is crucial, and thus characterised in the novel as "the central image of the story, Dorian's immutable portrait, as having become ultimately the whole book itself."[8] In other words, the novel with its verbal qualities is able to construct a painting of Dorian which stands as a pictorial narrative. In this sense, the dialogue between image and text signifies Dorian's construction of his identity which fluctuates between the real and the illusionary.

Henry states, "Some, day, when you are old and wrinkled and ugly, when thought has seared your forehead with its lines, and passion branded your lips with its hideous fires, you will feel it terribly", because Dorian has "the most marvellous youth, and youth is the one thing worth having" (26). When the painting is complete and Dorian sees it, "[a] look of joy came into his eyes, as if he had recognized himself for the first time" (29). On the other hand, he also thinks of his old and aging body in the future. At this moment, which is described as a revelation in the novel, Dorian reflects, "How sad it is! I shall grow old, and horrible, and dreadful. But this picture will remain always young. It will never be older than this particular day of June. … If it were only the other way!"(30). His desire highlights the fact that art is immortal, therefore endures time. That is why he wishes to be immortal: "If it were I who was to be always young, and the picture that was to grow old! For that—for that—I would give everything! […] I would give my soul for that!"(30) His desire represents his fantasy of remaining young and beautiful like the image in the painting. This desire also reveals the ekphrastic encounter in that Dorian's painting starts to dominate the verbal fiction. It is centralised by Dorian's illusionary self who is attached to the painting and its unchanged status.

The exchange between Dorian and his artistic representation is based upon a fantasy in which Dorian's wish to remain young and beautiful is fulfilled. When he discovers that the portrait starts to change, he supposes that "it was merely an illusion wrought on the troubled senses" (99). As far as Dorian's wish and the fulfilment of this wish are concerned, it is true to suggest that Dorian projects his unwanted desires of aging and ugliness onto the painting, and thus forms a self which stands for the "Ideal-I" in Lacanian terms. Lacan, in "The Mirror Stage," theorises that the mirror stage acts as an identification process.[9] Dorian's identification process results from his experience of the painting while constituting an "Ideal-I" which completes

---

[8] Epifanio San Juan, Jr., "The Picture of Dorian Gray and the Form of Fiction," in Epifanio San Juan, Jr., *The Art of Oscar Wilde* (Princeton: Princeton University Press, 1967), 50.

[9] Jacques Lacan, "The Mirror Stage," in Paul du Gay, Jessica Evans, and Peter Redman, eds., *Identity: A Reader* (London: Sage Publications, 2004).

what he lacks in selfhood. The portrait is "the most magical of mirrors" for Dorian. [10] When Dorian sees the complete painting for the first time, he is startled like an infant positioned in front of a mirror and feels "jubilant". [11] The artistic experience is repetitively cut by Lord Henry Wotton's warnings about the passing of time and old age, which influences Dorian. Dorian's inability to resist passing time and old age forces him to find a way to complete the lack. In this sense, his desire is imaginary and serves as a dramatic function in that "The mirror stage is a drama whose internal thrust is precipitated from insufficiency to anticipation." [12] It means that Dorian forms an illusionary self that anticipates immortal youth and beauty. Until the "Ideal-I" confronts the other—the "social-I"—which destroys the misrecognition produced by the identification, the illusionary self dominates. In this sense, Dorian's wish is fulfilled with his identification with the image in the painting that stands for his actual identity. At this point, the function of the painting reveals itself in that the intersection between art and life is transmuted into an opposition between immortal art versus mortal life. Therefore, "[o]nly art, through its ability to objectify inner experience, projecting it into the external world where each man can find his own reflection on its surface, can serve as communication between the encapsulated lives of Wilde's world." [13] Dorian's inner desire is impersonated by the painting. The painting becomes a part of himself, which shows his illusionary self and therefore, accentuates the power of the image from the very beginning.

Lord Henry Wotton is also influential on Dorian, as his remarks about the passing of time address the lack in Dorian's self, which in turn produces a negative effect on Dorian. Even though Basil does not want Henry to be introduced to Dorian owing to his belief that Henry's "influence would be bad" (18) and warns Dorian by stating, "You mustn't believe a word that he says" (24), Dorian is influenced by Henry's ideas on youth and beauty negatively. Henry repetitively reminds him of transitory beauty and youth. Alison Milbank suggests that "The novel is a pass-the-parcel game of influence and substitution, whereby characters infect each other with ideas like a disease. Lord Henry starts the game by infecting Dorian." [14] Dorian wishes to be young after he looks at the painting, and remembers that "[t]hen

---

[10] Wilde, *Dorian Gray*, 114.
[11] Lacan, "The Mirror Stage", 44.
[12] Ibid., 47.
[13] Robert Keefe, "Artist and Model in 'The Picture of Dorian Gray'," *Studies in the Novel*, No. 5.1 (Spring 1973): 67. https://www.jstor.org/stable/29531571.
[14] Alison Milbank, "Positive Duality in *The Picture of Dorian Gray*," *The Wildean*, No. 44 (January 2014): 21. https://www.jstor.org/stable/48569039.

had come Lord Henry Wotton with his strange panegyric on youth, his terrible warning of its brevity" (29). The duality between the real and the illusionary self is exposed when Basil calls the image of Dorian on canvas "real," and Dorian wonders if this image is really like him. The ideal self acts as a duplicate self, and therefore presents the power of language in Dorian's construction of the illusionary self. Both the image on the canvas and Henry's poisonous words are the indicators of Dorian's mortality, so that he is influenced by the image and the word simultaneously.

What problematizes the concept of the formation of the "Ideal-I" in *The Picture of Dorian Gray* is Basil's idealisation of Dorian. Since Basil produces a work of art which is inspired by Dorian's beauty and youth, there is a paradox of identification. Even though the painting plays the role of the mirror in Dorian's identification process, it must be noted that Basil is the creator of the painting. Saying that "I have put too much of myself into it", Basil rejects exhibiting the painting at first even though Henry insists (7). Basil's idealisation of Dorian results from his artistic motivation as Basil states that "Dorian Gray is to me simply a motive in art. You [Henry] might see nothing in him. He is never more present in my work than when no image of him is there"(15). Liebman writes that "As an artist, Basil is an idealist, whose goal is not to provide pleasure either to himself or to others—but to inspire people with an art that portrays the union of feeling and form."[15] Whether Basil idealises Dorian, or Dorian constructs his own illusionary self remains obscure until Basil explains that artists are the creators of beautiful things, and they must not put their own lives into their paintings (15). That is why he rejects exhibiting the painting at first since he puts too much of himself regarding Dorian into the painting. Basil's idealisation of Dorian, on the other hand, is resolved when Basil visits him in order to take the painting to exhibit it in Paris. While Dorian refuses to show him the painting, Basil explains that "You became to me the visible incarnation of that unseen ideal whose memory haunts us artists like an exquisite dream" (123). However, he also explains that "Art is always more abstract than we fancy" (124), which refers to Basil's belief that one cannot put feelings into one's works of art. Therefore, Dorian does not allow him to look at the picture and decides to hide it as if hiding Basil's idealisation of him as he forms his own "Ideal-I" by identifying with the image. This demonstrates that there is a rivalry between the image as representation by Basil and as self-identification by Dorian. While the image stands for Basil's unification of feeling and form to express his emotions, the same

---

[15] Sheldon W. Liebman, "Character Design in 'The Picture of Dorian Gray'," *Studies in the Novel*, No. 31.3 (Fall 1999): 304. https://www.jstor.org/stable/29533343.

image represents Dorian's misrecognition of the self, and the formation of an illusionary self. In this sense, the change in the painting is Dorian's objectification of his desires. It is a material copy of his changing body, and yet, it also embodies his desire for immortal youth and stability.

The alteration in the painting displays the fulfilment of Dorian's wish and the formation of the illusionary self. Discovering that the painting has altered, Dorian hides it as if he also hid his true self. He believes that "The portrait must be hidden away at all costs"(126). Since the painting carries the traces of his aging body and fading beauty instead of him, he isolates himself from the society. He does not leave his studio, or attend any parties, and people who meet him at parties leave the rooms (214). There are scandals about him, and these scandals irritate him. On the other hand, on his thirty-eighth birthday, Dorian comes across Basil who forces him to face the reality of these scandals. This confrontation is a reminder of the clash between the "Ideal-I" and the "social-I" in that Basil reveals the true nature of Dorian and questions his secret: "I wonder do I know you? Before I could answer that, I should have to see your soul" (162). Basil insists on the truth of his change, and Dorian invites him to see the truth. When Basil sees the hideous face on the canvas, he feels horror, disgust, and loathing. On the other hand, the confrontation of the "Ideal-I" with the "social-I" reveals the imaginary self by re-highlighting a lack of selfhood. The scene portrays Dorian's neurotic upheaval as he "glanced at the picture, and suddenly an uncontrollable feeling of hatred for Basil Hallward came over him, as though it had been suggested to him by the image on the canvas, whispered into his ear by those grinning lips" (169). In this unsteady and gloomy mood, Dorian stabs Basil. This marks Dorian's strife of preserving the "Ideal-I" and eradicating the "social-I" that reminds him of his true self. The effect of the painted image, in this regard, represents the rivalry of Dorian with his hidden and unwanted self. It also maintains the power of the image that substitutes for Dorian's actual self.

Lacan suggests, in the mirror stage, the subject is "caught up in the lure of spatial identification, the succession of phantasies that extends from a fragmented body-image to a form of its totality" which is called "orthopaedic".[16] In Dorian's identification process, the painting has the role of a mirror whose spatiality not only reflects Dorian's self but also constructs an alternative self for him. The duality between spatiality and temporality in ekphrasis leads theorists to focus on the features of the visual and the verbal. While a painting is spatial due to its representation of the object that takes place in a space, a literary text is temporal since narrative

---

[16] Lacan, "The Mirror Stage," 47.

works in sequences. This distinction has been discussed since Gotthold Ephraim Lessing, who suggests that "painting employs wholly different signs or means of imitation from poetry,—the one using forms and colors in space, the other articulate sounds in time."[17] The distinction between spatial and temporal qualities is a key to my argument for the illusion of the self in the novel because the painting is spatial while the narrative in the novel is temporal. I propose that ekphrasis, which combines the stability of the image in the painting with the moving words in the narrative, allows us to understand the nature of Dorian's fluctuating self. The exchange between Dorian and the image on the canvas may suggest that a stable artistic image can gain mobility through words. It means that ekphrasis in the novel allows us to delve into the interplay between stasis and mobility, which reflects Dorian's oscillating self throughout the narrative. In this sense, Dorian's murder of Basil maintains the mobility of the stable image which is an illusion of the self. Since "*Dorian Gray* gives the object a subjective power,"[18] it allows the image to possess the qualities of time. As the painting changes in time, the mode of the novel changes because there is a momentum between the mobile self and the fixed image repetitively. Nonetheless, Dorian's wish stabilises his body and youth while endowing the image with mobility and change. It means that the stability and the spatiality of the image is temporalized whereas the moving and changing body is spatialized and immobilised. In this sense, Dorian's illusionary self is linked to his spatialised qualities borrowed from the painting.

In the ekphrastic encounter between the image and the text, W. J. T. Mitchell argues, there are three stages of ekphrasis: "ekphrastic indifference," "ekphrastic hope," and "ekphrastic fear." While "ekphrastic indifference" recognises the fact that the image and the text cannot meet as they are the distinct modes of representation, "ekphrastic hope" presupposes that there is a link between the image and the word, and they get closer to each other. "Ekphrastic fear," on the other hand, refers to the idea that that "the difference between the verbal and visual representation might collapse and the figurative, imaginary desire of ekphrasis might be realized literally and actually."[19] The imaginary desire of ekphrasis is to produce an illusion that takes the place of the actual form, and acts like it. In a Lacanian sense, the imaginary desire can refer to the imaginary phase or the mirror stage in which the infant regards the self as separate from the other; while it has a

---

[17] Gotthold Ephraim Lessing, *Laocoon: An Essay upon the Limits of Painting and Poetry,* trans. Ellen Frothingham (New York: The Noonday Press, 1957), 91.

[18] Humphreys, "The Artistic Exchange," 527.

[19] W. J. T. Mitchell, *Picture Theory: Essays on Verbal and Visual Representation* (London: The University of Chicago Press, 1994), 154.

desire to be united with it, there is also a fear of returning to the neonatal stage or the real phase. The replacement of the actual image with the illusionary and represented image ends in ekphrastic fear. In these phases of ekphrasis, the novel moves from ekphrastic indifference to ekphrastic hope since the exchange between Dorian's actual self and the painted image precipitates an exchange between the stability of the image and the mobility of the word. On the other hand, the novel cannot perform the third phase of ekphrastic fascination, which is ekphrastic fear, since the relationship between the image and the word is broken and destroyed. Basil's intrusion into the illusion of Dorian's self, or into his illusionary ideal world not only destroys the ekphrastic encounter but also results in his death. Since Dorian finds Basil responsible for his own fatal change, Dorian kills him, and thinks that "The friend who had painted the fatal portrait to which all his misery had been due, had gone out of his life. That was enough" (170). The death of Basil is the death of the artist who ignites the exchange between the image and the text. Dorian disposes of the body with the help of his friend, Alan Campbell, who shoots himself in his laboratory after the act (181-82). Since Dorian wants a new life and to get rid of his misery and guilt, he decides to destroy the painting. He believes that he must destroy the picture as it is evidence for his frightful and guilty acts, since "[i]t would kill the past, and when that was dead he would be free. It would kill this monstrous soul-life, and without its hideous warnings, he would be at peace" (238). He stabs the painting with the same knife that killed Basil. The destruction of the painting is in fact the destruction of his illusionary self because when the police arrive and the servants enter the room, "they found hanging upon the wall a splendid portrait of their master as they had last seen him, in all the wonder of his exquisite youth and beauty" (239). Nevertheless, there is a contrast between the image of Dorian in the painting and the dead Dorian that "was withered, wrinkled, and loathsome of visage"(239). The contrast enables us to grasp the fact that Dorian's illusionary self is destroyed while the painting is transformed into its former status. Another contrast that this scene presents is that Dorian is seen in his real status by the police and the servants. Thus, while his illusionary self is disrupted, the police and the servants seeing him in his real condition for the first time underlines the complex construction of his self. In this sense, the image regains its stability. This means that while the painting is immortal, beautiful and stable, Dorian is ugly and mortal. This ending explains that the immobility of painting is reinstated while Dorian's temporary life is accentuated. It also reveals that ekphrasis, which represents Dorian's painting verbally, cannot stabilise Dorian's self as the painting does. In other words, the text's capacity for mobility contributes to the action of painting from which Dorian's imaginary self springs. Therefore, when the novel ends, "they [the servants] found hanging upon the wall a splendid portrait of their master as they had last seen him" (239). The painting remains as it is while Dorian is found old and wrinkled.

The anti-realist attitude in *The Picture of Dorian Gray* cements the idea of the illusionary self since Dorian's portrait is narrated in the form of a "magic-portrait story" in which "a male artist paints a masterful portrait of a beautiful young muse who inspires him. The process corrupts both the sitter and the artist, empowering only the spectators."[20] This quality presents Wilde's "emphasis on imaginative power in literature."[21] The magical exchange between Dorian's actual self and the imaginary self articulates the power of ekphrasis which translates image into a verbal form. In this sense, "ekphrasis can be thought of as being akin to the practices of translation."[22] The ekphrastic translation not only means that the image is translated into a verbal form but also implies that the verbal form is grasped like a painting since the text acts like a magical portrait that takes the form of a text. In this regard, Dorian's fascination with his portrait produces the illusion of the self which is reflected by the image on canvas that is narrated by words. This distorts the paragonal model which refers to the idea that "word and image compete with each other for artistic supremacy."[23] Until Dorian's death, there is no paragonal activity in the novel as the novel produces an amalgamation of the textual and the visual. This harmonious blending falls apart at the end of the novel as the ekphrastic encounter between text and image is disrupted by Dorian himself, and the ekphrastic fear cannot be observed. In this sense, when Dorian dies in an old and decayed form, the painting remains young and immortal, which in turn, highlights that there is a dialogue between text and image; however, this is not perpetual. According to Uzundemir, Wilde tries to eliminate the dualities between the text and the image by exchanging their features; on the other hand, by

---

[20] Diana E. Bellonby, "A Secret History of Aestheticism: Magic-Portrait Fiction, 1829-1929." Phd. Diss. (Vanderbilt University, 2012), 1.
[21] Özlem Uzundemir, "Art Criticism Veiled in Fiction: Oscar Wilde's Views on Art and Literature in *The Picture of Dorian Gray*". In Burçin Erol, ed., *One Day, Oscar Wilde: Irish Writer Series: 4* (Ankara: Bizim Büro, 2016), 67.
[22] David Kennedy and Richard Meek, "Introduction: from Paragone to Encounter," in David Kennedy and Richard Meek, eds., *Ekphrastic Encounters: New Interdisciplinary Essays on Literature and the Visual Arts* (Manchester: Manchester University Press, 2019), 12.
[23] Kennedy and Meek, "Paragone to Encounter," 3.

reinstating the image, he makes Dorian's strife seem futile.[24] This demonstrates that the textual medium is unable to incorporate the visual medium. It only interacts with it in the novel to a limited extent.

In conclusion, *The Picture of Dorian Gray* is an ekphrastic novel in which character and image exchange roles. The intersectionality between the image and the word reflects the idea that Dorian forms an illusionary self that consolidates the power of the pictorial image in the text. While Dorian forms his illusionary self by identifying himself with the image in the painting, the novel does not allow him to lithify the borrowed features of the painting. The death of Dorian, therefore, terminates the fanciful relationship between image and word. The painting in the novel acts like a mirror, and it stipulates that its pictorial and immortal qualities can only be borrowed until the character is dead and these qualities are restored by any means. Even though the relationship between the painting and the novel demonstrates the novel's aptitude in employing pictorial qualities, the valence between the text and image endures to a certain extent, and it is the death of Dorian Gray. In this sense, the illusionary self is also impermanent. The interchangeability between Dorian and the image also reverses the values and the characteristics of the originals, which exhibit that there is "the impossibility of locating authenticity in either [the character or the portrait]."[25] The death of Dorian reassigns authenticity to the original painting, and his own undesired mortality is also returned. The illusionary self is lost, the actual self is dead; what remains stable, and immortal is the painting and its own truth. Therefore, the novel's conclusion implies that the self is unprincipled, unlike the painting, which has stable and spatial characteristics. The fluctuating mode of the self, which is analysed here as the illusionary self, is a reduplication like ekphrasis which produces an illusion of the painting.

---

[24] Uzundemir, Özlem. "Oscar Wilde'ın Roman: Dorian Gray' in Portresi". In *İmgeyi Konuşturmak: İngiliz Yazınında Görsel Sanatlar* (İstanbul: Boğaziçi Üniversitesi Yayınevi, 2010), 129.
[25] Humphreys, "The Artistic Exchange," 533.

Figure 4.1 Paul Thiriat, Frontispiece to Oscar Wilde's *The Picture of Dorian Gray*, wood-engraved illustration (1908). Wikimedia Commons. Public domain.

Bibliography

Bellonby, Diana E. "A Secret History of Aestheticism: Magic-Portrait Fiction, 1829-1929." PhD diss., Vanderbilt University, 2012. http://hdl.handle.net/1803/13773

du Gay, Paul, Jessica Evans, and Peter Redman, eds. *Identity: A Reader*. London: Sage Publications, 2004.

Heffernan, James A. W. *Museum of Words: The Poetics of Ekphrasis from Homer to Ashbery*. London: The University of Chicago Press, 1993.

Hollander, John. "The Poetics of Ekphrasis," *Word & Image*, No. 4.1 (1988): 209-219. http://dx.doi.org/10.1080/02666286.1988.10436238.

Humphreys, Kathryn. "The Artistic Exchange: *Dorian Gray* at the *Sacred Fount*." *Texas Studies in Literature and Language*, No. 32.4 (Winter 1990): 522-535. https://www.jstor.org/stable/40754949.

Keefe, Robert. "Artist and Model in 'The Picture of Dorian Gray'". *Studies in the Novel*, No. 5.1 (Spring 1973): 63-70. https://www.jstor.org/stable/29531571.

Kennedy, David and Richard Meek. "Introduction: from Paragone to Encounter" in *Ekphrastic Encounters: New Interdisciplinary Essays on Literature and the Visual Arts*, edited by David Kennedy and Richard Meek, 1-24. Manchester: Manchester University Press, 2019.

Krieger, Murray. *Ekphrasis: The Illusion of the Natural Sign*. London: The John Hopkins University Press,1992.

Lacan, Jacques. "The Mirror Stage" in *Identity: A Reader*, edited by Paul du Gay, Jessica Evans, and Peter Redman, 44-50. London: Sage Publications, 2004. Originally published in *Revue Francais de Psychanalyse*, 1949; first published in English translation by Alan Sheridan in as "The Mirror Stage as Formative of the Function of the I as Revealed in Prychoanalytic Experience" (1949) in *Ecrits: A Selection*. New York: Columbia University Press, 1977.

Lessing, Gotthold Ephraim. *Laocoon: An Essay upon the Limits of Painting and Poetry*. Translated by Ellen Frothingham. New York: The Noonday Press,1957.

Liebman, Sheldon W. "Character Design in 'The Picture of Dorian Gray'". *Studies in the Novel*, No. 31.3 (Fall 1999): 296-316. https://www.jstor.org/stable/29533343.

Milbank, Alison. "Positive Duality in *The Picture of Dorian Gray*". *The Wildean*, No. 44 (January 2014): 24-36. https://www.jstor.org/stable/48569039.

Mitchell, W. J. T. *Picture Theory: Essays on Verbal and Visual Representation*. London: The University of Chicago Press, 1994.

San Juan, Epifanio, Jr. "The Picture of Dorian Gray and the Form of Fiction". In Epifanio San Juan, Jr. *The Art of Oscar Wilde*. Princeton: Princeton University Press, 1967.

—. *The Art of Oscar Wilde*. Princeton: Princeton University Press, 1967.

Uzundemir, Özlem. "Art Criticism Veiled in Fiction: Oscar Wilde's Views on Art and Literature in *The Picture of Dorian Gray*". In *One Day, Oscar Wilde: Irısh Writer Series: 4*, edited by Burçin Erol, 63-71. Ankara: Bizim Büro, 2016.

—. "Oscar Wilde'ın Roman: Dorian Gray'in Portresi". In *İmgeyi Konuşturmak: İngiliz Yazınında Görsel Sanatlar*. 93-129. (İstanbul: Boğaziçi Üniversitesi Yayınevi, 2010).

—. *İmgeyi Konuşturmak: İngiliz Yazınında Görsel Sanatlar* (İstanbul: Boğaziçi Üniversitesi Yayınevi, 2010).

Wilde, Oscar. *The Picture of Dorian Gray and Other Writings*. New York: Pocket Books, 2005. Originally published London, New York and Melbourne: Ward, Lock and Co., 1891.

CHAPTER FIVE

THE SENSUOUS PASTORAL:
VISION AND TEXT IN PRE-RAPHAELITE ART

RICHARD LEAHY

The Pre-Raphaelites were at first criticised for their lasciviousness: the incredible detail wrought in their paintings was lamented for being too "extravagant" and "outrageous": an *Athenaeum* review from 1850 argued that "[a]bruptness, singularity, uncouthness, are the counters by which they play for fame. Their trick is, to defy the principles of beauty and the recognised axioms of taste."[1] In 1851, the *Athenaeum* expanded on its criticism and suggested,

> The botanical predominates altogether over the artistical—and to a vicious and mistaken extreme. In nature there is air as well as earth—she masses and generalises where these facsimile makers split hairs and particularize. They take a branch, a flower, a blade of grass, place it close before them and closely copy it, forgetting that these objects, at the distance imagined in the picture, could by no means be seen with such hortus siccus minuteness.[2]

The newspaper picks up on the predilection of the Pre-Raphaelites to elaborate on intimate details in a way that goes against their resolution to show the *truth to nature*. The minutiae of idealised detail identified by *The Athenaeum* is also reminiscent of criticism levelled against Pre-Raphaelite depictions of women in art. Their works have been criticized by more contemporary commentators as being celebrated for their representations of beautiful idealised women and the overt sexualisation of the female body. At the centre of both of these accounts of Pre-Raphaelitism, in its overwhelming detail and later assessments of their depiction of the female

---

[1] "Fine Arts: Royal Academy", *The Athenaeum: Journal of Literature, Science, and the Fine Arts*, no. 1179 (1 June 1850), 590-91: 590.
[2] "Fine Arts: Royal Academy", *The Athenaeum: Journal of Literature, Science, and the Fine Arts*, no. 1282 (22 May 1852), 581-83: 582.

form, is the notion of the *ideal*. This chapter will examine the relationship between patterns of idealised natural imagery and overtly sensualised images of the body in Pre-Raphaelite poetry. This I term the sensuous pastoral; it is a process crucial to the ekphrastic tendencies of the Pre-Raphaelites. This attention to detail, the "hortus siccus minuteness" often leads to an alienated subject as they are pared down into their constituent parts. It is as if, with the focus so thoroughly on the detail, the whole fades into the background. The Pre-Raphaelite poets attempt a similar technique in their verse; the narrative eye fixes on minute details of both nature and body, which often has a dehumanising and objectifying effect.

Richard L. Stein explores this shared "formal assumption" of Dante Gabriel Rossetti's portraiture and poetry:

> Like his own painting and the medieval art he admired, his poetry involves sharp juxtapositions of narrative and decorative material, as well as shifts between physical description and symbolic details. Rossetti organises his poems around these oppositions, most self-consciously the poems referring to painting. His poetry dramatizes the interrelation between alternate views of experience, between figurative and literalistic treatments of a given subject.[3]

It is in these "sharp juxtapositions of narrative and decorative material" that we can find the sensuous pastoral. Rossetti achieves his effects through the intensely intimate focus from which he examines issues of nature and desire. Much of the sultry headiness of Pre-Raphaelite art and poetry may be seen to originate from the overabundance of minute detail. The important idea to acknowledge, however, is that much of this detail was created or conjured from the imaginary. The minutiae are often, in some way, *imagined*. Dinah Roe raises an important and corroborating idea, essential to understanding the idealised nature of Pre-Raphaelite art and poetry:

> The poems are generally set in rural landscapes whose natural details, true to PRB principles, are minutely expressed [...] Curiously, while most of the poetry focuses on rural scenes, Pre-Raphaelitism was an urban movement. The natural world to which it swore fealty was not experienced on a daily basis, but was a landscape remembered, imagined or conjured out of time spent in London's parks and green spaces or the rural retreats of friends, reached by the ever-expanding network of the new railway.[4]

---

[3] Richard L. Stein, "Dante Gabriel Rossetti: Painting and the Problem of Poetic Form", *Studies in English Literature, 1500-1900* 10, no. 4 (1970), 775-792: 775.

[4] Dinah Roe, "Introduction" in Dinah Roe, ed., *The Pre-Raphaelites: From Rossetti to Ruskin* (London: Penguin, 2010), xxi-xxii.

It is significant that Roe states the Pre-Raphaelite landscape was "remembered, imagined and conjured" as it highlights the altered sense of reality caused by the hyper-focused detail outlined in early reviews of their art. This imagined landscape is crucial to the effectiveness of the idealised representations of desire and the muse in Pre-Raphaelite art. In their attempts to find truth in nature, artists and poets of the Pre-Raphaelite Brotherhood (PRB) instead presented a falsely idealised image of the natural, something Nicholas Jagger touches on in his discussion of background imagery in Pre-Raphaelite painting:

> Simple objects and the demotic are central to the performance of the real, felt if not analysed, by the reader. […] What I suggest is that backgrounds in Pre-Raphaelite painting are important in two aspects; firstly they help to naturalise the impact of the implied narrative represented by the subject, and secondly, with reference to nature, they disarm the viewer's critical faculties by implying a truthfulness to nature.[5]

This operates similarly to the use of minute detail in PRB poetry. The intimacy of the depictions of nature, and the implied idealism of the poetry's subjects, combine to create an experience of sensuality and desire. As John Dixon Hunt suggests, "From its earliest stages the Pre-Raphaelite Brotherhood used exact and detailed representation of objects less as an end in itself than as a vision of suggestion of greater things."[6] The hyper-realised minutiae of description leant PRB poetry a certain tactility, emphasising the sensuous desires explored in their works. Alison Smith states that "Just as art critics could not help but compare the intense detail of Pre-Raphaelite paintings with that attained by photography, so parallels were also drawn with the microscope to suggest that such excessive concentration on a particular detail created a sense of hyper-reality that went beyond accepted notions of realism in art."[7] This technique may also be noticed in PRB poetry, where the hyper-reality of detail is used to elevate the subject of the poem to fantastical levels.

David Peters Corbett engages with this idea in *Writing the Pre-Raphaelites,* where he considers F. G. Stephens's analysis of Rossetti's paintings:

---

[5] Nicholas Jagger, "The Complexity of Nature in Pre-Raphaelite Ideals", in Paul Hardwick, Martin Hewitt, eds., *The Pre-Raphaelite Ideal* (Leeds: Leeds Centre for Victorian Studies, 2004), 33.

[6] John Dixon Hunt, *The Pre-Raphaelite Imagination* (London: Routledge, 1968), 129.

[7] Alison Smith, *Reflections: Van Eyck and the Pre-Raphaelites* (New Haven: Yale University Press, 2017), 15.

Stephens imagines the painter, spiritually honed and refined by a "firm attachment" to truth in every point of representation, "delineating the reality of experience, cultivating the power of representing an object, that its entire intention may be visible, its lesson felt." His model, the same one which operates subterraneously in his reminiscence of Rossetti as a student, is therefore one of the penetration of analysis into reality through an inward purity and innocence of the self [...] The key is that, in order to release its yield of significance, the leaf has to be "earnestly studied", unlocked through the artist's inner attention.[8]

What Corbett identifies in his investigation into Stephens's reactions is the value of the "yield of significance" that can be garnered by exploring the intimate details of the subject. This is an idea that is just as true in terms of the minutely explored landscape detail as in the depictions of the Pre-Raphaelite body. The idea that attention to detail could unlock something valuable in terms of meaning and impact was highly significant to the Pre-Raphaelites, particularly to their progenitor, Dante Gabriel Rossetti. In their attention paid to the micro level, the Brotherhood moved beyond true representation and into a level of heightened analytical detail. Corbett expands upon these ideas as he states,

Such ambitions raise the central questions which confronted the PRB. If the role of their new art was to provide a new order of visual representation which could deal with modern experience in this revelatory way, then how was that goal to be achieved? In what sense could the visual arts diagnose, communicate, and reform the lived realities of mid-nineteenth-century life? (83)

This concept is perhaps most succinctly explored in Dante Gabriel Rosetti's poem "The Portrait", where he writes: "In painting her I shrined her face / Mid mystic trees, where light falls in / Hardly at all" (lines 19-21).[9] These lines acknowledge the connection between the intimate natural detail and the bodily physicality of Rossetti's muses, while also suggesting the paradox at the heart of the Pre-Raphaelite desire for the ideal of *truth to nature*. Rossetti, potentially addressing Jane Morris or Elizabeth Siddal, states that he "shrined" the model's face in painting her. This elevates and enshrines the figure of the artistic muse to something above pure reality. Again, this is achieved partly due to the situating of the model "[m]id mystic trees." The adjective "mystic" distances the imagery from reality, while also

---

[8] David Peters Corbett, "A Soul of the Age" in Tim Barringer, ed., *Writing the Pre-Raphaelites: Text, Context, Subtext* (Farnham: Ashgate, 2009), 84.
[9] Dante Gabriel Rossetti, "The Portrait" in Roe, *The Pre-Raphaelites.*

suggesting the influence of romantic medievalism. The model is framed by the natural, pastoral imagery, but in a way that elevates their subjectivity. This type of framing emphasises the intimacy of her "enshrined" face. Stein argues that the metaphors at work in "The Portrait" are used by Rossetti to "dramatize his role as a creator of symbols, mediating between emotional states and a physical world. By considering painting in this way, he calls our attention to the active processes needed to give experience artistic form."[10] So, to Rossetti, the intimacy and nuance of the incredibly detailed depictions of nature and muse help him to express the all-consuming emotions and desires he was experiencing in the affection and attraction felt towards his muses. He was trying to encapsulate the nature of his love, and did so through his elevated exploration of detail. This phenomenon is also something that may be witnessed in "Jenny", an oft-reworked Rossetti poem that was finally published in 1881. In yet another dedication to beauty and the divine, Rossetti writes "You know not what a book you seem, / Half-read by lightning in a dream" (lines 51-52).[11] Here, Rossetti explicitly makes clear the connection between woman and text. Jenny, a figure often conceived of as a fallen woman yet treated with a level of sympathy by Rossetti, is described in a textual sense, something only furthered by the suggestion of enlightenment and imagination in "half-read by lightning in a dream". This concept is further complicated by the lines "Fair shines the gilded aureole / In which our highest painters place / Some living woman's simple face" (lines 230-233). It is clear how Rossetti views his role and responsibility, as he does other members of his peer group; they are in some ways providing a holy service, as they enshrine unsuspecting women's faces in the annals of history. Woman is "simple", yet the painter is positioned as the "higher" power. The simple face becomes significant when examined through the Pre-Raphaelite gaze.

This is, in many ways, what led to the criticism of the Pre-Raphaelite Brotherhood as being exclusionary to women. These imagined micro-details did not represent reality, and instead led to women in Pre-Raphaelite art and poetry seeming objectified and limited in their agency. Andrea Henderson argues that

> Rossetti is doing more than offering a critique of gender roles here; the ubiquity of these powerful but confined women in Rossetti's *oeuvre* speaks, among other things, to the difficulty of producing art the significance and value of which is at once objectively verifiable and rooted in subjective perception. The women Rossetti celebrates in his poems and paintings seem

---

[10] Stein, "Dante Gabriel Rossetti", 777.
[11] Dante Gabriel Rossetti, "Jenny" in Roe, *The Pre-Raphaelites*.

quite literally inflated, the receptacles of both explicit and unspoken powers. By implication, their attractiveness is not merely a subjective matter—they seem objectively to demand the admiration of their viewers.[12]

Women, like the imagined and conjured landscapes of Pre-Raphaelite portraiture, were "inflated", becoming "receptacles" of power and desire. Henderson goes on to exemplify the heightened aggrandization of women in PRB art: "they are women who have the power to suspend subjectivity or self-consciousness as they enforce submission to their sublime charms" (913). She also explores the altered nature of subject and object within the dynamic of the sensuous pastoral: "Rossetti recognized that this effort to rescue objective value by aggrandizing the object, precisely because it had its origins in the subjective desires and motives of the artist, was always in fact an imposition upon the object" (913). Pre-Raphaelite women appear to operate under a Medusa complex when considering their objectification and subsequent limiting of agency. As much as Rossetti tries to make them idolatrous through the sculptor's eye he demonstrates in the micro-elements of his portraiture and poetry, he self-consciously represents them as being obstructed by patriarchal gazes and desires. Henderson uses the term "monumental" to describe Rossetti's women in a way that suggests the solidity of the Muse/Medusa dynamic. This was amplified by the often-described fascination Rossetti had with the hair of his sitters.

Anne de Long dissects the Medusa myth in a way reminiscent of the Rossetti's hair-based discourse:

> These Medusan features dramatise and heighten inspirational anxieties about evanescence and passivity, for when one's muse is Medusa, one must look quickly or risk paralysis. Self-possession, or the traditional Romantic tendency to "other" the muse, forbids braving the Medusa's stare, preferring to decapitate and objectify or fetishise her, freezing or killing her into art.[13]

In both Rossetti's, and his sister Christina's, poetry, we are presented with this type of Medusan muse, who possesses via her inspiration yet is othered in the objective fetishisation of hair. Descriptions in "Goblin Market" of the wand-like Lizzie and Laura and their magic golden tresses, Rossetti's obsession with the magic of Lilith's hair, as well as his devoutness to many of his sitters', relate to de Long's notions of Medusan qualities—"flashing eyes and floating hair"—that can other the muse through freezing them as

---

[12] Andrea Henderson, "The 'Gold Bar of Heaven': Framing Objectivity in D.G. Rossetti's Poetry and Painting", *ELH* 76, no. 4 (Winter 2009), 911-29: 913.

[13] Anne de Long, *Mesmerism, Medusa, and the Muse: The Romantic Discourse of Spontaneous Creativity* (Lanham: Lexington Books, 2012), 102.

artistic object. It was in this dichotomy that the Rossettis discovered an ideal means of expressing their differing ideals on the treatment of women as art; Christina took issue with the commodification of women as an artistic object, and the objectification of hair; Dante Gabriel, on the other hand, found Medusa-based imagery provided him with a way of portraying the obsession he had with his sitters, and the powerlessness he himself felt through the possession of his muses upon him. They are caught by Rossetti, captured and twisted into a consumable form, and yet through this form they hold power and draw the attraction of gazes, both male and artistic. They are confined by male desire, but can also influence male desire. Kate Flint has suggested that for the Victorians "to make something visible is to gain not just understanding of it, but control over it."[14] Rossetti, and other members of his peer group, are an example of this understanding of ownership. Indeed, *Sister Helen*—in which he employed pencil, followed by pen, to form the character of the central figure of his poem between the two major textual revisions of 1868-69 and 1879—is an example of what Flint describes. In the recreation of the microcosmic details of hair and nature, the Pre-Raphaelites—especially their leader Dante Gabriel Rossetti—fused image and text to create an intimate sense of sensual pastoral.

Stein's analysis of Rossetti as "mediating between emotional states and a physical world" can be seen in subsequent stanzas in "The Portrait": "A deep dim wood; and there she stands / As in that wood that day: for so / Was the still movement of her hands / And such the pure line's gracious flow" (lines 28-31). Rossetti's adoration of his muse is conflated with the composition of the natural environment. The movement of her hands becomes the "pure line's gracious flow". Again, detail is explored specifically and minutely to the point where muse becomes part of the natural imagery. In elevating his muse's beauty, Rossetti attempts to immortalise, or "enshrine" her through the conflation of patterns of natural imagery with patterns of sensuality. Rossetti's imagined idealism may be seen in the depiction of both of these things, encapsulated in the lines "Next day the memories of these things, / Like leaves through which a bird has flown, / Still vibrated with Love's warm wings; / Till I must make them all my own / And paint this picture" (lines 55-59). There is a sense of ownership to Rossetti's words; in his attempts to capture his overwhelming desire for his muse, he elevates both nature and his lover to levels remembered and idealised in comparison to reality. The enjambment and deviation from the

---

[14] Kate Flint, *The Victorians and the Visual Imagination* (Cambridge: Cambridge University Press, 2009), 7.

Ronsardian rhyme scheme in this stanza around the words "ease" and "silences" (lines 59-60) help to isolate the visual quality of the imagery. Rossetti claims that "the memories of these things […] vibrated with love's warm wings." The verbal quality of this emotion details the visuality of motion and the techniques of ekphrasis. It emphasises the paradoxical nature of the Pre-Raphaelite's idealised vision of *truth to nature*. These are natures and muses that are caught by memory, the "vibrations" of Rossetti's visual imagery evoking the ekphrastic difficulty of trying to capture an instance of fleeting emotion in painting and poetry. This is something Rossetti directly acknowledges in the final stanza as he writes "here with her face doth memory sit / Meanwhile and wait the day's decline" (lines 100-101). Just as Dinah Roe suggests the Pre-Raphaelite landscape is one "remembered" and "conjured", so too is the artist's muse. Corbett also calls attention to this idea, terming it "glossing". He clarifies the paradox of imagined truth: "The implication of this gesture is that the visual is prior to the linguistic register, which exists in order to explicate it […] The result of this is to complicate the claim that the visual provides access to reality. The ontological complexities of the relationship between language and visual understanding underline how problematic any such claim must be."[15] The concept of glossing itself raises these issues. Rossetti's poems seem to assume what Michael Baxendall has called an "ostensive" relationship to the image,[16] that is they point out, explicitly, the important aspects of the painting. Both sonnets begin with this ostensive gesture towards the work: "This is that blessed Mary", "These are the symbols." Sir John Everett Millais engaged with the problematic nature of Rossetti's idealised depictions as he wrote: "D. G. Rossetti, you must understand, was a queer fellow, and impossible as a boon companion—so dogmatic and imitable when opposed. His aims and ideals in art were also widely different from ours, and it was not long before he drifted away from us to follow his own peculiar fancies."[17] These ideals may be witnessed in the composition of his poetry and portraiture.

Dante Gabriel Rossetti's "The Blessed Damozel" offers an insight into this process, as it was painted while his adoration of Elizabeth Siddal grew. The poem, unusual in that its original composition predated that of its companion painting, features a number of instances where related patterns of minute pastoral sensuality and fetishisation of the muse intersect. "Her

---

[15] Corbett, "Soul of the Age," 86.

[16] Michael Baxendall, *Patterns of Intention* (New Haven and London: Yale University Press, 1985), 23.

[17] John Everett Millais, *The Life and Letters of John Everett Millais,* ed. John Guille Millais (London: Methuen & Co, 1905), 26.

hair that lay along her back / Was yellow like ripe corn" (lines11-12), writes Rossetti in an ideal example of the combination of natural and idealised imagery. [18] This is furthered in lines 85-90, as we may witness the PRB technique of intently focusing on minute detail to evoke an aura of intimacy: "We two will lie i' the shadow of / That living mystic tree / Within whose secret growth the Dove / Is sometimes felt to be, / While every leaf that His plumes touch, / Saith His Name audibly" (lines 85-90). Again, Rossetti uses an intensely focused yet shifting narrative gaze to visually represent the intimate attention to detail. He moves between the "mystic" tree to the "every leaf" that decks it. It is clear to see the similarity between this poem and "The Portrait", where Rossetti "shrined her face / Mid mystic trees", especially when considering the preceding stanza of "The Blessed Damozel" where he states: "We two will stand beside that shrine." The consistent references to "shrines" elevate the dedication felt towards the muse, while the comparisons drawn between these religious sites of dedication and the natural pastoral imagery indicate the similar patterns of representation in each concept. They both use types of intimate intensity to evoke a sensuous atmosphere. Take, for example, "Silent Noon", where the lovers' bodies entwine with nature as much as they do each other: "Your hands lie open in the long fresh grass, - / The finger-points look through like rosy blooms" (lines 11-12).[19] In this simile, body and nature are blurred through Rossetti's creation of the microcosm; the hands of his muse lie open, but the narrative gaze focuses on the intimacy of the fingertips and flower blooms. The sensuality in this poem comes from the intimacy of the detail. The precise focusing of the narrative gaze occurs throughout the poem; in the second half of the first stanza, Rossetti creates the image by at first being all-encompassing in his vision: "All round our nest, far as the eye can pass." After suggesting this omniscient ekphrastic horizon though, Rossetti focuses in yet again on the intimate details of the scene, the "golden kingcup-fields with silver edge" and the "cow-parsley [which] skirts the hawthorn-hedge" (lines 6-7). He opens the stanza with an image of a wide visual horizon, but then moves in to examine the details at the margins of vision. This level of micro-detail Rossetti engages with also aids the idea of "visible silence" acknowledged in the final line of the stanza.

There are striking similarities between this poem and the earlier "A Silent Wood" by Rossetti's muse Elizabeth Siddal. Rossetti's poem was composed in Kelmscott while he was staying with Jane Morris following Siddal's death, but we can discern many similarities in Siddal's melancholic

---

[18] Dante Gabriel Rossetti, "The Blessed Damozel," in Roe, *The Pre-Raphaelites.*
[19] Dante Gabriel Rossetti, "The Silent Noon" in Roe, *The Pre-Raphaelites.*

poem that further outline the relationship between artist and muse, and the sensuous pastoral that is at the centre of its representation. Lizzie writes: "O silent wood, I enter thee" (lines 1-2)[20]—creating a similar atmosphere to Dante Gabriel Rossetti's entrance into a scene from an objective position. From this all-encompassing narrative gaze, Siddal follows conventional Rossettian technique as she moves inward to examine the minutiae of the scene. She closely discusses "the ferns that cling about my knees" (line 4) at the close of the first stanza in a metaphor that evokes both the intimate sensuousness of nature, but also the constricted role that Siddal was to play when "enshrined" in portrait and poetry. In the final rhyming couplet of the poem, the similarities are clear to see between Siddal and Rossetti's techniques: "Can God bring back the day when we stood / Beneath the clinging trees in that dark wood?" (13-14). The wood is the scene but the "clinging trees" are the object. The wood frames the two lovers, and the "clinging" trees function in a way that yet again blurs images of nature and desire. The "clinging" trees are reminiscent of the lovers' fingertips entwined in the grass in "Silent Noon". The interaction between natural imagery and the enshrined muse was suggested by William Holman Hunt in the preface to *Pre-Raphaelites and the Pre-Raphaelite Brotherhood,* where he uses a quotation from *King Lear* to suggest the PRB ideal: "Thou, Nature, art my Goddess; / To thy law my services are bound."[21] In Rossetti's and Siddal's poetry, we can understand the elevated subjectivity of both muse and nature; in a way, they both become goddesses. Griselda Pollock and Deborah Cherry have similarly explored the "textuality" of Siddal's construction in their essay "Woman as sign in Pre-Raphaelite literature", concluding that what we have come to identify as "Siddal" is a collection of tropes dominated by "passivity", but including a whole host of other associations such as "fragility", "incapacity", "inactivity" and "suffering". And Beatrice is, inevitably the literary heroine in which all these traits are brought (all too literally) to rest: " 'Siddal' becomes Beatrice, the beautiful, adored, and yet unattainable image for the masculine artist inspired by her beauty, a beauty which he [Rossetti] fabricates in the 'beautiful' drawings he makes."[22] They were highly imaginative and original, and not without elements of beauty, but they were not Nature.

---

[20] Elizabeth Siddal, "A Silent Wood" in Roe, *The Pre-Raphaelites.*
[21] William Holman Hunt, *Pre-Raphaelitism and the Pre-Raphaelite Brotherhood* (London: E.P. Dutton and Co, 1914),1.
[22] Deborah Cherry and Griselda Pollock, "Woman as Sign in Pre-Raphaelite Literature: A Study of the Representation of Elizabeth Siddall", *Art History* 7, no. 2. (June 1984), 206-227: 210.

The Pre-Raphaelite body, just like the image of Nature, was one remembered, imagined and conjured. This is what gives Pre-Raphaelite art its heady sensuousness; in the attention paid to the microcosmic intimacy of both body and nature, patterns of idealised reality come into focus. Ontologically, trying to capture these feelings and emotions in words or paint leads to a sort of paradoxical hyper-reality. Lynn Pearce suggests something similar as she comments on Elizabeth Siddal and Beata Beatrix: "[…] Not single enough to be an ideal, an Abstraction, she is thus the archetypal floating signifier; the textual identity that Elizabeth Siddal was supposedly mythologised into was no more substantial than the mythologies themselves."[23] This "floating textual signifier" occurs out of Rossetti's desire to elevate the muse; he attempted to visually embellish her while trying to stay true to nature. See fig. 5.1. William Rossetti outlines his brother's technique as he reflects on how "In all these descriptive verses, about railway-travelling, etc., the reader will readily perceive that the writer was bent on the Pre-Raphaelite plan—that of sharply realizing an impression on the eye, and through the eye of the mind."[24] The objectivity of truth within the Pre-Raphaelite artistic ideology, caused by the difficulty of attempting to recreate truth to nature, while also idealising through memory, leads to an explanation of both the praise Pre-Raphaelite art has encountered (beauty, detail, nature), but also the criticisms (objectification, sensuousness, etc.). In both circumstances, the Natural and the Muse are interconnected by the intimacy of the sensuous pastoral, as both may be considered to be not as they are, "but as she fills his dream." As Andrea Rose states: "Their sole code of operation was Truth to Nature. But what is Nature? Is it the woodspurge by the forest's edge or one's own inner nature—one's imagination and feelings—sometimes as unnatural and unreal as the chimera of the ancients?"[25]

Elizabeth Siddal also makes clear her sense of the objectification and limited agency felt in her poem "The Lust of the Eyes". In the opening lines, Siddal writes: "I care not for my lady's soul, / Though I worship before her smile"(lines 1-2).[26] This clearly engages with the same lexical and semantic field as Rossetti's venerating verse and the enshrining of his portraiture; what he sees as a noble and almost religious devotion to capture the beauty

---

[23] Lynne Pearce, *Woman/Image/Text: Readings in Pre-Raphaelite Art and Literature* (Toronto: Univeristy of Toronto Press, 1991), 50.

[24] Dante Gabriel Rossetti, *Dante Gabriel Rossetti: His Family Letters with a Memoir*, vol. 2, ed. William Michael Rossetti (London: Ellis & Co., 1895), 56.

[25] Andrea Rose, *The Pre-Raphaelites: Colour Library* (London and New York: Phaidon, 1998), 8-9.

[26] Elizabeth Siddal, "The Lust of the Eyes" in Roe, *The Pre-Raphaelites*.

he saw in his sitters—particularly Siddal—she sees instead as a sense of worship that blinds him. She acknowledges the power dynamics which see the Pre-Raphaelite Brotherhood above their subjects, akin to how Rossetti envisioned the "highest painters" that enshrine women's faces, as she reverses the gaze mechanic: "Low sit I down at my lady's feet, / Gazing through her wild eyes, / Smiling to think how my love will fleet, / When their starlike beauty dies." (ll. 5-8) In Siddal's poem, the typical Pre-Raphaelite gaze is subverted. The painter sits "low" at his lady's feet. Note as well how the sitter here is elevated to the position of "lady". The inverted sense of visual authority may also be seen in the next line as the painter gazes "through" her wild eyes. There is a potential dual meaning here, as Siddal refocuses the powerful gaze of the painter to emphasise how empty it is. The painter looks "through" his sitter, in a description that emphasises the alienating sense of limited agency that women feel as products of the Pre-Raphaelite Brotherhood. Rossetti's 1853 sketch of Lizzie drawing his portrait further complicates this matrixial gaze. See fig 5.2. There is also a suggestion of the vision of the painter and the sitter becoming blurred here, especially when taken into consideration alongside the following lines; again, Siddal challenges the elevation of women and their "starlike beauty" and the flippant love of Rossetti once this beauty fades.

In these examples from the Pre-Raphaelite oeuvre, we can see the significance of interactions between text and image. They were an artistic movement obsessed with the ekphrastic nature of representing what they deemed to be "truth" in art. Yet, in a Keatsian manner, this truth they represent is often confused with elevated beauty. It results in images and text becoming imagined, conjured, and remembered rather than truly represented. It is the Pre-Raphaelite tendency to inspect and reflect on the micro level, be that in the backgrounds of their portraiture and landscapes, or in the description of the minutiae of the sitter's bodies in their poetry, or indeed the combination of the two. Coventry Patmore saw similar ideas within the material composition of Rossetti's work: "It appeared sweet and bright and pure […] and yet, if closely looked into, there is scarcely a square inch of all those hundred square feet of colour which has not half a dozen tints in it."[27] They strive to portray truth to nature, yet they constantly elevate nature beyond the realms of true portrayal. The colours and composition of the portraits and poetry draw the gaze, and the micro detail maintains it. This is also what happens to Rossetti's muses—he attempts to capture their beauty in both image and text, but the desperation he shows in

---

[27] Coventry Patmore, *Memoirs and Correspondences of Coventry Patmore* (Harvard: G. Bell and Sons, 1900), 283.

attempting to elevate his sitters actually leads them to become objectified and take an active stance against the Pre-Raphaelite gaze in their own poetry. Words try to reclaim an agency taken by the enshrining portraits.

Figure 5.1. Dante Gabriel Rossetti, *Beata Beatrix* (1877). Oil on canvas. 88 cm x 69 cm. Birmingham Museum and Art Gallery. Photo by Birmingham Museums Trust. Public domain.

Figure 5.2. Dante Gabriel Rossetti, *Elizabeth Siddal drawing Rossetti* (1853). Birmingham Museum and Art Gallery. Photo by Birmingham Museums Trust. Public domain.

Bibliography

Anon. "Fine Arts: Royal Academy", *The Athenaeum: Journal of Literature, Science, and the Fine Arts*, no. 1179 (1 June 1850), 590-91.

—. "Fine Arts: Royal Academy", *The Athenaeum: Journal of Literature, Science, and the Fine Arts*, no. 1282 (22 May 1852), 581-83.

Baxendall, Michael, *Patterns of Intention.* New Haven and London: Yale University Press, 1985.

Braganza, Vanessa M. "The Search for Utopia: Charles Dickens' Hard Times and Alfred Tennyson's Mariana," *Inquiries Journal/Student Pulse* 6, no. 10 (2014): 1-2. http://www.inquiriesjournal.com/a?id=926

Cherry, Deborah, and Griselda Pollock. "Woman as Sign in Pre-Raphaelite Literature: A Study of the Representation of Elizabeth Siddal". *Art History* 7, no. 2. (June 1984), 206-227.

Corbett, David Peters. "A Soul of the Age," in *Writing the Pre-Raphaelites: Text, Context, Subtext.* Farnham: Ashgate, 2009.

de Long, Anne. *Mesmerism, Medusa, and the* Muse*: The Romantic Discourse of Spontaneous Creativity.* Lanham: Lexington Books, 2012.

Flint, Kate. *The Victorians and the Visual Imagination.* Cambridge: Cambridge University Press, 2009.

Hardwick, Paul, and Martin Hewitt, eds. *The Pre-Raphaelite Ideal.* Leeds: Leeds Centre for Victorian Studies, 2004.

Henderson, Andrea. "The 'Gold Bar of Heaven': Framing Objectivity in D.G. Rossetti's Poetry and Painting." *ELH* 76, no. 4 (2009):911-29. doi.org/10.1353/elh.0.0063.

Hunt, William Holman. *Pre-Raphaelitism and the Pre-Raphaelite Brotherhood.* London: E.P. Dutton and Co., 1914.

Hunt, John Dixon. *The Pre-Raphaelite Imagination.* London: Routledge, 1968).

Jagger, Nicholas. "The Complexity of Nature in Pre-Raphaelite Ideals", in *The Pre-Raphaelite Ideal,* edited by Paul Hardwick, Martin Hewitt. Leeds: Leeds Centre for Victorian Studies, 2004.

Millais, John Guille. *The Life and Letters of John Everett Millais.* London: Methuen & Co, 1905. Originally published in 2 vols., London: Methuen & Co, 1899.

Roe, Dinah, ed. *The Pre-Raphaelites: From Rosetti to Ruskin.* London: Penguin, 2010.

Rose, Andrea. *The Pre-Raphaelites: Colour Library.* London and New York: Phaidon, 1998.

Rossetti, Dante Gabriel. *Dante Gabriel Rossetti: His Family Letters with a Memoir*, vol. 2. Edited by William Michael Rossetti. London: Ellis & Co., 1895.

Pearce, Lynne. *Woman/Image/Text: Readings in Pre-Raphaelite Art and Literature.*

Smith, Alison. *Reflections: Van Eyck and the Pre-Raphaelites.* New Haven and London: Yale University Press, 2017.

Stein, Richard L. "Dante Gabriel Rossetti: Painting and the Problem of Poetic Form". *Studies in English Literature, 1500-1900* 10, no. 4 (1970), 775-792.

CHAPTER SIX

"HALF-SICK OF SHADOWS": IMAGINING WOMEN, REVERSE EKPHRASIS AND THE LADY OF SHALOTT

PAUL HETHERINGTON AND CASSANDRA ATHERTON

Victorian poetry and representations of women

Alfred Tennyson's extended and beguiling lyrical ballad, "The Lady of Shalott" (1833 and 1842) is an important text for understanding representations of women in Victorian literature and visual art. The poem depicts a version of the Romantic ideal of a largely inaccessible woman who is irreproachable because she is imprisoned away from human affairs. The poem starkly emphasises the divide between public and private spaces, and how perilous it was for Victorian women to attempt to cross this divide. As Alison Westwood argues, the Lady of Shalott suggests "a nineteenth-century notion that the boundary separating the private and public spheres is safest left unbreached".[1] In this respect, the curse placed on the Lady of Shalott exemplifies the Victorian idealisation of women who were chaste until marriage and who eschewed any thought of a career—to the extent that careers were even available to Victorian women—or any public role that reached beyond a dutiful socialising. This illustrates the "Woman Question" that, even during the Victorian era, came under increasing scrutiny, where women's domestic roles were associated with limits on their political and legal rights.

---

[1] Alison Westwood, "Between the Spheres: Breaking the Boundary Between Private and Public Spheres in Wilkie Collins's *The Woman in White* and William Holman Hunt's *The Lady Of Shalott*," Open Educational Resources, University of Oxford, 89. https://open.conted.ox.ac.uk/sites/open.conted.ox.ac.uk/files/resources/Create%20 Document/VIDES%202014%20section%20016%20Alison%20Westwood.pdf.

Although Victorian views about women were often taken for granted by the men and women who held them, various texts make them explicit. For instance, Rachael Zeleny draws attention to the ubiquity of Coventry Patmore's representation of the woman as "The Angel in the House" in his poem of that name.[2] It was considered that a woman's duty was to please men and Zeleny argues that this notion was pervasive; that "[i]terations of the pleasant and subservient Angel virtually flooded Victorian culture ... alternative models of feminine behaviour were rarely offered or if they were, they were not embraced".[3] Importantly, against this backdrop, Dante Gabriel Rossetti coined the expression, the "Pre-Raphaelite stunner" as a dark counterpart to the Angel in the House. While the "stunner" is often presented by the Pre-Raphaelites as a stronger woman than the Victorian stereotype of the passive and masochistic Angel—she is identifiable by her "statuesque physique, large eyes, thick hair, and sensuous lips"[4]—her sexualisation and festishisation undermine any sense of her autonomy.

With such issues in mind, this chapter examines well-known examples of Pre-Raphaelite, and Pre-Raphaelite-influenced, paintings of reverse ekphrasis that response to "The Lady of Shalott". These are paintings by William Holman Hunt, John William Waterhouse and Sidney Harold Meteyard, and a drawing by Elizabeth Siddal. While Tennyson's revised 1842 version of his poem ties the Lady of Shalott's identity to Lancelot and concludes with him musing over her corpse's "lovely face", the Pre-Raphaelites appear to imbue her with greater power, representing her in bright bursts of colour. However, despite the vibrancy of their images, the Pre-Raphaelites also invest her with a conspicuous remoteness and sexual allure, positing such women as doomed femme fatales. It is only Elizabeth Siddal's drawing that demonstrates a sympathetic and "feminist" portrayal of the character, and which gives real priority to female agency. As we discuss below, this drawing makes use of a reverse ekphrasis to open new conceptual spaces in a way that deserves greater acknowledgement.

Boundary crossings: the Lady of Shalott

John Ruskin (1819–1900), a powerful influence on the Pre-Raphaelites, encapsulates various idealistic notions of womanhood in an essay originally published in 1865, "Lilies: Of Queens' Gardens". As recently as 1977,

---

[2] Coventry Patmore, *The Angel in the House* (London and Cambridge: Macmillan and Co., 1863). Originally published in four parts between 1854 and 1862.
[3] Rachael Zeleny, "'She Left the Window': Challenging Domestic Ethos in Wilkie Collins's *The Woman in White*," *Peitho Journal* 21, no. 1 (2018): 61–62.
[4] Zeleny, "'She Left the Window'," 63.

David Sonstroem claimed that Ruskin's essay supports "the fullest exercise of women's influence and authority—indeed dominion of women over men".[5] Sonstroem also writes that Ruskin's essay demonstrates "views [that are] are evidently not an anathema to all strains of the feminist movement".[6] Yet, despite Sonstroem's encomium, Ruskin remarks in his essay that

> [t]he man's power is active, progressive, defensive. He is eminently the doer, the creator, the discoverer, the defender. His intellect is for speculation and invention; his energy for adventure, for war, and for conquest, wherever war is just, wherever conquest necessary. But the woman's power is for rule, not for battle, —and her intellect is not for invention or creation, but for sweet ordering, arrangement, and decision … And wherever a true wife comes, this home is always round her. The stars only may be over her head; the glow-worm in the night-cold grass may be the only fire at her foot; but home is yet wherever she is.[7]

Kate Millett explores and critiques Ruskin's judgements in this work in the light of John Stuart Mill's 1869 essay "The Subjection of Women", asserting that

> if we are to accept Ruskin's vision, the grief of the world is on the heads of women, so powerful are they in their secluded bowers, those shadowy corners of "higher mystery" where masculine power "bows itself and will forever bow, before the myrtle crown and the stainless sceptre of womanhood."[8]

More generally, Millett critiques the Victorian stereotypes of women that Ruskin invokes and praises on the basis that they are regressive, paternalistic and confine women to a *male* vision of what is right and proper for them.

The Lady of Shalott, who is confined to a private tower where she "weaves by night and day / A magic web with colours gay" (lines II.1-2),[9] metaphorically illustrates and exposes the nature of Victorian public and

---

[5] David Sonstroem, "Millett versus Ruskin: A Defense of Ruskin's 'Of Queens' Gardens'," *Victorian Studies* 20, no. 3 (Spring 1977): 297.

[6] Sonstroem, "Millett versus Ruskin," 296.

[7] John Ruskin, "Lilies: Of Queens' Gardens," in *Sesame and Lilies and the Crown of Wild Olive* (1865; reis., New York: Century, 1901), 101–03.

[8] Kate Millett, "The Debate Over Women: Ruskin vs. Mill," in Martha Vicinus, ed., *Suffer and Be Still: Women in the Victorian Age* (London: Routledge, 2013), 137.

[9] Alfred Tennyson, *The Poetical Works of Alfred Lord Tennyson* (1864; reiss., London: Macmillan and Co., 1899). "The Lady of Shalott" was first published in Alfred Tennyson, *Poems* (London: Edward Moxon, 1832).

private spaces for women—and, indeed, those spaces in-between. Although Tennyson represents the Lady of Shalott as a skilled weaver and singer—a true, if domesticated, maker—she is unable to extend these skills into the world at large. Crossing over from the private to the public realm occasions rupture and death. While Tennyson acknowledges her abilities in his poem, at least in passing—and in much the same tone of nodding approval as Ruskin uses when remarking on women's capacities for "sweet ordering, arrangement, and decision"—she cannot fully exercise these powers. Kate Green and Hilary Lim observe that

> [t]he feminist story goes that women originated weaving, and the cloth (the curtain) was then turned around against them, folding them away from the "real" world of men, the spaces of money and power. Thus, weaving can be used to symbolise the world of men and how they have used women […] Our favourite [example] is Tennyson's *Lady of Shalott*, alone in her solitary tower, "imbowered" in a "silent isle".[10]

Green and Lim also comment that the "boundaries between private and public are not solid walls but, at most, curtains of thought, woven from racist, capitalist and patriarchal abstraction" (88).

Thus, the Lady of Shalott is defined by boundaries that are designed to defeat her. She is confined to an entirely private space that the poem suggests is unfathomable to men and in which they have little real interest. Although she is active and relatively independent within the extreme constraints of her environment, she is also a kind of sleepwalker—someone only able to garner power and agency providing she does not look directly on, or engage directly with, the world or intimate human relationships. Ambiguously, she embodies a prevalent Victorian trope of female desirability—someone who is simultaneously mysterious, admirable, unknowable and doomed—much like a revenant returned, via poetry, from the legends of a remote chivalric past. She is a strange combination of the unreal and enchanting—a fantastic projection of a literary culture that was in thrall to the unwieldy drama and pathos of poems such as John Keats's "The Eve of St. Agnes" and Shakespeare's depiction of a suicidal Ophelia beset by Hamlet's madness and neglect.[11]

---

[10] Kate Green and Hilary Lim, "Weaving Along the Borders: Public and Private, Women and Banks," in Susan Scott-Hunt and Hilary, ed., Lim *Feminist Perspectives on Equity and Trusts*, (London: Cavendish, 2001), 89.

[11] John Keats, "The Eve of St. Agnes," in John Keats, *Lamia, Isabella, The Eve of St Agnes, and Other Poems* (London: Taylor and Hessey, 1820). William

With respect to Ophelia, Ana Peluffo writes that "Ophelia's suicide in an aquatic tomb surrounded by floating flowers was depicted over and over again in the paintings of the members of the [Pre-Raphaelite] brotherhood",[12] and Mary Balestraci's study of Victorian attitudes to Shakespeare's female characters concludes: "[a]mong Shakespeare's tragic innocents, Ophelia stands out as the paragon of idealized traits that the Victorians typically associated with women. She is loyal, obedient, deferential, and passive, yet she is seemingly punished for these traits".[13] In his discussion of Keats's poetry, Stephen Prickett writes that "[n]ot for nothing is Keats the most potent single poetic influence upon the art of the Victorian era", adding that "it was to the work of Blake, Coleridge, and Keats that the Victorians turned in search of a language to describe the complexities of the irrational".[14] Such female characters partly realised and embodied destructive male sexual fantasies during this period, where women were truly desirable in a public sense only as long as they were notionally untouched and, preferably, also somewhat remote and exotic— at least to the gaze of Victorian men. In "The Eve of St. Agnes", for example, the heroine is imagined as no real woman at all: "on her hair a glory, like a saint: / She seem'd a splendid angel, newly drest, / Save wings, for heaven:—Porphyro grew faint: / She knelt, so pure a thing, so free from mortal taint" (lines XXV.6-9).

Prickett states that "the Gothic romances of Morris and Tennyson have a sexuality that is usually dreamy, languid, remote, and stylized"— compared to what he calls the "suggestion of unnamed vice and sexual unwholesomeness"[15] in William Morris's story, "Lindenborg Pool"—but this is not to say that such "sexuality" is in any way benign. Kathryn Sullivan Kruger points out that while "The Lady of Shalott" has "been read […] as the (non-gendered) artist's struggle between the public and private spheres", it has also "been read as a warning of what awaits women who try

---

Shakespeare, *Hamlet, Prince of Denmark*, edited with an introduction and notes by Heather Hirschfield, further edited by Philip Edwards, 3rd ed., (Cambridge: Cambridge University Press, 2019), IV.7.166-83. doi:10.10117/9781316594117.

[12] Ana Peluffo, "Latin American Ophelias: The Aesthetisation of Female Death in Nineteenth-Century Poetry," *Latin American Literary Review* 32, no. 64 (July–December 2004): 64.

[13] Mary Balestraci, "Victorian Voices: Gender Ideology and Shakespeare's Female Characters" (PhD diss., Northeastern University, 2012), 29.

[14] Stephen Prickett, *Victorian Fantasy*, 2nd edition (Waco, Texas: Baylor University Press, 2005), 31.

[15] Prickett, *Victorian Fantasy*, 95.

to exercise artistic autonomy in a strictly patriarchal culture".[16] Jennifer A. Gehrman and Elizabeth Stuart Phelps observe that "[a]s the extreme version of the angel in the house, the Lady of Shalott embodied the ideal of Victorian womanhood […]. To rebel, to look upon the world directly, meant instant punishment by death".[17] Furthermore, in her rebellion, the Lady of Shalott is sexualised and represented as salaciously dangerous, but only insofar as the viewer understands that she is sailing to her death. In this way, her insurgency is ultimately harmless and her boldness is undercut; she is safe to gaze at because she is already bound to be punished for her transgression.

In its revised and best-known 1842 version, the poem begins by setting the scene. It presents a river, fields of barley and rye, and a road running to Camelot, and the island of Shalott. Camelot is bustling and surrounded by natural beauty but the island of Shalott is silent except when reapers hear a song in the very early morning. The Lady of Shalott, weaving and singing, is cursed and cannot look on the town which, instead, she views via reflections in her mirror. She is alone and apparently untroubled by her predicament:

> Only reapers, reaping early
> In among the bearded barley,
> Hear a song that echoes cheerly
> From the river winding clearly,
>   Down to tower'd Camelot: (lines 37-41)

However, by the end of part two of the poem, she is said to be "half sick of shadows" (line II.44). With the arrival of Lancelot—or, more precisely, his image in her mirror—she becomes seriously discombobulated, leaving her loom and looking directly at Camelot. The curse is enacted and she is carried down to Camelot in a boat, singing her final song, after which she dies and is admired by Lancelot for her "lovely face" (lines IV.61).

This is undoubtedly a complex, ambiguous and subtle poem. It retains a great deal of power, partly because of the uncanniness of its representation of its central character who, in one sense, is a death-in-life figure transported from the repertoire of folklore and fairy tales. As A.S. Byatt writes, "the Lady has things in common with the frozen death-in-life states of Snow White and of the lady and her castle [in the Brothers Grimm's story, 'Glass

---

[16] Kathryn Sullivan Kruger, *Weaving the Word: The Metaphorics of Weaving and Female Textual Production* (Selinsgrove: Susquehanna University Press, 2001), 48.
[17] Jennifer A. Gehrman and Elizabeth Stuart Phelps, "'I am half-sick of shadows': Elizabeth Stuart Phelps's Ladies of Shalott," *Legacy* 14, no. 2 (1997): 123–24.

Coffin']",[18] and Christine Poulson views the poem as one of Tennyson's "counter-fairy-tales, in which the heroines do not have to grow up and there is no happy ending".[19] However, no matter how complex and well-wrought the poem is, it was also just one of innumerable nineteenth-century literary affirmations of women's powerlessness in the face of patriarchy's social straitening.

Nina Auerbach observes that

> Victorian culture abounds in icons of beautiful corpselike women and in women—such as Dickens's Little Nell Trent, George Eliot's Maggie Tulliver, Tennyson's Mariana and the Lady of Shalott, Millais's Ophelia—who are transfigured in trance, sleep, lifelike death, or embalmed life. These figures come as close as possible to palpable realization in the animated Sleeping Beauty which drew unprecedented crowds to Madame Tussaud's waxworks exhibition.[20]

The poem presents a protagonist who encapsulates pressing existential issues for Victorian women while failing to explicitly identify those issues or critique the parlous situations they confronted. And, in presenting its protagonist in an idealised, backward-looking world, it attempts to make a kind of charm and self-conscious eloquence out of its protagonist's mortal crisis. Perhaps for this reason, the poem simultaneously tantalised and captivated the imagination of various, mostly male, painters, especially members of the self-styled Pre-Raphaelites, who considered themselves progressive. This was potentially an opportunity for those artists to directly address the plight of their female contemporaries, even if in their paintings they employed and fetishised "stunners", inviting the male gaze.

The Pre-Raphaelites, literature and *reverse ekphrasis*

As the Pre-Raphaelite painters, in particular, took up the challenge of producing images of women they believed ran counter to staid Victorian stereotypes, they often turned to subjects from literature. Indeed, the imaginations of the Pre-Raphaelite artists were so connected to the literary that Elizabeth Prettejohn writes, "Pre-Raphaelitism as we now understand it designates a movement in English literature as much as it does the

---

[18] A.S Byatt, *On Histories and Stories: Selected Essays* (London: Vintage, 2001), 157.
[19] Christine Poulson, *The Quest for the Grail: Arthurian Legend in British Art 1840–1920* (Manchester: Manchester University Press, 1999), 196.
[20] Nina Auerbach, *Women and the Demon: The Life of a Victorian Myth* (Cambridge, MA: Harvard University Press, 1982), 41.

corresponding movement in the visual arts".[21] Isobel Armstrong states, "[i]t was over Keats that the Pre-Raphaelites bonded [and t]hey also bonded over Tennyson, particularly the Lady of Shalott". She adds that "Tennyson was the poet who made possible what Ruskin asked for—a poet on canvas".[22]

This literary bent was so ingrained that it was not always easy to interpret Pre-Raphaelite paintings without having read the books to which they referred—the works were "often reliant on a further text to explain the pictorial symbolism and detail".[23] Furthermore, Heather Bozant Witcher and Amy Kahrmann Huseby comment that "all of the members were practising a form of literary Pre-Raphaelitism" and "at the inaugural meeting of the Pre-Raphaelite Brotherhood, [John Everett] Millais was working on a poem, while [Dante Gabriel] Rossetti read aloud from one of his poems-in-progress".[24] Witcher and Huseby also contend that, through their art, "Pre-Raphaelite painters were […] interpreting poetry, close reading it, and then offering their own 'readings' of poetry in a visual format" (49).

Thus, the Pre-Raphaelite painters produced numerous examples of what is often termed *reverse ekphrasis*—works of (usually) visual or plastic art that respond to pre-existing literary works. While, in one sense, this may be understood as an extension of the practice of many visual artists throughout history who have depicted scenes from culturally important stories, including mythological and biblical subjects, the Pre-Raphaelites were engaged in a close artistic dialogue with a variety of contemporary and near-contemporary poets they admired, thus actively contributing to and modifying understandings of these texts. Cathy Callaway contends that "the act of reverse ekphrasis is […] a representation of the poem down to the yoke"[25] that goes beyond mere illustration. Furthermore, Maria Aline Seabra Ferreira argues that "[i]f ekphrasis is the art of portraying works of

---

[21] Elizabeth Prettejohn, "Introduction," in *The Cambridge Companion to the Pre-Raphaelites*, edited by Elizabeth Prettejohn (New York: Cambridge University Press, 2012), 2.

[22] Isobel Armstrong, "The Pre-Raphaelites and Literature," in *The Cambridge Companion to the Pre-Raphaelites*, edited by Elizabeth Prettejohn (New York: Cambridge University Press, 2012), 20–21.

[23] Tim Barringer, *Reading the Pre-Raphaelites* (New Haven: Yale University Press, 1999), 150.

[24] Heather Bozant Witcher and Amy Kahrmann Huseby, "Gender Work: The Political Stakes of Pre-Raphaelitism," in Heather Bozant Witcher and Amy Kahrmann, ed., *Defining Pre-Raphaelite Poetics* (Cham, Switzerland: Palgrave Macmillan, 2020), 48.

[25] Cathy Callaway, "Reverse Ekphrasis," *Afro-Hispanic Review* 36, no. 2 (Fall 2017), 53.

art through verbal representation" reverse ekphrasis generates "a re-reading of […texts] through the lens of visual culture".[26]

As the Pre-Raphaelites engaged with literary works in this way, they were aware of the tradition of poetic ekphrasis—the term from which the notion of reverse ekphrasis derives—which had for millennia seen poets create strong visual imagery and lively descriptions, often conjuring—as if placing it before the reader's eyes—a known work of visual art. Most famously and influentially, Homer evokes Achilles's Shield in the *Iliad*. He uses his depiction of the highly-wrought and illustrated shield as a way of reflecting at some length on archaic Greek social norms and aspirations and also to problematise his text, opening up spaces that cast the rest of the *Iliad*'s action into new light.[27] The Pre-Raphaelites, too, employed their (reverse) ekphrasis to open up spaces that complicate and, to some extent, reinterpret the poetic imagery they refer to, creating an eddying dynamic that potentially opens spaces between the poem and the ekphrastic work.

However, the Pre-Raphaelites were very selective indeed in their choices of literary subjects. When Auerbach mentions, in the passage quoted above, that Millais's painting, *Ophelia* (1851–52) represents an image of a woman "transfigured in trance, sleep, lifelike death, or embalmed life",[28] she highlights that their paintings provide a keen insight into the Pre-Raphaelites's particular predilections, tastes, values and proclivities. Although they aimed to depict their subjects more realistically than was the fashion in mid-nineteenth century England—Susan P. Casteras notes that in the nineteenth century one of the "areas of greatest vulnerability [for their work] was its flouting of prevailing standards of beauty and decorum"[29]— they replaced one form of stylisation with another. Casteras observes that "Hunt, Millais, and Rossetti […] all broke through certain barriers of form and style, reinventing the insipidness of contemporary beauty and substituting a more uncompromising, unsentimental—if extravagantly

---

[26] Maria Aline Seabra Ferreira, "Paula Rego's Painterly Narratives: *Jane Eyre* and *Wide Sargasso Sea—A* Dictionary of Images," in Rui Carvalho Homem and Maria de Fátima Lambert, ed., *Writing and Seeing: Essays on Word and Image* (Amsterdam: Rodopi, 2006), 184.

[27] For further discussion of these matters, see Cassandra Atherton and Paul Hetherington, "Ekphrastic Spaces: The Tug, Pull, Collision and Merging of the In-between," *New Writing* (2022): 1–16. doi.org/10.1080/14790726.2022.2025850.

[28] Auerbach, *Women and the Demon*, 41.

[29] Susan P. Casteras, "Pre-Raphaelite Challenges to Victorian Canons of Beauty," *Huntington Library Quarterly* 55, no. 1 (Winter, 1992): 480-84,13. doi.org/10.1353/vic.2001.0047

personal—vision".[30] In this way, the Pre-Raphaelites were significant innovators but hardly revolutionary in terms of social values or sexual politics, and their realism was compromised by a powerful interest in idealistic notions of the past. They were drawn to female literary characters who were strange, doomed or fantastical, thus endorsing—even as they may have seemed to oppose—many of the most conventional values of Victorian society.

There are many Pre-Raphaelite works of visual art, expressing a variety of preoccupations. We will concentrate on selected images by William Holman Hunt, John William Waterhouse and Sidney Harold Meteyard—a member of the Birmingham Group rather than a Pre-Raphaelite, per se— and Elizabeth Siddal. In particular, we are interested in the ways in which their paintings of the Lady of Shalott imagine and depict their subject. It should also be noted that these painters never adopted a single or unified position about art and none of them strictly conformed to Pre-Raphaelite ideas and practices as originally articulated in rather vague terms by the Pre-Raphaelite Brotherhood at their formation in 1848:

> 1, to have genuine ideas to express; 2, to study Nature attentively, so as to know how to express them; 3, to sympathize with what is direct and serious and heartfelt in previous art, to the exclusion of what is conventional and self-parading and learned by rote; and 4, most indispensable of all, to produce thoroughly good pictures and statues.[31]

We do not attempt to generalise about the artists we discuss beyond what we find in the works we have selected to analyse.

Reimaging, and failing to reimagine women

William Holman Hunt's *The Lady of Shalott* was painted between 1888 and 1905. It is a late painting in his oeuvre, and its finalisation extends into the Edwardian period, but it is partly based on two earlier drawings of the Lady of Shalott he made in the 1850s and thus derives its inspiration from the early decades of the Victorian era. Hunt's painting (there are two versions, one smaller than the other, and we focus on the larger of the two) is more detailed than both of these drawings but, as with them, it depicts the Lady of Shalott at the poem's chief moment of crisis. See fig. 6.1.

---

[30] Casteras, "Pre-Raphaelite Challenges," 32.

[31] Quoted in David Latham, "Haunted Texts: The Invention of Pre-Raphaelite Studies," in David Latham, ed., *Haunted Texts: Studies in Pre-Raphaelitism* (Toronto: University of Toronto Press, 2003), 12.

She left the web, she left the loom,
She made three paces thro' the room,
She saw the water-lily bloom,
She saw the helmet and the plume,
    She look'd down to Camelot.
Out flew the web and floated wide;
The mirror crack'd from side to side;
"The curse is come upon me," cried
    The Lady of Shalott (lines 46-54).

Hunt elaborates on the poem, not only depicting the poem's protagonist in a state of extreme perturbation but encircling her with her broken loom and entangling her body in its threads. Furthermore, as Allyson McMahon Bourke observes,

> [b]ehind The Lady's head, a frieze of cherubs reminds her of her female duties. An angel on the right steps with her foot upon a red serpent—just as Eve should have done. The frieze as a whole depicts the music of the spheres and indicates the social harmony that results when women observe social boundaries and serve God as they should […]. Other details in the tapestry foreshadow The Lady's fall into sin.[32]

There is also a good deal of other religious imagery, and irises on the floor, representing sullied virtue. Hunt stated that his work depicts a woman who "casts aside duty to her spiritual self [… as a result of which] destruction and confusion overtake her".[33] In other words, the painting may be understood to be one of Hunt's representations of "allegorical or mythic figures who are not literal women but aspects of humanity as a whole".[34]

No matter how one interprets this moralising work, it unequivocally buys into and promotes repressive ideas concerning women and their place in the world. As an example of reverse ekphrasis, it provides new interpretations of Tennyson's work, pinning its morality down and taking pleasure in the crisis it depicts—the work is deliberately sensual and detailed. Sharyn R. Udall wonders "why this high-born lady, described by

---

[32] Allyson McMahon Bourke, "Tennyson's Lady of Shalott in Pre-Raphaelite Art: Exonerated Artist or Fallen Woman" (Dissertations, Theses, and Masters Projects, Paper 1539626054 (1996), 41–42, https://dx.doi.org/doi:10.21220/s2-eybx-jm55.

[33] Quoted in George P. Landow, "Shadows Cast by *The Light of the World:* William Holman Hunt's Religious Paintings, 1893–1905," The Victorian Web, n.p., https://victorianweb.org/painting/whh/shadlow/shadows.html.

[34] George P. Landow, *William Holman Hunt and Typological Symbolism* (London: Routledge, 2015), 46.

Hunt as 'intelligent,' condemns herself to a life lived at second hand",[35] adding that "[i]mplicit in Tennyson's scenario and in Hunt's drawing are the empty flattery and internalized acceptance [...] that kept Victorian women at their handwork".[36] However, Hunt's painting does not allow the Lady of Shalott any say in the matter. It is nothing less than an insistence on consigning women to the limited roles and unrealistic expectations—and desires—of men who cannot and will not see them other than through their own projections.

Figure 6.1. William Holman Hunt, *The Lady of Shalott* (c. 1890-1905). Wadsworth Athenaeum, Hartford CT. Wikimedia Commons. Public domain.

---

[35] Sharyn R. Udall, "Between Dream and Shadow: William Holman Hunt's 'Lady of Shalott'," *Woman's Art Journal* 11, no. 1 (Spring–Summer 1990): 34.
[36] Udall, "Between Dream and Shadow," 5.

This painting, skilful and evocative as it is, is backward-looking and pernicious in its implications. It demonstrates that one aspect of the Pre-Raphaelite Brotherhood was to envision women in a way that tantalised with the idea of female agency and independence while simultaneously insisting that, really, they had none at all. With its wild flourish of the Lady of Shalott's red hair, along with its window's appealing and receding perspective, Hunt represents his subject as sexually alive and literally bound, experiencing utter frustration, tantalisation and abnegation. She is also shown to be dangerously Maenad-like—Christiane Hertel discusses this aspect of the image, characterising Hunt's 1857 drawing of the Lady of Shalott as dramatically depicting "her censured freedom".[37] There can be little doubt that the idea of a powerful, unconstrained women was anathema to Hunt and his overwrought endorsement of conservative Victorian religious and social values.

John William Waterhouse produced three paintings based on "The Lady of Shalott" poem, and a great number of other paintings as well. Simon Goldhill comments on Waterhouse's representation "of the male subject of desire, and how his representational devices position, manipulate, and implicate the viewer [… part of] a Victorian worry about male self-control and erotic openness"[38]—and these comments apply to the paintings based on Tennyson's poem. We will confine our discussion to the most famous of these images, entitled *The Lady of Shalott* (1888)[39]—the other two paintings are *The Lady of Shalott Looking at Lancelot* (1894) and *I Am Half-Sick of Shadows, Said the Lady of Shalott* (1915). The 1888 painting illustrates the following stanza from part IV of Tennyson's poem:

> And down the river's dim expanse
> Like some bold seër in a trance,
> Seeing all his own mischance—
> With a glassy countenance
>   Did she look to Camelot.

---

[37] Christine Hertel, "Disruption and Entanglement: Maenadism in William Holman Hunt's 'The Lady of Shalott' and Max Klinger's 'Temptation'," *Studies in Iconography* 15 (1993): 234–35.

[38] Simon Goldhill, *Victorian Culture and Classical Antiquity: Art, Opera, Fiction, and the Proclamation of Modernity* (Princeton, NJ: Princeton University Press, 2011), 25.

[39] John William Waterhouse, *The Lady of Shalott* (1888). Oil on canvas, 1530 x 2000 mm. Tate Britain, London. Presented by Sir Henry Tate. 1894. The painting may be searched and viewed on www.tate.org.uk.

> And at the closing of the day
> She loosed the chain, and down she lay;
> The broad stream bore her far away,
>   The Lady of Shalott (lines IV.10-18).

Waterhouse's image emphasises the trance-like and disturbed nature of the Lady of Shalott's experience and, significantly, he moralises in his painting in a way that, while sparer and less insistent than Hunt's image, nevertheless consigns his subject to the same broad set of judgements. He wants to be clear that she has transgressed and is doomed, perhaps even mad. Her face, as she seems to sing, certainly reveals her to be strangely distraught.

In this instance, the Lady of Shalott is explicitly depicted as a virgin, leaving the viewer in no doubt that they are witnessing the destruction of one who has stepped away from her destined role as an uncomplaining nun-like devotee of her domestic arts—the visual iconography is unambiguous. Hodder notes that Waterhouse gives "the Lady a number of ... traditional attributes of maidenhood: long, flowing hair, a simple white garment, and pearls, which together with the foreground waterlilies, are highly suggestive. He has also [...] placed a crucifix in the bow of the boat".[40] However, paradoxically, her flowing red hair and tight bodice in the boat also mark her as a kind of temptress, encouraging voyeurism. In this way, she is exposed to the male gaze in a manner consistent with Emily J. Orlando's comment that "in the paintings by Waterhouse and his nineteenth-century peers, the Lady of Shalott is translated as an exquisite corpse to be gazed upon and mourned".[41] In a moment twinned with Lancelot's comments on her beauty in death in Tennyson's poem, the painting illustrates the enduring misogynistic idea, posited by Edgar Allan Poe, that "[t]he death [...] of a beautiful woman is unquestionably, the most poetical topic in the world".[42]

Furthermore, Poulson writes that the painting's eroticism lies "in the sensuousness of the handling and the vulnerability of the Lady's gaze", also observing that, as in Hunt's painting, "the viewpoint gives the spectator the sense of intruding on a scene of violent disruption, appearing, indeed, in the case of the Waterhouse, to be the cause of it".[43] The Lady of Shalott is once

---

[40] Karen Hodder, "The Lady of Shalott in Art and Literature," in Susan Mendus and Jane Rendall, ed., *Sexuality and Subordination: Interdisciplinary Studies of Gender in the Nineteenth Century* (London: Routledge, 1989), 73.

[41] Emily J. Orlando, "That I may not faint, or die, or swoon," *Women's Studies* 38 (2009): 632, doi.org/10.1080/00497870903021505.

[42] Edgar Allen Poe, "The Philosophy of Composition," in *Poe's Works, Vol. III, Poems and Essays* (1846; reis., London: A. & C. Black, 1899), 272.

[43] Poulson, *Quest for the Grail*, 187.

again characterised as a deserving victim of patriarchal norms, and as someone who has, in a rather clouded way, been violated and destroyed. The frisson of pathos that informs the work is of the kind associated with one who has no power over her own decisions or, eventually, even over her body. Therefore, this is an evocation of women as what we would call "desirable victim"—although this desirability only works for those who like their desired objects ruined. Waterhouse cannot allow the Lady of Shalott to be any more than a cipher that rather painfully gestures at destructive Victorian values. She is exotic, strange and unapproachable, a figure to be seen by men who refuse, in fact, to "see" women at all except through their projections.

Sidney Harold Meteyard, a painter and stained-glass designer was not strictly speaking a Pre-Raphaelite, partly because he was younger than the members of the Pre-Raphaelite Brotherhood. However, he was friendly with William Morris and the Pre-Raphaelite, Edward Burne-Jones, and his painting was heavily influenced by Pre-Raphaelite precepts and examples. His well-known painting depicting the Lady of Shalott is entitled, like one of Waterhouse's works, "*I Am Half-Sick of Shadows," Said the Lady of Shalott* (1913). See fig. 6.2. Elizabeth Nelson eloquently sums up this painting's main preoccupations, suggesting that Meteyard "emphasizes the sensual mood of the Lady's newly awakened sexual desire" while he "confines his embowered Lady in a narrow, cramped space in which her semireclining figure, her tapestry, and her mirror fill the picture plane".[44]

This work voyeuristically emphasises the power of the male gaze as it depicts a woman reclining languorously in her private sphere with her eyes closed, as if unconscious of being seen. It is also dominated by the colour blue, which Kruger contends becomes "the painting's main subject […] These shades of blue are both oppressive and enigmatic".[45] Bourke goes even further in her characterisation of this work, writing that

> Meteyard's Lady is … the Victorian archetype of Eve. She reclines on lush purple pillows surrounded by dark purple drapes and leans her full figure toward her "mirror blue". Her blue dress reveals more than it conceals, and Meteyard even taints the white lilies with a purplish hue … The fingers of

---

[44] Elizabeth Nelson, "The Embowered Woman: Pictorial Interpretations of 'The Lady of Shalott'," The Victorian Web,
 https://victorianweb.org/authors/tennyson/losbower.html.
[45] Kathryn Sullivan Kruger, *Weaving the Word: The Metaphorics of Weaving and Female Textual Production* (Selinsgrove: Susquehanna University Press, 2001), 124.

her right hand toy idly with a strand of thread, and with her eyes half closed
and her bare white neck exposed, she is deep in sexual fantasy.[46]

Kruger observes that Meteyard—as well as others such as Hunt and
Waterhouse—"seem unable to escape both their own history (as male
painters) as well as the history of art that fosters representations of the
female body as containers for (male) desire".[47] More generally, Casteras
argues that in Pre-Raphaelite images "women were generally distorted as
passive visual objects, dominated by the gaze of the men who made and
stared at them in real life and on canvas".[48]

Figure 6.2. Sidney Harold Meteyard, *I am Half Sick of Shadows, Said the Lady of
Shalott* (1913). Oil on canvas 30 x 45 inches. Private Collection, Europe [as of
1985]. Victorian Web. Public domain.

This was never more true than for Elizabeth Siddal, who is famous as
the model, muse and quintessential "stunner" for a number of male Pre-
Raphaelite artists—particularly Dante Gabriel Rossetti, whom she married.

[46] Bourke, "Tennyson's Lady of Shalott in Pre-Raphaelite Art," 33.
[47] Kruger, *Weaving the Word*, 134.
[48] Susan P. Casteras, "Pre-Raphaelite Portraiture: A Strangely Disordered Vision,"
in Margaretta Frederick Watson, ed., *Collecting the Pre-Raphaelites: The Anglo-
American Enchantment* (Aldershot: Ashgate, 1997), 146.

However, she was a visual artist and a poet in her own right, notwithstanding that fact that, over time, her talent as an artist and writer has been subjugated to her role as model and muse. This process was started by contemporary critiques by men, including painter Arthur Hughes who stated, "[h]er drawings were beautiful but without force" and historian William Michael Rossetti (brother of Dante) who argued, "[h]er designs resembled those of Dante Rossetti at the same date: He had his defects and she had the deficiencies of these defects".[49]

Siddal produced one of the first illustrations of *The Lady of Shalott*—a pen and ink drawing from 1853. See fig. 6.3. Her representation of this subject differs markedly from those of the male artists discussed because the emphasis of the picture is not on the contours of the woman's body—although that is placed centrally—but on the Lady of Shalott's act of making and observing. Thomas L. Jeffers suggests that: "Her rendering of the weaver is the only Pre-Raphaelite image to show correctly the probable medieval technique, with a high-warp loom [...] and with a mirror that allows the Lady [...] to see [...] the scene out her window, and [...] the right side of her tapestry".[50] Elaine Shefer remarks that

> calmness, order, and quiet pervade the Siddal work [...] The furniture—the chair she sits upon, the loom she works on, the table that holds the crucifix for her personal devotion as well as the perched bird that is her companion— all are pedestrian elements that locate the woman's action in the present.[51]

Siddal is primarily interested in the moments that lie between the Lady of Shalott's acceptance of her existence immured in her tower and what is yet to come. Her drawing does not explore a fantasy, even though it is based on a scene from Tennyson's rather fantastical poem but, instead, functions very much as a visual query. Although Siddal knew the catastrophic outcome of the lady of Shalott's predicament as Tennyson detailed it in his poem, she nevertheless uses her drawing to separately interrogate and question the purport of encountering a collision between innocence and knowledge. She asks calmly and observantly what all women are likely to ask in a patriarchal society after they have dared to face the world—"what now?"

Importantly, as Orlando argues,

---

[49] Hughes and Rossetti both quoted in Orlando, "That I may not faint," 627.
[50] Thomas L. Jeffers, "Tennyson's Lady of Shalott and Pre-Raphaelite Renderings: Statement and Counter-Statement," *Religion and the Arts* 6, no. 3 (2002): 232.
[51] Elaine Shefer, "Elizabeth Siddal's *Lady of Shalott*," *Woman's Art Journal* 9, no. 1 (Spring–Summer 1988): 25.

Siddall, herself a woman who has been most remembered as an object of the gaze rather than an agent of it, significantly has positioned her subject actively looking. It is the subject's most assertive act in the poem, and Siddall's decision to depict the lady's activity rather than her beautiful passivity (as a corpse) is an important step forward (629).

Figure 6.3. Elizabeth Siddal, *The Lady of Shallot* (1853). Pen, black ink, sepia and pencil 16.5 cm x 22.3 cm. Copyright © the Maas Gallery.

In her drawing, Siddal's Lady of Shalott not only looks firmly and with a healthy curiosity out of the window, but she eschews the unwanted gaze. It is even possible that this image was one way of demonstrating, as Orlando argues, "a shrewd awareness of, and distaste for, the passive, disempowering ways that she and other Pre-Raphaelite women were recorded in visual culture".[52] Siddal knew firsthand the kind of predicaments faced by capable, intelligent women in Victorian society, and how the gaze of men could be persistent, intrusive and disquietening. Her drawing challenges the apparent compulsion, so prevalent among Victorian male artists, to represent women in strange crises, contortions and wild throes, implicitly asking the viewer, "what is it that you see?"

---

[52] Orlando, "That I may not faint," 629.

Spaces of Doubt and Becoming

We have written elsewhere that "in ekphrasis, the reader-viewer will often cross into an indeterminate and unspecified place that does not entirely rest with language or another form of artistic representation".[53] This is because the two artworks involved in ekphrasis are never entirely congruent and, as it were, sit apart from one another despite their close relationship. Furthermore, in light of Victor W. Turner's conceptualisation of the liminal—he comments that "during the [...] liminal period, the state of the ritual subject (the 'passenger') is ambiguous; he passes through a realm that has few or none of the attributes of the past or coming state"[54]—we have argued that the ekphrastic process requires "a new imaginative proposition in order to arrive at a fresh state of understanding or representation".[55]

All of the images of the Lady of Shalott we have discussed take a notionally liminal moment as their subject matter—although Waterhouse's *The Lady of Shalott* is more aftermath than truly liminal. Yet in their paintings, Hunt, Waterhouse and Meteyard do not recognise the liminal space as one of ambiguity and genuine uncertainty—as a place of great, if often difficult potential and coming-into-being. Rather, they moralise this space out of its liminality, fixing it in their own time-bound preconceptions. Although their reverse ekphrasis creates a notional third space that exists between the poem and their paintings, they refuse the opportunity to dwell openly in this space. Instead, they create images where, although the depiction of space eddies, it turns back upon itself in a profoundly claustrophobic manner. In the case of Waterhouse, this claustrophobia occurs despite the outdoor setting, as the Lady of Shalott is closely confined to the quarters of her boat, dislocated and lost in a space that is both enclosing and strangely dissipated. One can speculate that such works were a defensive response, as Orlando argues, to the "escalating debates encircling the 'Woman Question,'".[56]

Only Siddal's image allows her subject to occupy a true liminality— even in defiance of Tennyson's language—and, in doing so, to open up the possibilities that belong to ekphrasis of all kinds, reverse or otherwise. Between Siddal's drawing and Tennyson's poem, the act of reverse ekphrasis opens a gap in which paternalistic and conservative views of

---

[53] Atherton and Hetherington, "Ekphrastic Spaces", 7.
[54] Victor W. Turner, "Betwixt and Between: The Liminal Period in *Rites de Passage*," in W.A. Lessa and E.Z. Vogt, ed., *Reader in Comparative Religion: An Anthropological Approach* (New York: Harper and Row, 1979), 235.
[55] Atherton and Hetherington, "Ekphrastic Spaces," 8.
[56] Orlando, "That I may not faint," 621.

women swirl and are subverted. It is not entirely sufficient to say, as Elaine Shefer does, that "the drawing has little to do with Tennyson's poem"[57] because the point of Siddal's drawing is it "reads" the poem from a woman's point of view, and challenges its laboured, only half-admitted moralising. Siddal does nothing less than re-image and re-envision Tennyson's heroine in a way that suggests women are capable of responding thoughtfully, independently and actively to crisis and doubt, and that men did not need to be a central part of such a picture—in her drawing, Lancelot is merely a fugitive image in a badly cracked mirror. It may be understandable that Pre-Raphaelite male painters failed to escape repressive Victorian stereotypes of women when depicting the Lady of Shalott's allure but their inability to do so remains a significant imaginative and artistic failure.

Bibliography

Armstrong, Isobel. "The Pre-Raphaelites and Literature." In *The Cambridge Companion to the Pre-Raphaelites*, edited by Elizabeth Prettejohn, 15–31. New York: Cambridge University Press, 2012.

Atherton, Cassandra and Paul Hetherington. "Ekphrastic Spaces: The Tug, Pull, Collision and Merging of the In-between." *New Writing* (2022): 1–16. https://doi.org/10.1080/14790726.2022.2025850.

Auerbach, Nina. *Women and the Demon: The Life of a Victorian Myth*. Cambridge, MA: Harvard University Press, 1982.

Barringer, Tim. *Reading the Pre-Raphaelites*. New Haven: Yale University Press, 1999.

Balestraci, Mary. "Victorian Voices: Gender Ideology and Shakespeare's Female Characters." PhD diss., Northeastern University, 2012.

Bourke, Allyson McMahon. "Tennyson's Lady of Shalott in Pre-Raphaelite Art: Exonerated Artist or Fallen Woman." Dissertations, Theses, and Masters Projects, Paper 1539626054 (1996), https://dx.doi.org/doi:10.21220/s2-eybx-jm55.

Byatt, A.S. *On Histories and Stories: Selected Essays*. London: Vintage, 2001.

Callaway, Cathy. "Reverse Ekphrasis" *Afro-Hispanic Review* 36, no. 2 (Fall 2017): 50–59.

Casteras, Susan P. "Pre-Raphaelite Challenges to Victorian Canons of Beauty." *Huntington Library Quarterly* 55, no. 1 (Winter, 1992): 13-35.

Casteras, Susan P. "Pre-Raphaelite Portraiture: A Strangely Disordered Vision." In *Collecting the Pre-Raphaelites: The Anglo-American*

---

[57] Shefer, "Elizabeth Siddal's *Lady of Shalott*," 26.

Enchantment, edited by Margaretta Frederick Watson, 139–48. Aldershot: Ashgate, 1997.

Ferreira, Maria Aline Seabra. "Paula Rego's Painterly Narratives: *Jane Eyre* and *Wide Sargasso Sea*—A Dictionary of Images." In Carvalho and Lambert, *Writing and Seeing.*

Gehrman Jennifer A. and Elizabeth Stuart Phelps. "'I am half-sick of shadows': Elizabeth Stuart Phelps's Ladies of Shalott." *Legacy* 14, no. 2 (1997): 123–36.

Goldhill, Simon. *Victorian Culture and Classical Antiquity: Art, Opera, Fiction, and the Proclamation of Modernity.* Princeton, NJ: Princeton University Press, 2011.

Green, Kate and Hilary Lim. "Weaving Along the Borders: Public and Private, Women and Banks." In *Feminist Perspectives on Equity and Trusts*, edited by Susan Scott-Hunt and Hilary Lim, 85–110. London: Cavendish, 2001.

Hertel, Christiane. "Disruption and Entanglement: Maenadism in William Holman Hunt's 'The Lady of Shalott' and Max Klinger's 'Temptation'." *Studies in Iconography* 15 (1993): 227–60.

Hodder, Karen. "The Lady of Shalott in Art and Literature." In *Sexuality and Subordination: Interdisciplinary Studies of Gender in the Nineteenth Century*, edited by Susan Mendus and Jane Rendall, 60–88. London: Routledge, 1989.

Homem, Rui Carvalho, and Maria de Fátima Lambert, eds. *Writing and Seeing: Essays on Word and Image.* Amsterdam: Rodopi, 2006.

Inglis, Alison and Cecilia O'Brien. "'The Breaking of the Web': William Holman Hunt's Two Early Versions of The Lady of Shalott." NGV *Art Journal* 32: n.p., https://www.ngv.vic.gov.au/essay/the-breaking-of-the-web-william-holman-hunts-two-early-versions-of-the-lady-of-shallot/.

Jeffers, Thomas L. "Tennyson's Lady of Shalott and Pre-Raphaelite Renderings: Statement and Counter-Statement." *Religion and the Arts* 6, no. 3 (2002): 231–56.

Keats, John. *Lamia, Isabella, The Eve of St Agnes, and Other Poems* (London: Taylor and Hessey, 1820).

Kruger, Kathryn Sullivan. *Weaving the Word: The Metaphorics of Weaving and Female Textual Production.* Selinsgrove: Susquehanna University Press, 2001.

Landow, George P. *William Holman Hunt and Typological Symbolism.* London: Routledge, 2015.

—. "Shadows Cast by *The Light of the World:* William Holman Hunt's Religious Paintings, 1893–1905." The Victorian Web.

https://victorianweb.org/painting/whh/shadlow/shadows.html.

Latham, David. "Haunted Texts: The Invention of Pre-Raphaelite Studies."
     In Latham, *Haunted Texts.*

—. ed. *Haunted Texts: Studies in Pre-Raphaelitism.* Toronto: University of
     Toronto Press, 2003.

Millett, Kate. "The Debate Over Women: Ruskin vs. Mill." In Vicinus,
     Suffer and Be Still.

Nelson, Elizabeth. "The Embowered Woman: Pictorial Interpretations of
     'The Lady of Shalott'." The Victorian Web.

https://victorianweb.org/authors/tennyson/losbower.html.

Orlando, Emily J. "That I may not faint, or die, or swoon." *Women's Studies*
     38 (2009): 611–46. https://doi.org/10.1080/00497870903021505.

Patmore, Coventry. *The Angel in the House.* London and Cambridge:
     Macmillan and Co., 1863. Originally published in four parts between
     1854 and 1862.

Peluffo, Ana. "Latin American Ophelias: The Aesthetisation of Female
     Death in Nineteenth-Century Poetry." *Latin American Literary Review*
     32, no. 64 (July–December 2004): 63–78.

Plasa, Carl. "'Cracked from Side to Side': Sexual Politics in 'The Lady of
     Shalott'." *Victorian Poetry* 30, no. 3/4 (Autumn–Winter 1992): 247–63.

Poe, Edgar Allen "The Philosophy of Composition." In *Poe's Works, Vol.
     III, Poems and Essays*, 266–78. London: A. & C. Black, 1899.
     Originally published in *Graham's American Monthly Magazine of
     Literature and Art*, April 1846, No. 245, 163-67.

Poulson, Christine. *The Quest for the Grail: Arthurian Legend in British Art
     1840–1920.* Manchester: Manchester University Press, 1999.

Prettejohn, Elizabeth. "Introduction." In *The Cambridge Companion to the
     Pre-Raphaelites*, edited by Elizabeth Prettejohn, 1–12. New York:
     Cambridge University Press, 2012.

Prickett, Stephen. *Victorian Fantasy.* 2nd edition. Waco, TX: Baylor
     University Press, 2005.

Ruskin, John. "Lilies: Of Queens' Gardens." In *Sesame and Lilies and the
     Crown of Wild Olive.* 81–134. New York: Century, 1901. Originally
     published in John Ruskin, *Sesame and Lilies* (New York: John Wiley
     and Sons, 1865).

Shakespeare, William. *Hamlet, Prince of Denmark*, edited with an
     introduction and notes by Heather Hirschfield, further edited by Philip
     Edwards, 3rd ed. (Cambridge: Cambridge University Press, 2019),
     IV.7.166-83. doi:10.10117/9781316594117.
     Originally published London: N.L. and John Trundell, 1603.

Shefer, Elaine. "Elizabeth Siddal's *Lady of Shalott*." *Woman's Art Journal* 9, no. 1 (Spring–Summer 1988): 21–29.

Sonstroem, David. "Millett versus Ruskin: A Defense of Ruskin's 'Of Queens' Gardens'." *Victorian Studies* 20, no. 3 (Spring 1977): 283–97.

Tennyson, Alfred. *The Poetical Works of Alfred Lord Tennyson*. London: Macmillan and Co., 1899. Originally published London: macmillan and Co., 1864.

Turner, Victor W. "Betwixt and Between: The Liminal Period in *Rites de Passage*." In *Reader in Comparative Religion: An Anthropological Approach*, edited by W.A. Lessa and E.Z. Vogt, 234–43. New York: Harper and Row, 1979.

Udall, Sharyn R. "Between Dream and Shadow: William Holman Hunt's 'Lady of Shalott'." *Woman's Art Journal* 11, no. 1 (Spring–Summer 1990): 34-38.

Vicinus. Martha, ed. In *Suffer and Be Still: Women in the Victorian Age*. London: Routledge, 2013.

Westwood, Alison. "Between the Spheres: Breaking the Boundary Between Private and Public Spheres in Wilkie Collins's *The Woman in White* and William Holman Hunt's *The Lady Of Shalott*." Open Educational Resources, University of Oxford. https://open.conted.ox.ac.uk/sites/open.conted.ox.ac.uk/files/resources/Create%20Document/VIDES%202014%20section%20016%20Alison%20Westwood.pdf.

Witcher, Heather Bozant and Amy Kahrmann Huseby. "Gender Work: The Political Stakes of Pre-Raphaelitism." In Witcher and Huseby, *Defining Pre-Raphaelite Poetics.*

—. *Defining Pre-Raphaelite Poetics*, edited by Heather Bozant Witcher and Amy Kahrmann, 27–54. Cham, Switzerland: Palgrave Macmillan, 2020.

Zeleny, Rachael. "'She Left the Window': Challenging Domestic Ethos in Wilkie Collins's *The Woman in White*." *Peitho Journal* 21, no. 1 (2018): 61–80.

CHAPTER SEVEN

OLIVER TWIST AND THE TRANSPORTABILITY OF THE IMAGE

COURTNEY KROLCZYK

When *Oliver Twist* was first published in the late 1830s, the text of Dickens's novel was just one of several ways this enormously popular narrative entered into the public consciousness.[1] *Oliver Twist*'s serial publication presents us with two important moments of adaption, and the earliest "adaptations" of the novel proved to be just as crucial to *Twist*'s popularity as the novel itself. Both forms of adaptation could be said to have appeared almost simultaneously with the novel. The first, George Cruikshank's illustrations, were necessarily created immediately prior to the novel's gradual publication in *Bentley's Miscellany*, and the second, the novel's many theatrical adaptations, appeared sometimes only days after the novel's serial parts were published. Though the reading public would have first come in contact with Cruikshank's illustrations at the same time they were introduced to Dickens's text, I consider these illustrations to be the novel's first adaptations. These illustrations are packaged with the novel to form a single literary object, but nevertheless they are ultimately the product of another artist, and can be hermeneutically separated from the text with relative ease. These images had a "life of their own" beyond the confines of the text, but they also played a crucial role in defining the text itself in the public consciousness. As early as 1840, William Makepeace Thackeray wrote of the "wonderful assistance" given to Dickens by Cruikshank, "who has given us the portraits of his ideal personages, and made them familiar to all the world. Once seen, these figures remain impressed on the memory, which otherwise would have had no hold on them, and the Jew and Bumble […] become personal acquaintances to each of us."[2] Though the lasting

---

[1] Charles Dickens, *Oliver Twist*. 3 vols. (London: Richard Bentley, 1838).
[2] William Makepeace Thackeray, "George Cruikshank," *The Westminster Review* 34, no. 1 (June 1840): 53.

impressions created by these particular images may indeed be owing to some quality that is peculiar to Cruikshank, the idea that a visual accompaniment to a novel can make its characters more memorable and even personal has a much broader applicability.

This chapter will examine *Oliver Twist* (the novel), its illustrations, and its theatrical adaptations to explain what I am calling the transportability of the image. Early melodramatic adaptations heavily utilized Cruikshank's illustrations when bringing the novel to the stage, and my claim is that this is due to the image's inherent transportability: its ability to be easily extracted and adapted from its original narrative context. When I refer to "the image" in this sense, I am not only referencing the physical illustration bound into the book. Rather, I am using "image" here to refer to visuality more generally. A piece of prose can be, to a greater or lesser degree, visually oriented in its concrete description of persons, things, places, and actions. In this chapter, I will also argue that certain narrative genres have a tendency to be, to varying extents, visually or textually oriented. It is my claim that genres that are more visually oriented are the ones that are more inherently transportable and adaptable. A single image, such as any one of the twenty-four illustrations Cruikshank created for *Oliver Twist*, is, in this sense, easily transportable and thus easy to adapt into another medium, but so are certain narrative threads in the novel. Dickens's novels may be faulted for perceived aesthetic failings caused by the lack of unity and internal coherence among their multitudinous plot lines. But it is precisely this lack of unity, which I will refer to as the incidental nature of certain aspects of both the novel and its illustrations, that helps facilitate the novel's transportability into other media, thereby expanding its reach and cultural relevancy.

Not only did Cruikshank's illustrations assist the transition from the page of Dickens's text to the contemporary melodramatic stage by providing dramatic adaptors with ready-made tableaux, the images themselves rely on the kind of dramatic realization that would have been seen in contemporary stage melodramas as the primary method of text to image translation. My work in this chapter is obviously indebted to Martin Meisel's landmark work, *Realizations*, which studies the formal similarities and narrative conventions that fiction, painting, and drama shared. The "realizations" of Meisel's title refers to a "literal re-creation and translation into a more visual, that is more vivid, physically present medium", and is also a technical term that applies to basing theatrical tableaux on well-known pictures.[3] The more vivid physical presence of the image, whether that image be rendered on paper, by bodies on the stage, or in language, is what gives the image its transportability. And it is this transportability that allows the novel to achieve a greater relevance in the minds of its reading and theatre-going public.

Stylistic Adaptation and Illustrative Independence

When discussing illustrated novels, it is only natural, and generally necessary, to give the text of the novel more attention than its accompanying illustrations. These images, by virtue of being illustrations, would necessarily seem to be secondary to the novel they accompany because they were created in response to a pre-existing text. But the history of *Oliver Twist*'s composition in particular, and the conditions of serial publication more generally, call this supposition into question. In 1871, more than three decades after the novel was published, and a year after Dickens's death, Cruikshank published a letter in *The Times*, claiming that the idea for *Oliver Twist* was originally his own, and that he was the originator of many of the story's characters, incidents, and settings.[4] Even if Cruikshank's much later account is to be viewed with considerable suspicion, as early as 1840, William Makepeace Thackeray wrote that he could "hardly believe [Dickens] implicitly when he tells us that the artists designed *after* his hints. In fact, many of his sketches are little more than catalogues of what we find in the pictures," and in the case of *Oliver Twist*, the artist "wanted the attractive subject of a boy growing up from the meagre poverty of workhouse childhood to the graceful beauty of happy youth, and the letterpress was written 'to match, as per order.'"[5] The "hints" refer to Dickens's well-established practice of providing his illustrator with his manuscript pages along with some suggestions about what would be a good subject to illustrate. Thackeray's assessment frames the claim that

---

[3] Martin Meisel, *Realizations: Narrative, Pictorial, and Theatrical Arts in Nineteenth-Century England* (Princeton, NJ: Princeton University Press, 1983), 30.
[4] Robert L. Patten, *George Cruikshank's Life, Times, and Art* (New Brunswick, NJ: Rutgers University Press, 1996), 2:56.
[5] William Makepeace Thackeray, "Charles Dickens and his Works," *Fraser's Magazine* 21, no. 124 (April 1840): 400. In his biography of Cruikshank, Robert Patten suggests that, while not all the facts given by Cruikshank are "precisely accurate," his version of events cannot be entirely discounted, as it was by John Forster and most subsequent commentators. Cruikshank had, apparently, pitched a novel about the life of a thief to at least one other author prior to Dickens (Patten, *George Cruikshank's Life*, 53).

Cruikshank himself would make a few decades later, that he in fact was the originator of the Hogarthian progress narrative at the heart of *Oliver Twist*, in terms of the relationship between the completed text and its illustrations, slighting Dickens's authorial authority by positioning him as the journeyman working "per order" to Cruikshank's creative genius, and likely referencing the origin of Dickens's career as a novelist, where he was indeed originally hired to provide text to match, or to "write up to," Robert Seymour's sporting plates, in a project that would become *The Posthumous Papers of the Pickwick Club*.[6]

While the idea that Dickens created the text of *Oliver Twist* to match a pre-existing illustration is demonstrably false, Thackeray's reason for alleging this, that Dickens's writing is too much like a description, or a "catalogue," of the details in an image, is not as completely without merit. In his biography of Cruikshank, Robert Patten does identify at least one instance where a plate was most likely designed before the chapter it illustrated was written.[7] The illustration for the number published in May of 1838, hardly one of Cruikshank's most spirited productions, depicts two new characters: the two police officers, who are shown being presented to a convalescent Oliver by Mr. Losberne. See fig. 7.1. On the first page of the number, Dickens describes Blathers and Duff as follows: "The man who had knocked at the door was a stout personage of middle height, aged about fifty, with shiny black hair cropped pretty close, half-whiskers, a round face, and sharp eyes. The other was a red-headed, bony man, in top-boots, with a rather ill-favoured countenance, and a turned-up sinister-looking nose."[8] Dickens description of the first man adheres fairly closely to the image created by Cruikshank. Though the second description seems like it *could* be a perfunctory description of an image, the actual figure that Cruikshank drew is partially obscured and cast in shadows, and therefore cannot be clearly discerned as bony, in top boots, or in possession of "turned-up sinister-looking nose." In other words, the text of the novel provides a "visual" realization beyond or even distinct from that found in the illustration. The portion of the text closest to the exact moment illustrated in the image is also highly visual without being simply a catalogue of details that appear in *this* image:

> 'This,' said Mr. Losberne, speaking softly, but with great vehemence notwithstanding, 'this is the lad, who […] comes to the house for assistance this morning, and is immediately laid hold of, and maltreated by that

---

[6] Michael Steig, *Dickens and Phiz* (Bloomington: Indiana University Press, 1978), 7.

[7] Patten, *George Cruikshank's Life*, 2:76.

[8] Charles Dickens, *Oliver Twist* (London: Richard Bentley, 1838), 2:179.

ingenious gentleman with the candle in his hand' […] Messrs. Blathers and Duff looked at Mr. Giles as he was thus recommended to their notice, and the bewildered butler gazed from them towards Oliver, and from Oliver towards Mr. Losberne, with a most ludicrous mixture of fear and perplexity.[9]

Figure 7.1. George Cruikshank, "Oliver waited on by the Bow Street Runners" (1838), etching, in Charles Dickens, *Oliver Twist* (London: Richard Bentley, 1838), 2: facing page 196. Internet Archive. Public domain.

---

[9] Dickens, *Oliver Twist*, 2:195-6.

The refence to the candle in Mr. Giles's hand is likely a concrete detail that was taken from the image, but other descriptive elements, such as Losberne's vehemence and the butler's ludicrous look of bewilderment, do not match the relatively expressionless image. The passivity of this illustration is something of an outlier when compared to Cruikshank's other work, which typically features highly expressive figures and dramatic gestures. In the above description, it is as if Dickens is providing a "catalogue" for a Cruikshank illustration that easily could, but in fact does not, exist by creating a sort of verbal tableau that mimics Cruikshank's well-established style of depicting figures and action.

Though Cruikshank's style was highly distinctive, his work also exists within a larger tradition of non-verbal serial storytelling. For instance, William Hogarth's serial narrative engravings obviously influenced Cruikshank greatly, spurring him to create two Hogarthian progresses, *The Bottle* and *The Drunkard's Children*, in 1847 and 1848. Meisel examines the "translation" of Hogarth's progresses into Cruikshank's, and the latter's translation into stage melodramas, claiming that this translation reveals an "irreducible tension" which "suggests that genre and style in the end are *not* fully transferable."[10] Though Cruikshank's progresses were already heavily influenced by domestic melodrama, when transformed into melodramas themselves, they required just as much "time-filling elaboration" as Hogarth's did when adapted for the stage.[11] My argument, on the other hand, is that some generic and stylistic components are more effectively transferred than others. It was the narrative elements of Cruikshank's progresses that needed further elaboration when they were turned into melodrama, and not so much his style of representation. In the review by Warren, quoted above, we can see that contemporary reviewers felt that Cruikshank's style, characterized by caricature and exaggeration, carried over almost too well into Dickens's highly visual prose. While the serious moral messaging of Cruikshank's two Hogarthian progresses did not translate as easily to stage melodrama, the same cannot be said for Cruikshank's considerably more comedic illustrations of *Oliver Twist*, which materially assisted in bringing the novel to the stage. While the *Twist* illustrations, when viewed as a group, also follow something of a Hogarthian progress narrative (after all, the subtitle of the novel was "The Parish Boy's Progress"), they have the freedom to be much more incidental, since they, as book illustrations, did not have to shoulder the burden of

---

[10] Meisel, *Realizations*, 98.
[11] Ibid., 125.

conveying a completely coherent narrative in the way that Cruikshank's six-part Hogarthian progresses did. A book illustration is not meant or expected, like the plates that make up one of Hogarth's progresses, to tell the whole story.

The incidental nature of Cruikshank's designs for *Oliver Twist* is not as pronounced in all works of book illustration, or even in illustrative work produced by Cruikshank in the same period. William Harrison Ainsworth's *Jack Sheppard*, a historical novel in the same "Newgate novel" genre as *Oliver Twist*, overlapped with the last four months of *Twist*'s publication in *Bentley's Miscellany*, and was also illustrated by Cruikshank. The format of the *Sheppard* illustrations differ markedly from those of *Twist* in their presentation: while the *Twist* illustrations are presented in a vignette style, with rounded edges and etching marks that taper off into the blank space of the page, the *Sheppard* illustrations are evenly rectangular and framed by a thick black line. The overall effect of the *Twist* illustrations is considerably more sketch-like, and the *Sheppard* illustrations, with their sharp edges and detailed, highly finished backgrounds, more closely resemble Cruikshank's independently published plates, like *The Bottle*, or Hogarth's own engravings. The thick lines of the *Sheppard* illustrations highlight their *independence* as etchings, conceptually separating them from the accompanying letterpress.[12] At the same time, their resemblance to the Hogarthian series also suggests a greater degree of narrative enmeshment than the vignette-style illustrations of *Twist*. I am referring not so much to their greater enmeshment within the narrative of the letterpress as to the suggestion that the plates could come together to form a coherent narrative of their own.

The sense that the plates might come together to form a narrative comes to fruition in the illustrations that accompany the third volume of *Jack Sheppard*. Cruikshank depicts Jack Sheppard's escape from Newgate prison in ten separate images spread across three pages: each step of the escape process is presented in a comic-strip-like panel, with four panels on the first two pages and two wider panels on the third page. Similarly, the plate entitled "The Last Scene" is in fact made up of three separate images, which avoid depicting the actual moment of Sheppard's execution by instead depicting his arrival at the gallows, his body being cut down, and his corpse being carried away by the mob. See fig. 7.2. Compare this plate to the similarly titled "Last Chance" of *Oliver Twist* which depicts a single, frozen moment of action before Bill Sykes accidently hangs himself in his attempt to escape from Jacob's Island. See fig. 7.3. In the *Sheppard* plate, the focus

---

[12] Patten, *George Cruikshank's Life*, 2:100.

is on the overall scene, with the central figure of Sheppard enmeshed within a sea of other bodies. Though the textual scene illustrated by "The Last Chance" also includes a large crowd, the focus of the illustration is squarely placed on the soon-to-be-hanged man as an individual. Its focus is in every way more "singular," in both its attention to a single individual and its depiction of a single moment, which then gives the plate its incidental quality.

Figure 7.2. George Cruikshank, "The Last Scene" (1839), etching, in W. Harrison Ainsworth, *Jack Sheppard* (London: Richard Bentley, 1839), 3: facing page 311. Internet Archive. Public domain.

Figure 7.3. George Cruikshank, "The Last Chance," 1838, etching, in Charles Dickens, *Oliver Twist* (London: Richard Bentley, 1838), 3: frontispiece. Internet Archive. Public domain.

Cruikshank's *Twist* illustrations in fact begin to make *less* sense as a narrative unit as the novel goes on. The first ten of the novel's twenty-four illustrations all feature Oliver, and when viewed in succession, provide a reasonably coherent summary of the events of the first part of the novel. We see Oliver at the workhouse, Oliver begging not to be apprenticed to the chimney sweep, Oliver finally "plucking up spirit" and attacking his fellow apprentice at the Sowerberry's, his arrival at Fagin's hideout in London, his horror at the robbery of Brownlow and his subsequent convalescence at Brownlow's home, his recapture by and reintroduction to the gang, and finally, Oliver being shot during the robbery of the Maylie home. This sequence of illustrations testifies to the dominance of Cruikshank's original suggestion of a Hogarthian progress narrative in the first part of the novel. The illustrations for Book II and III, on the other hand, indicate a decided shift away from the centrality of Oliver, as the title character only appears in four of the last fourteen of the illustrations. The last illustration to Book I, "The Burglary," literally shows Oliver in the center of the composition. See fig. 7.4. It also freezes a moment of violent action, complete with a smoking gun, and leaves this narrative thread in a state of extreme suspense. Readers of the original serialization would have had to wait three months for the resolution of this image, which would not come until Part XIII, which begins with a plate showing Oliver kneeling at the Maylie's front door. The plate that opens the next Book, "Mr. Bumble and Mrs. Corney Taking Tea," represents a pointed shift away from the earlier Oliver-centered images and a pointed refusal to satisfy the suspense established in the previous image. See fig. 7.5.

This shift in the illustrations necessarily follows a shift in the novel, which begins to focus less on Oliver as more plots and characters are introduced. The illustrations for Parts XI and XII could not possibly have shown Oliver, since Oliver is not mentioned in the text of those chapters. Over the course of the next two books, the various plot lines make it impossible for illustrations to form a cumulative narrative sequence. For instance, a series of four illustrations that move from Mr. Bumble being chastised by his wife, Nancy fainting and being revived by Fagin and the boys, Fagin meeting Noah and Charlotte, and the Bumbles meeting with Monks to destroy the locket do not work together to develop a clear narrative. This does not mean they are any less effective as individual illustrations, or as visual realizations, of individual moments in the text. But it does indicate a shift in the power dynamics of text and image, or of author and illustrator, as the illustrations become less of a coherent narrative structure undergirding the novel's progress narrative and more incidental in relationship to each other. If the genesis of *Oliver Twist* was indeed in Cruikshank's request for a narrative about "a boy growing up from the meagre poverty of workhouse childhood to the graceful beauty of happy youth," then the illustrations for the second half of the book demonstrate that the project's narrative energy began to rapidly expand beyond those specifications.

Figure 7.4. George Cruikshank, "The Burglary," 1838, etching, in Charles Dickens, *Oliver Twist* (London: Richard Bentley, 1838), 2: frontispiece. Internet Archive. Public domain.

Figure 7.5. George Cruikshank, "Mr. Bumble and Mrs. Corney taking tea," 1838, etching, in Charles Dickens, *Oliver Twist* (London: Richard Bentley, 1838), 2: facing page 61. Internet Archive. Public domain.

Whether or not a novel's illustrations exist in a coherent relationship to each other, the illustrations and the text they represent already exist in a relationship that is more or less incidental. By incidental, I mean that an illustration can only highlight a single instance out of a much larger constellation of connected narrative events. They already exist as dramatic "realizations" in their own right, pausing the larger narrative they are imbedded within in order to make a particular incident more vivid and physically present. It is this already incidental nature that primes them to be easily extracted and resituated within the new context of a theatrical adaptation. At the same time, the *Twist* illustrations are still narrative *enough* to be understood once reinserted into the new dramatic context, in part owing to the late eighteenth-century tradition of caricature that Cruikshank was influenced by, or according to some, was in fact the last practitioner of.[13] Both Hogarth's narrative series and the satirical etchings created by James Gillray and Thomas Rowlandson (as well as Cruikshank's own father, Isaac, and, in the nineteenth century, by Cruikshank himself) can be "read" with limited textual accompaniment because they utilized "a recognizable visual vocabulary of gesture, expression, and interior decoration," which was in turn drawn upon by nineteenth-century illustrators.[14] Stylistically, Cruikshank's figures, whose faces and bodies often verge on the exaggerated and even the grotesque, more closely resemble the fantastical work of late eighteenth-century satirists than the "realist tradition" of Hogarth.[15] This genre of satiric etching, as argued by Ian Haywood, translates "political processes into a compelling, comprehensible and critical visual language" through its "textual and visual allusiveness."[16] Book illustrations, which bear a direct, rather than allusive, relation to their source material, can also create a comprehensible visual language. Of course, the simplest way to understand a single book illustration is to view it in relation to the portion of the narrative it purports to illustrate. But many of Cruikshank's illustrations can still be understood, to a certain degree, once removed from the text they accompany. Both

---

[13] Frederic G. Stephens, *A Memoir of George Cruikshank*, (New York: Scribner and Welford, 1891), 2-3.

[14] Catherine J. Golden, *Serials to Graphic Novels: The Evolution of the Victorian Illustrated Book* (Gainesville: University Press of Florida, 2017), 66.

[15] Louis James, "Cruikshank and Early Victorian Caricature," *History Workshop* 6, no. 1 (Autumn 1978): 108. For comparison, *The Bottle* and *The Drunkard's Children*, the two narrative series where Cruikshank is most consciously emulating Hogarth, are much more "realistic" in their style of representation.

[16] Ian Haywood, *Romanticism and Caricature* (Cambridge and New York: Cambridge University Press, 2013), 8.

satirical etchings and Cruikshank's *Twist* illustrations use an exaggerated style of representation to instruct the reader on how they are meant to feel about the persons depicted. While the satirical etching relies on a dense allusiveness to concurrent political and social events to make meaning (for instance, a political satire by Gillray is unintelligible if the viewer lacks knowledge about the figures or events depicted), Cruikshank's book illustrations instead lean more on the meaningful gestures and postures of the stage. In a plate like "The Meeting", the characters could not specifically be identified without a knowledge of the text, but even an uninformed observer could understand that the figure representing Noah Claypole is clearly differentiated from the other figures by his more exaggerated features, like his comically flattened face and excessively thin legs, because of the conventions of caricature. See fig. 7.6. On the other hand, his pose, pressed against the wall and noticeably leaning forward, indicates the act of eavesdropping, and is readable in the same way that the "conventionalized language of facial expression, pose, and gesture" on the melodramatic stage was readable to its audience.[17] The lines of influence between the drama and book illustrations, illustrations and the novel, and the novel and the drama all ran in both directions, as each of these forms relied on the others to make meaning, and even to make meaning that could be understood once a work is separated from the form it was originally developed alongside.

Dramatic Adaptation and Genre Transportability

When George Cruikshank produced the illustrations that accompanied *Oliver Twist*, he did so with the knowledge and approval of Dickens and his publisher, Richard Bentley, though this relationship was not without conflict. The novel's early theatrical adaptations, on the other hand, were produced under considerably different circumstances. The unauthorized theatrical reproduction of novels was a contentious issue, as authors would have received no profit from versions of their novels that appeared on stage. Dickens was one of the most vocal proponents for the protection of intellectual property via copyright, particularly when it came to the reprinting of his work for the American market. In a letter to actor-manager Frederick Yates regarding a production of *Nicholas Nickleby* that had opened at the Adelphi Theatre in November of 1838, Dickens indicates that he had less of a problem with the concept of adaptation itself, and more of an issue with the adaptation of an as yet unfinished work. He wrote that such adaptations "vulgarize the characters, [and] destroy or weaken in the minds

---

[17] Meisel, *Realizations*, 5.

of those who see them the impressions I have endeavoured to create." But he then tells Yates that "no such objection can exist for a moment where the thing is so admirably done in every respect as you have done it in this instance."[18] In an unfinished work, Dickens suggests, the reader's impressions of the characters are not yet formalized, and they run the risk of being usurped by the vulgar misrepresentations of the characters on the stage. As long as the original work itself was complete, or the adaptation was "admirably done" and not a vulgar misrepresentation, Dickens seemed to be willing to participate in what Monica Cohen calls a "culture of reuse," where each play involved the (conscious or unconscious) collaboration of multiple writers (the original author and their adaptors or translators), just as the physical performance of a play could necessitate the collaboration of actors, dancers, clowns, and so forth.[19] Though these novelistic adaptations indeed tend to be extremely derivative and overtly commercial, I still want to consider these plays not only as brazen acts at textual appropriation, but also as legitimate attempts to reinterpret a literary work from one narrative genre into another, in the same way that book illustrations represent an interpretive translation of incidents in the novel that required the collaboration of multiple parties.

The novel itself was published in twenty-four monthly parts between February of 1837 and April of 1839, and a three-volume book version of the completed novel was published in November of 1838, five months before the final part was issued. Published over the course of two years, its slow and steady progression though serial publication did not deter the London theaters from attempting to capitalize on the novel's popularity. The first theatrical adaptation of *Oliver Twist* was mounted at the St. James's Theatre in March of 1838, an entire year before the novel's serialization ended.[20] In May, another adaptation appeared at the Pavilion Theatre, which would have given the author, C. Z. Barnett, only fourteen out of twenty-four monthly parts to work from.[21] Though neither of these preemptive productions remained on the stage for long, George Almar's version at the Surrey Theatre, which premiered on November 19, 1838, was far more popular. *Oliver Twist: A Serio-Comic Burletta in Three Acts* continued to be performed throughout the nineteenth century, and editions were

---

[18] Charles Dickens, *The Letters of Charles Dickens* (Oxford: Clarendon Press: 1965-2002), 1:463.
[19] Cohen, Monica F., *Pirating Fictions: Ownership and Creativity in Nineteenth-Century Popular Culture* (Charlottesville: University of Virginia Press, 2017), 132.
[20] Malcolm Morley, "Early Dramas of *Oliver Twist*," *The Dickensian* 43 (Spring 1947): 75.
[21] Ibid., 77.

published as late as 1920. But even this version was partially preemptive, since it was first performed only ten days after the complete novel had been published in volume form, with five more months of serialization remaining.[22]

Perhaps the most surprising aspect of Almar's adaptation of *Oliver Twist* is his erasure of the portions of the novel set in the workhouse. His version begins in Mrs. Corney's cottage, a scene that happens about halfway through the novel. This scene occurs somewhat anachronistically in the play as well, since the next scene, which takes place in Sowerberry's shop, backtracks considerably. By positioning this scene first, Almar is able to avoid setting any scenes in the workhouse. Bumble bypasses young Oliver's time at the workhouse by telling Mrs. Corney not the names of the parochial foundlings, but of the parochial apprentices, ending with Oliver Twist: "Ah! That's the last parochial orphan the parish—thanks to Mr. Sowerberry, the undertaker—has thrown off its shoulders."[23] Because it is a "realization," we have a very good idea of how the scene Almar chose to open the play with would have appeared on stage. Almar's stage direction describe "*the house of* Mrs. Corney, *an interior, fireplace on one side,* R.H.*, with glass over the mantel-piece, according to the etching of the history*" (5). The etching that Almar is referencing is "Mr. Bumble and Mrs. Corney Taking Tea," one of Cruikshank's illustrations to the novel. See fig. 7.5. This means that the image the play opens with is one of warm domesticity. In the Cruikshank etching, the figures are thrown into shadow by the light from the fireplace; a tea kettle boils, and a mother cat and her three kittens frolic in the warmth. In the novel, this illustration opens first chapter of Book II, and, as another scene of consumption, acts as an ironic parallel to the grim "Oliver Asking for More," the first illustration presented in Book I. Though Act III is set in "The workhouse parlour,"[24] there are no indications of the carceral in this domestic space, nor are there any pauper characters present here or anywhere else in the play.

Though Almar did remove the workhouse from his play, he did not remove all traces of more private poverty and abject social conditions. We do hear about Oliver accompanying Mr. Sowerberry to the home of a poor family for the first time, and the stage direction describing the family's apartment is virtually identical to the description in the novel, all the way down to the "low stool," "the cold hearth," and "the small recess opposite

---

[22] Meisel, *Realizations*, 252-3.

[23] George Almar*, Oliver Twist. A Serio-Comic Burletta, in Three Acts.* (London: Chapman and Hall, n.d), 8.

[24] Ibid., 42.

the door."[25] Almar even invents an additional scene to add to the family's dejected conditions. In the novel, we simply hear that "the family [had] been meanwhile relieved with a half-quartern loaf and a piece of cheese" (1:86). In the play, we see a parish officer give the man some bread, and watch him as "*he pounces on the contents of the basket, tears a loaf into several pieces—throwing them around—children eagerly pick them up—kneeling and bursting into an hysterical laugh*" (15). While this highly visual and non-verbal scene is actually more shockingly abject than the corresponding scene in the novel, the scene of poverty that Almar chose to highlight and even expand upon is one that is removed from the institutional structure of the workhouse. This starkly contrasts to the workhouse setting that Dickens gives us the novel, where we hear that "the room in which the boys were fed, was a large stone hall, with a copper at one end, out of which the master, dressed in an apron for the purpose, and assisted by one or two women, ladled the gruel at mealtimes" (1:27). His description, especially when compared to Almar's adaptation, emphasizes the carceral nature of the institution by focusing on the largeness and the coldness of the room in which a mass of people are served in a disciplinary manner: each boy must walk to the front of the room to receive his gruel from "the master". The privacy and domesticity of the equivalent spaces in the melodramatic adaptation de-systematizes the institutional social problem of the novel. The necessity of representing the social problem through individualized bodies on a stage (or individualized figures in an illustration) means that such adaptations will inevitably lack the discursive explication that the genre of the social problem novel relies upon.

Like most novels written in the nineteenth century, a period which, according to Alastair Fowler, was one of the most prolific in terms of genre experimentation and combination,[26] *Oliver Twist* is made up of multiple interacting genres. Its two most important generic categories are the social problem novel and the Newgate (or crime) novel, though only the second would have been recognized or articulated *as* a genre at the time the novel was written. Genre, as theorized by Mikhail Bakhtin and the later generations of genre theorists influenced by him, is much more than a classificatory system. Rather, genres determine the content of the works themselves by knitting language together with "specific points of view, specific approaches, forms of thinking, nuances and accents characteristic

---

[25] Ibid., 13; Dickens, *Oliver Twist*, 1:82-3.
[26] Alastair Fowler, *Kinds of Literature: An Introduction to the Theory of Genres and Modes* (Cambridge, MA: Harvard University Press, 1982), 206.

of the given genre."[27] Though both the social problem novel and the Newgate novel are operating within the larger genre of prose fiction, they each necessitate different approaches and forms of thinking. Dickens's critique of the workhouse system cannot rely on the visually oriented scenes of action that, as will be further explained below, the Newgate novel primarily uses to convey meaning. The point of view from which the issue at hand, here the workhouse, is approached needs to be wide-ranging and systematic in order to situate it as a social problem. Melodrama, as a genre that must render everything in either dialogue or image, is therefore unsuited for this systematic point of view.

Figure 7.6. George Cruikshank, "Oliver asking for more," 1837, etching, in Charles Dickens, *Oliver Twist* (London: Richard Bentley, 1838), 1: facing page 29. Internet Archive. Public domain.

---

[27] M. M. Bakhtin, *The Dialogic Imagination: Four Essays*, trans. Caryl Emerson and Michael Holquist (Austin: University of Texas Press, 1981), 189.

Because it needs to create a more wide-ranging, systematized problem, the social problem novel must rely on textual explication in addition to textual (or visual) description. The scene where "Oliver asks for more" accrues meaning not only from Dickens's description of the carceral nature of the physical institution, but also from his reflections on the philosophy of the board members who run it:

> The members of this board were very sage, deep, philosophical men; and when they came to turn their attention to the workhouse, they found out at once, what ordinary folks would never have discovered—the poor people liked it! [...] So, they established the rule, that all poor people should have the alternative (for they would compel nobody, not they,) of being starved by a gradual process in the house, or by a quick one out of it [...] For the first six months after Oliver Twist was removed, the system was in full operation (1:24-6).

This description emphasizes that the injustice committed against the workhouse inmates is not simply the result of individual cruelty or incompetence. Instead, Oliver is the victim of a "system" and a "process" instituted as part of an intentional, "philosophical" method of dealing with the poor. Though George Cruikshank did provide an illustration for this scene (in fact, it is the novel's first illustration), "Oliver asking for more" is unable to convey this structural and systematic perspective. See fig. 7.6. It, in comparison to Dicken's description of the workhouse, is comparatively intimate, featuring only around ten boys in a relatively small space. It must sacrifice the "large stone hall" of the description in order to achieve a focus on the individualized appearance and expressions of Oliver, the master, and the other boys. On the other hand, Cruikshank is able much more easily to encapsulate the criminal aspects of the novel, such as the Artful Dodger and Charley Bates stealing Mr. Brownlow's handkerchief or Oliver being shot during the robbery of the Maylie home, in a single image because these plot points are able to be encapsulated in a single action, and are themselves already incidental in nature. Unlike Dickens's description of the workhouse, his description of the robbery of Brownlow's handkerchief does not necessitate the same type of omniscient explication. It is this inherently action-oriented, *and therefore visual*, aspect that makes the Newgate novel the more transportable, and illustratable, genre. This same emphasis on action and visuality is what makes melodrama such a transportable genre, or mode, as well.

Studying the ways in which a single work is translated back and forth between different media ultimately reveals a relationship among genre forms that is more lateral than hierarchical. Though Dickens's novel remains the source text (later claims made by Cruikshank about his role in originating the novel's characters and incidents notwithstanding) that adaptations both visual and theatrical can ultimately be traced back to, it does not follow that "the novel" as a genre retains a similar precedence over media. Illustrations and dramas must adapt and to varying degrees transform the content of *Oliver Twist* into their own particular forms, the content of the novel itself has already drawn from the conventions of both image-making and melodrama, adapting and transforming these conventions to fit its own textual form.

Bibliography

Almar, George. *Oliver Twist. A Serio-Comic Burletta, in Three Acts.* London: Chapman and Hall, n.d.

Bakhtin, M. M. *The Dialogic Imagination: Four Essays.* Translated by Caryl Emerson and Michael Holquist. Austin: University of Texas Press, 1981.

Cohen, Monica F. *Pirating Fictions: Ownership and Creativity in Nineteenth-Century Popular Culture.* Charlottesville: University of Virginia Press, 2017.

Dickens, Charles. *The Letters of Charles Dickens.* 12 vols. Oxford: Clarendon Press: 1965-2002.

—. *Oliver Twist.* 3 vols. London: Richard Bentley, 1838.

Fowler, Alastair. *Kinds of Literature: An Introduction to the Theory of Genres and Modes.* Cambridge, MA: Harvard University Press, 1982.

Golden, Catherine J. *Serials to Graphic Novels: The Evolution of the Victorian Illustrated Book* Gainesville: University Press of Florida, 2017.

Haywood, Ian. *Romanticism and Caricature.* Cambridge and New York: Cambridge University Press, 2013.

James, Louis. "Cruikshank and Early Victorian Caricature." *History Workshop*, no. 6 (Autumn 1978): 107-120.

Meisel, Martin. *Realizations: Narrative, Pictorial, and Theatrical Arts in Nineteenth-Century England.* Princeton, NJ: Princeton University Press, 1983.

Morley, Malcolm. "Early Dramas of *Oliver Twist*," *The Dickensian* 43 (Spring 1947): 74-79.

Patten, Robert L. *George Cruikshank's Life, Times, and Art.* 2 vols. New Brunswick, NJ: Rutgers University Press, 1996.

Steig, Michael. *Dickens and Phiz.* Bloomington: Indiana University Press, 1978.

Stephens, Frederic G. *A Memoir of George Cruikshank*. New York: Scribner and Welford, 1891.

Thackeray, William Makepeace. "Charles Dickens and his Works." *Fraser's Magazine* 21, no. 124 (April 1840): 381-400.

—. "George Cruikshank." *The Westminster Review* 34 (June 1840): 1-60.

CHAPTER EIGHT

VISIONS OF LONG WILL:
LANGLAND AND *PIERS PLOWMAN*
FOR CHILDREN AT THE END OF THE
LONG NINETEENTH CENTURY

PAUL HARDWICK

Kathleen Scott, discussing the marginal illustrations of William Langland's fourteenth-century dream vision poem *Piers Plowman* in Bodley MS Douce 104, has noted that the illustrations do not seem to depend greatly upon traditional models; instead, they offer

> an immediate contemporary response to the text by the person who commissioned the manuscript and probably selected the subjects for illustration; they are also, to a certain extent, a reaction by the artist to the text, but probably through a screen of transmitted instructions.[1]

The images do not merely illustrate the figures encountered by the dreaming narrator, they also act as a gloss, telling us how to read the poem. In this chapter, I shall discuss some illustrations of Langland, his poem, and his world, in children's books of the first years of the twentieth century which act in a similar manner, offering a response to the accompanying text which creatively nuances our reading. I shall present these in the context of what we may think of as the "traditional" representations of the Middle Ages which formed and coalesced throughout the "long nineteenth century", in this case personified by representations of Chaucer for the same audience.

---

[1] Derek Pearsall and Kathleen Scott (ed.), *Piers Plowman: A Facsimile of Bodleian Library, Oxford, MS Douce 104* (Cambridge: D. S. Brewer, 1992), 28. The Bodleian Library has made all of the manuscript illustrations available at: https://digital.bodleian.ox.ac.uk/objects/e6865046-6257-4591-a731-548232c7c8dd/.

I have chosen Chaucer as my point of contrast for three reasons. First, he is Langland's contemporary;[2] secondly, Chaucer is generally the poet through which children are introduced to the literature of the Middle Ages;[3] finally, until recently studies of Langland invariably placed him in relation to Chaucer. Chaucer's status as the father of English poetry, almost as a matter of course, made him the yardstick against which other medieval writers were subsequently judged. In terms of poetry, Langland invariably fails to measure up—as early as 1778, Thomas Warton, in his *History of English Poetry*, characterises *Piers Plowman* as offering the reader, "not only striking specimens of our author's allegorical satire, but contain[ing] much sense and observation of life, with some strokes of poetry."[4]

Whilst containing only "some strokes of poetry", then, *Piers Plowman* could nonetheless offer an insight into fourteenth-century history. Specifically, in the words of J. R. Green,

> all the darker and sterner aspects of [the fourteenth century], its social revolt, its moral and religious awakening, the misery of the peasant, the protest of the Lollard, are painted with a terrible fidelity in the poem of William Longland [sic]. Nothing brings more vividly home to us the social chasm which in the fourteenth century severed the rich from the poor than the contrast between the "Complaint of Piers the Ploughman" and the "Canterbury Tales." The world of wealth and ease and laughter through which the courtly Chaucer moves with eyes downcast as in a pleasant dream is a far-off world of wrong and of ungodliness to the gaunt poet of the poor.[5]

It is also a far-off world when compared with the idealised medievalism of the nineteenth century.[6] Whilst what is seen as Langland's unsparing truth-

---

[2] I explore the suggestion that Chaucer may have been influenced by Langland's work in "Chaucer: The Poet as Ploughman," *The Chaucer Review* 33 (1998), 146-56.

[3] As Steve Ellis has argued, the first decade and a half of the twentieth century may be considered the "golden age of editions of Chaucer aimed at children": see Steve Ellis, *Chaucer at Large* (Minneapolis and London: University of Minnesota Press, 2000), 46-57. The Victorian and Edwardian eras are explored in Velma Bourgeois Richmond's *Chaucer as Children's Literature* (Jefferson, NC: McFarland, 2004).

[4] Thomas Warton, *The History of English Poetry, from the Eleventh to the Seventeenth Century* (London: Alex Murray and Son, 1778), v.

[5] John Richard Green, *A Short History of the English People* (London: Macmillan, 1876), 248.

[6] The rise of an idealised view of the Middle Ages, and its ideological representations in the nineteenth century, is discussed at length in Alice Chandler, *A Dream of Order* (London: Routledge and Kegan Paul, 1971) and Mark Girouard, *The Return to Camelot* (New Haven and London: Yale University Press, 1981). Richmond, in

telling may be considered admirable, it is rather less attractive than Chaucer's "wealth and ease and laughter" and, therefore, best consigned to the realm of historical curiosity. As Sarah A. Kelen has noted,

> Chaucer's works were directly imitated or translated by later writers from the fifteenth through the nineteenth centuries, but the early modern readers of *Piers Plowman*, particularly after the fifteenth century, rarely found in Langland's work a stylistic inspiration. More often they found political rhetoric, theological propaganda, linguistic evidence, and a milestone in the development of English Literary history.[7]

A notable exception, however, may be found in a fictional representation of Langland by the Christian Socialist children's author Florence Converse.[8] Although none of her works remain in print today, Converse was very successful in the early decades of the twentieth century, particularly for her "Sunday books", such as *The House of Prayer* (1908) and *The Blessed Birthday* (1917).[9] These are beautifully illustrated volumes of moral instruction for children, which frequently borrowed medieval motifs. Her most widely read work, however, is *Long Will* (1903)—a very popular children's novel in its time, which ran to numerous reprints in its Everyman edition, well into the 1940s.

Some synopsis of this largely forgotten work will be useful at this point. Set in the context of events surrounding the "Peasants' Revolt" of 1381, the novel offers a veritable "who's who" of late fourteenth-century literary and political characters. The main protagonist, however, is Langland's daughter Calote,[10] who spends much of the novel travelling the country, from Devon to Newcastle, in an attempt to rouse the downtrodden poor. This she does by reciting extracts from her father's Vision, after first drawing an attentive crowd with more immediately attractive tales of "Robin Hood, or Earl

---

Chaucer as Children's Literature, notes that "Chaucer for children [was] a part of this process of idealization directed to many audiences" (11).

[7] Sarah A. Kelen, *Langland's Early Modern Identities* (New York and Basingstoke: Palgrave Macmillan, 2007), 8.

[8] Regrettably little is known of the life of Converse. Some biographical detail may be gleaned from Theresa Corcoran's biography of her lifelong companion, Vida Dutton Scudder. Theresa Corcoran, *Vida Dutton Scudder* (Boston: Twayne, 1982).

[9] Florence Converse, *The House of Prayer* (New York and London: J. M. Dent and Sons, 1908); *The Blessed Birthday* (New York: E. P. Dutton, 1917).

[10] In *Piers Plowman* Will, the narrator, refers to "Kytte my wif and Calote my doghter": William Langland, *The Vision of Piers Plowman*, ed. A. V. C. Schmidt (London: J. M. Dent and Sons, 1995), B V.429.

Randle of Chester,"[11] on a mission half-heartedly supported by the petulant boy-king Richard II. It is a very engaging narrative, full of page-turning suspense, posing such questions as: will the rather unpleasant Jack Straw have his evil way with Calote? and who is the mysterious, chubby, bearded figure who saves Langland from Straw and Tyler's crazed throng of bloodthirsty weavers?

Whilst I of course do not wish to spoil the book for would-be readers, I would like to elaborate upon a couple of points. First, as I have already suggested, Jack Straw and Wat Tyler—recorded as rebel leaders by contemporary chronicles, though little is known about either of them—are portrayed in a very negative light throughout the book. Will himself realises their natures, pointedly asking his daughter, "dost believe Jack Straw and Wat Tyler seek Truth,—or their own glory?"[12] Converse, in painting the rebel leaders as self-seeking exploiters of their followers, who wilfully misrepresent Langland's message, alters the expected perspective on the Revolt. For Converse, the historical failure of the Rising is transformed from a tragic defeat under the might of the ruling classes into a self-defeat brought about through the inappropriate motives of the rebel leaders themselves. Thus, the ideals underpinning the Revolt live beyond its inglorious end, remaining embodied in an uncorrupted form in the person of Langland, in his poem, and in those who take his words to heart. Consequently, his message of social equality grounded firmly in Christian precepts remains valid beyond the failed rebellion and, implicitly, into the twentieth century.

The other revelation I would like to make is that the chubby stranger who comes to Will's aid is none other than Geoffrey Chaucer. Chaucer makes several appearances throughout the novel, initially representing the traditional world of "wealth and ease and laughter" we would expect. Young Chaucer and Langland first meet by chance in the Malvern Hills, as Will— to a suitably avian accompaniment—is composing an early draft of *Piers Plowman*. As the reader familiar with *Piers Plowman* may expect, he soon falls asleep. However, before he has the opportunity to dream a wondrous dream, he is awoken by "a gay lad in scarlet hosen and a short green coat, and shoes of fine leather" who, distracted by the composition of a roundel

---

[11] Florence Converse, *Long Will* (London: J. M. Dent and Sons, 1939), 165. In Passus V of *Piers Plowman*, the allegorical figure of Sloth, whilst unaware of his Paternoster, confesses, "But I kan rymes of Robyn Hood and Randolf Erl of Chestre": V.396. For examples of the appropriation of *Piers Plowman* by the rebels of 1381, see R. B. Dobson, *The Peasants' Revolt of 1381* (Basingstoke: Macmillan, 1983), 379-83.

[12] Converse, *Long Will*, 123.

to his lady, has become separated from the hunting party of Prince Lionel, himself currently a guest at Malvern Priory (4). The perceptive youngster almost immediately discerns that the "long brown man" must be a poet, and there follows a discussion between the two concerning what being a poet might actually mean. Naturally, the still unworldly Chaucer defines poetry as a noble, courtly pastime, and is rather perplexed by Langland's alliterative metre, interrupting the recitation of *Piers Plowman* after a mere half-dozen lines with an irritable urgency which echoes—albeit in more polite language for a young reader—Harry Bailley's exasperation at Chaucer's own "drasty speche" when he interrupts *The Tale of Sir Thopas* in *The Canterbury Tales*:

> "No, no! not thus, not thus! [...] never thus! An thou come to court they'll not hearken to thy long slow measures. Thou shalt make thy verses the French way, with rhyme. Needs must thou learn this manner of the French ere thou come to court."[13]

Already, we have a tension between the "merrie England" of Chaucer, prevalent in the early twentieth century,[14] and the poetry of "the poor folk in cots" provided by Langland. This contrast is reiterated later by a kind of medieval "battle of the bards" before Richard, in which Langland holds his own against Chaucer (John Gower is also present but is not considered to represent serious competition).

As Chaucer is waiting for this reading to begin, we have one of Converse's knowing touches, which is rather significant. Taking in the opulent surroundings, Calote wanders down the room, looking at the tapestries:

> And when she was nigh to where the little round gray man sat a-scribbling, nevertheless he was not so busy but he was 'ware of her and looked up sidewise with a smile. Then, on a sudden, he had taken the long rope of her hair, and he shook it gently and laughed.
> "Her yellow hair was braided in a tresse,
> Behind her back, a yarde long I guesse,"

---

[13] Converse, *Long Will*, 8. For Harry Bailey's interruption, see Geoffrey Chaucer *The Tale of Sir Thopas*, in *The Riverside Chaucer*, ed. Larry D. Benson (Oxford: Oxford University Press, 1988), VII (B^2) 919-25.

[14] On Chaucer as the embodiment of "merrie England" outside the academy, see Ellis, *Chaucer at Large*, 17-31.

Quoth he; and anon, "Saint Mary, –'t is a good line! I'll write it down."
Whereupon he did, and Calote ran back to her father, rosy flushed, yet no-
wise frighted – for this was a friendly wight.[15]

In this little vignette of Chaucer, we can recognise the influential philologist
and Chaucer scholar F. J. Furnivall's "most gracious and tender spirit, the
sweetest singer, the best pourtrayer ... and withal the most genial and
humourful healthy-souled man that England had ever seen,"[16] cheerfully
seizing inspiration from a passing attractive young girl for his description
of Emelye for his *Knight's Tale*.[17]

She thought of the two young princes who were prisoners there

Figure 8.1. W. Heath Robinson, "She thought of the two young princes there"
(1906). Image: Paul Hardwick. Public domain.

---

[15] Converse, *Long Will*, 246.
[16] F. J. Furnivall, "Recent Work at Chaucer," *Macmillan's Magazine* 27 (1872-73), 383.
[17] Chaucer, *The Knight's Tale*, in *The Riverside Chaucer*, I (A)1049-50.

This is just the sort of image we would expect of Chaucer in the early twentieth century, and just the sort of image that we would expect to attract illustrators of children's books. Indeed, W. Heath Robinson's illustration of Emelia—a vision of ideal, youthful, feminine beauty—is one of only two images used to illustrate the *Knight's Tale* (or, as it is called, "Emelia: The Story of the Man of Might") in Janet Harvey Kelman's *Stories from Chaucer* (1906).[18] See fig. 8.1. As Velma Bourgeois Richmond observes, Emelia here, with her "abundant auburn hair and long neck, emphasized by a necklace, and her green shawl suggest(s) the 'stunners' of Dante Gabriel Rossetti, albeit with softer colours,"[19] presenting the ideal Pre-Raphaelite dream, appropriately stripped of the intense sensuality characteristic of Rossetti and his followers. *Long Will*, however, offers no such idealism in its illustrations. The soft lines and muted tones of Chaucer's "world of wealth and ease and laughter" are eschewed in favour of Garth Jones's much harsher style. See fig. 8.2.

I will come down from the hill-top.

Figure 8.2. Garth Jones, "I will come down from the hill-top" (1903). Image: Paul Hardwick. Public domain.

---

[18] Janet Harvey Kelman, *Stories from Chaucer told to the Children* (London: T. C. and E. C. Jack, 1906).
[19] Richmond, *Chaucer as Children's Literature*, 85.

Greatly influenced by the woodcuts of Dürer, Jones sympathetically reinforces the austere political spiritual message of Converse's text, lest we should be seduced by the enticingly picturesque. After his first encounter with the boy Chaucer, who chides him for his lack of experience of the world, Will exclaims,

> "Now lead me down into the valley, O Truth, where the world dwelleth! I will follow. I will come down from the hill-top. Men shall be more than a name for me before I am done. A child hath found me out."[20]

Jones's illustration fills the frame with purpose and energy. There is no room for post-Pre-Raphaelite languor and "palely loitering". Though young, Converse's hero has the appearance of one who is facing an altogether more metaphorical valley. Jones, in all his illustrations throughout the novel, focuses on a harsh, very human, corporeal realism. This continues right up until the death of Langland, returned to Malvern Priory for one last encounter with his mentor, Brother Owen (the *Pearl*-poet in Converse's cast of characters). See fig. 8.3. In this final illustration, the drawn face and, particularly, the wasted hands, deliberately eschew the glamourisation of the Middle Ages that we find in most children's books of the period.

Significantly, Chaucer does not appear in any of the illustrations in *Long Will*. As mentioned earlier, in the chaos of the Revolt, Chaucer saves Langland from an angry mob with whom he is remonstrating about their violent misinterpretation of his message. The exchange between Langland and Chaucer following the incident is telling:

> "No friend of Gaunt is safe in London streets."
> "Who is safe?" asked Chaucer. "No friend of the people, neither."
> Langland groaned and clasped his head in his hands.
> "'T was said thou hadst made peace," said Chaucer. "Methought 't was ended, this rioting."
> "Peace!" cried Long Will. "There shall be no peace so long as men strive to be king. When they have forgot to add glory unto themselves, when they are content to serve their brothers, – then cometh peace."
> "Take heart, brother," said Dan Chaucer. "Here be two men that do not desire a kingdom, – thou, and I."[21]

Here we have Chaucer, not compromising himself in the least—he can still talk disparagingly of "Jakke Straw and his meynee" in his *Nun's Priest's*

---

[20] Converse, *Long Will*, 14.
[21] Converse, *Long Will*, 314.

Tale[22]—but nevertheless aligning himself with his "brother" Langland. In this relationship we see the Father of English Poetry authenticating Langland's revolutionary spirit, with Garth Jones's pictorial gloss stripping away the trappings of complacent, picturesque idealism and reinforcing the narrative's message in what Maria Nicolajeva and Carole Scott have usefully defined as a *symmetrical* interaction between words and pictures.[23]

It may well be for purely financial reasons that editions of *Long Will* after 1910 were not illustrated. However, at the same time, the novel also lost its sub-title, *A Romance of the Days of Piers Plowman*.[24] Could it be that the overt Socialist moralisation was deemed inappropriate for young readers? Certainly, by the time a specific schools edition was published in 1939, a note suggested that "You will find this book much more interesting if at the commencement you find out all you can about the reign of Richard II."[25] The novel is firmly captured in a period of political history far removed from the present, illustrating "all the darker and sterner aspects of [the fourteenth century], its social revolt, its moral and religious awakening, the misery of the peasant, the protest of the Lollard," and does nothing to disrupt the image of Chaucer's "world of wealth and ease and laughter" with which late nineteenth- and early twentieth-century England sought to align itself.[26]

---

[22] Chaucer *The Nun's Priest's Tale*, in *The Riverside Chaucer*, VII.3394.
[23] Maria Nicolajeva and Carole Scott, "The Dynamics of Picturebook Communication," *Children's Literature in Education* 31 (2000), 225.
[24] This sub-title, to my knowledge, only appeared on the first English illustrated edition of 1910.
[25] Converse, *Long Will*, 379. The 1939 schools edition is identical to earlier editions in text and pagination, with notes and questions appended at the end. The placing of *Long Will* in a "safe" historical context may also be seen in Sir John Marriott's *English History in English Fiction* (London: Blackie and Son, 1940), in which the highest praise reserved for Converse is that "The novelist adhered closely to history".
[26] Green, *A Short History of the English People*, 248.

Figure 8.3. Garth Jones, "Will Langland, art thou there?" (1903). Image: Paul Hardwick. Public domain.

Figure 8.4. John R. Skelton, "It is a company of pilgrims such as this that Chaucer paints for us, he himself being of the company" (1909). Image: Paul Hardwick. Public domain.

By way of a contrast, I would like to conclude by turning briefly to an illustration of Langland and his world from around the same time as Garth Jones's illustrations for *Long Will*. In her 1909 volume, *English Literature for Boys and Girls*, H. E. Marshall draws the familiar picture of the genial Chaucer, to whose life she devotes three chapters:

> But if Chaucer loved books he loved people too, and we may believe that he readily made friends, for there was a kindly humour about him that must have drawn people to him.[27]

John R. Skelton's accompanying illustrations perfectly complement the tone of the narrative of the genial, bumbling, yet important figure of Chaucer who, contrary to his own *General Prologue*, is depicted leading his company of pilgrims out into an idyllic English morning. See fig. 8.4. I am rather less sure, however, of Skelton's suitability for the figure of Langland who, we are told, "dreamed a wondrous dream". See fig. 8.5.

'Langland dreamed a wondrous dream.'

Figure 8.5. John R. Skelton, "Langland dreamed a wondrous dream" (1909). Image: Paul Hardwick. Public domain.

---

[27] H. E. Marshall, *English Literature for Boys and Girls* (London and New York: Thomas Nelson and Sons, 1909), 133.

In the illustration, we can see a "brood bank by a bourne syde", and a rather misty, romanticised "tour on a toft", in which, on a clear day, we may expect to see Palamon and Arcite pining, but there is no evidence of any "dongeon … With depe diches and derke and dredfulle of sighte".[28] We do have a suitably dark and haunting figure of Piers, but he is almost entirely lost in the Chaucerian "merry company" that surrounds him, the most prominent figure of whom is a fool in bright motley. Langland himself is a far cry from Jones's gaunt, almost apocalyptic figure descending from the hill-top. Indeed, he has more the pose we may expect of the languishing dreamer of a love-vision: we may compare him, for example, with Heath Robinson's other illustration from the *Knight's Tale*, depicting the pining Palamon. See fig. 8.6.

Palamon lay beside a pool of water

Figure 8.6.W. Heath Robinson, "Palamon lay beside a pool of water". (1906). Image: Paul Hardwick. Public domain.

---

[28] Langland, *Piers Plowman*, B Prol.1-16.

The image Skelton offers is one of comfort, of fantasy, of illusion. And, after all, as Marshall reminds us in her text, "the chief interest and value of *Piers Plowman* is that it is history".[29] In Marshall's work, the *contradictory* interaction of words and image ensures that Langland does not offer a contemporary message—he is safely consigned to the historical medieval past, as opposed to the ideal medieval past characterised by the "kindly humour" of Chaucer.[30] So, we see here a contrasting process of pictorial glossing to that of *Long Will*: whilst Marshall's text acknowledges Langland's unavoidable criticisms of society, placing him along with John Wyclif at the head of nascent Protestantism, Skelton's illustrations point the reader to the idyllic "world of wealth and ease and laughter" of the early twentieth-century Middle Ages.[31]

To return to my starting-point, Scott closes her discussion by emphasising the significance of the illustrator of Bodley Douce 104:

> The artist's ability […] to translate a written text (even if through instructions) into visual imagery that remains engaging and credible as an interpretation of the poem was exceptional; and his skill in rendering a variety and nuance of facial expression, animated bodily movement, detail of attribute and costume, and emotive power were particularly rare in this period of heavily outlined and painted, generally static, often stereotyped figures. The canny individualist who illustrated *Piers Plowman* in Douce 104 deserves recognition for a major contribution to the history of English art – for his lively characterisations that anticipate drawing and book illustration of the eighteenth and nineteenth centuries.[32]

What I hope my discussion has demonstrated is the way in which, some five hundred years later, the descendants of the Douce illuminator could either evoke or avoid stereotype in order to aid the "translation" of Langland for young readers in the early years of the twentieth century, according to differing ideological agendas.

---

[29] Marshall, *English Literature for Boys and Girls*, 121.
[30] Nicolajeva and Scott, "The Dynamics of Picturebook Communication," 226.
[31] Velma Bourgeois Richmond, *Chivalric Stories as Children's Literature: Edwardian Retellings in Words and Pictures* (Jefferson, NC: McFarland, 2014), 316-9, comments upon the quality of Skelton's illustrations—particularly that of Wyclif—but does not explore the dynamic between them and Marshall's text.
[32] Pearsall and Scott (ed.), *Piers Plowman: A Facsimile*, xxxii.

Bibliography

Chandler, Alice. *A Dream of Order*. London: Routledge and Kegan Paul, 1971.

Chaucer, Geoffrey. *The Riverside Chaucer*. Edited by Larry D. Benson. Oxford: Oxford University Press, 1988.

Corcoran, Theresa. *Vida Dutton Scudder*. Boston: Twayne, 1982.

Converse, Florence. *Long Will*. Boston and New York: J. M. Dent and Sons, 1903.

—. *The House of Prayer*. New York and London: J. M. Dent and Sons, 1908.

—. *The Blessed Birthday*. New York: E. P. Dutton, 1917.

—. *Long Will*. London: J. M. Dent and Sons, 1939.

Dobson, R. B. *The Peasants' Revolt of 1381*. Basingstoke: Macmillan, 1983.

Ellis, Steve. *Chaucer at Large*. Minneapolis and London: University of Minnesota Press, 2000.

Furnivall, F. J. "Recent Work at Chaucer," *Macmillan's Magazine* 27 (1872-73), 383-88.

Girouard, Mark. *The Return to Camelot*. New Haven and London: Yale University Press, 1981.

Green, John Richard. *A Short History of the English People*. London: Macmillan, 1876.

Hardwick, Paul. "Chaucer: The Poet as Ploughman" *The Chaucer Review* 33 (1998): 146-56.

Hunt, Peter. "Retreatism and Advance (1914-1945)," in *Children's Literature: An Illustrated History*. Edited by Peter Hunt. Oxford: Oxford University Press, 1995.

Kelen, Sarah A. *Langland's Early Modern Identities*. New York and Basingstoke: Palgrave, 2007.

Kelman, Janet Harvey. *Stories from Chaucer told to the Children*. London: T. C. and E. C. Jack, 1906.

Langland, William. *The Vision of Piers Plowman*. Edited by A. V. C. Schmidt. London: J. M. Dent and Sons, 1995

Marriott, Sir John. *English History in English Fiction*. London: Blackie and Son, 1940.

Marshall, H. E. *English Literature for Boys and Girls*. London and New York: Thomas Nelson and Sons, 1909.

Nicolajeva, Maria and Scott, Carole. "The Dynamics of Picturebook Communication," *Children's Literature in Education* 31 (2000): 225-239.

Pearsall, Derek, and Kathleen Scott, ed. *Piers Plowman: A Facsimile of Bodleian Library, Oxford, MS Douce 104.* Cambridge: D. S. Brewer, 1992.

Richmond, Velma Bourgeois. *Chaucer as Children's Literature.* Jefferson, NC: McFarland, 2004.

—. *Chivalric Stories as Children's Literature: Edwardian Retellings in Words and Pictures.* Jefferson, NC: McFarland, 2014.

Warton, Thomas. *The History of English Poetry, from the Eleventh to the Seventeenth Century.* Reprint. London: Alex Murray and Son, 1778.

Chapter Nine

"La Torgue was Monarchy; the Guillotine was Revolution": Anti-Medievalism in Victor Hugo's *Ninety-Three* (*Quatrevingt-Treize*)

Stephen Basdeo

Introduction

"Thus the guillotine had a right to say to the tower: I am thy daughter"[1]

…So wrote the visionary French author Victor Hugo in *Ninety-Three* (*Quatre-Vingt Treize*) (1874), his final novel. By the time that Hugo had published *Ninety-Three*, he had been witness to some of the defining events of nineteenth-century French history such as the French Revolution of 1848 and the *coup d'état* of Napoleon III in 1852. This passage, and indeed the entire novel, illustrates Hugo's own reservations towards the idea of revolutionary violence and the battle for the destruction of the *ancien regime*, expressed through his novel which was published in the aftermath of the Paris Commune of 1871. Yet this conflicted attitude towards ideas of revolution in the novel—which result in Hugo's coming out firmly in favour of revolution via several justifications of it—were not only expressed in the text of Hugo's novel but also the illustrations produced for the second French and English editions in 1874.[2] I use the second editions here because—and interestingly for a volume whose focus is that of text and image—Hugo staunchly opposed the inclusion of images in first editions of

---

[1] Victor Hugo, *Ninety-Three* (London: Richard Edward King, c.1890), 246.
[2] Victor Hugo, *Ninety-Three*, 2 vols (London: George Routledge, 1889). For reproductions of the illustrations I have used this fine library edition which is seemingly only available in rare book libraries. For quotations from the text itself, I have used a different edition by Richard Edward King published in the late 1890s which is more accessible.

his works, wanting the text to stand on its own, but he willingly allowed images to be included in subsequent editions of his works.[3] Only once the text of the message in his novel had been available to the public for some time did he allow artists to contribute to this.

It is an analysis of the recurrent imagery and motifs in *Ninety-Three*— of civilization and barbarism; progress and backwardness; the "old" world and the new—and selections of its accompanying images, which are the focus of this chapter. The combined message in both the texts and the images is one of what I shall call "Revolutionary Anti-Medievalism". This anti-medievalism is the use of the Middle Ages to deride the medieval past and foreground the progressive nature of the French Revolution, even if that revolution, as Hugo illustrates, was "the daughter" of the feudal world.[4]

Victor Hugo

Jean Cocteau once quipped that "Victor Hugo was a madman who thought he was Victor Hugo".[5] Many of his literary contemporaries indeed thought that Hugo was a little eccentric, perhaps bordering on "mad", but Cocteau meant something different. Hugo's talent was, as one critic put it, of a mythopoetic nature; he was able to convert his own inner "psychodrama" over artistic, cultural, social, and political questions, express them through the medium of print, and in the process fashion himself as a grand sage or "prodigious pyrotechnist posing as God's special interlocutor".[6] Of course, in fashioning himself thus, Hugo was imitating the British novelist Walter Scott (1771–1832), whom Hugo praised for leading the reader "at his will into all places and into all times [and who] unveils for him with ease the most secret recesses of the heart, as well as the most mysterious phenomena of nature, as well as the obscurest pages of history". [7]

Yet it was not only that Hugo sought to emulate and surpass Scott's literary talent but also, much like Scott, to become a French version of the author-as-national-hero. The message that Hugo took from reading Scott's novels is that fiction and those who write it should always have one eye on

---

[3] *Maisons Victor Hugo* (n.d.), https://www.maisonsvictorhugo.paris.fr/.
[4] A version of this chapter originally appeared as a short blog: Stephen Basdeo, "Victor Hugo's Ninety-Three (1874)." *Reynolds's News and Miscellany*, 27 September 2021, https://reynolds-news.com.
[5] Victor Brombert, *Victor Hugo and the Visionary Novel* (Harvard University Press, 1984), 4.
[6] Ibid. 5.
[7] Victor Hugo, "Walter Scott," in *Things Seen (Choses Vue): Essays* (Boston, MA: Estes and Lauriat, n.d.), 310.

entertaining the audience but also have another eye firmly on national concerns and try, if possible, to solve the country's problems. Just as Scott's *Ivanhoe* was a call for national unity in the post-Napoleonic War period, so Hugo wished that French authors, and he humbly offered himself, would do the same.

Just as in Walter Scott's novels, Hugo's early works betray (small 'c') conservative, romantic, and medievalist sentiments. The work which first brought Hugo to public notice was his play *Hernani* (*Hernani, ou l'Honneur Castillan*) (1830). Set in early modern Spain, and therefore not a typical "classicist" play of the type usually featured in contemporary French theatre, and featuring a "king and commoner" plot, the work was a direct assault on the values of the classicists who had long dominated the French stage. Shortly afterwards Hugo published further medievalist romances such as the famous *Hunchback of Notre Dame* (*Notre Dame de Paris*) (1833), a book in which he lamented France's neglect of the great edifice of Notre Dame Cathedral and "the mutilations which time and man have inflicted on the structure".[8] He was above all, however, a patriot—a sentiment that shines through in several poems in his *Songs of Twilight* (*Les Chants du Crepuscule*) (1835). He truly wanted the best for France and by 1848, after the previous Restoration of the monarchy in 1815 and a subsequent change of king of 1830, France's future, so he thought, lay in becoming a republic. Having participated in the French Revolution of 1848, after the foundation of the Second French Republic he became a politician. He was elected to the French legislative assembly, as a member of the conservative-republican Parti de l'Ordre (referred to in English radical newspapers as the Party of Law and Order).[9] Consistently presenting himself as the defender of republican order against Red Republican anarchy, Hugo in fact had many reservations about being a member of the Parti de l'Ordre. Yet his political career was not to last long. His opposition to Napoleon III meant that he was forced into exile (a fate which befell his fellow author and contemporary Eugene Sue; the two men's careers, in terms of their literary output, activism, and eventual exile were in fact very similar).

It was during his exile in Jersey, and later Guernsey, between 1852 and 1870, that Hugo embraced socialism and produced his finest work: *Les Miserables* (1862). This story of redeemed criminal named Jean Valjean, who becomes mixed up in the 1832 student rebellion, was published to huge

---

[8] Victor Hugo, *The Hunchback of Notre Dame* (London: Milner, n.d.), 63.
[9] Jonathan Beecher, *Writers and Revolution: Intellectuals and the French Revolution of 1848* (Cambridge University Press, 2021), 185.

critical acclaim, although it was not without its detractors.[10] This was followed by another masterpiece, *The Toilers of the Sea* (*Les Travailleurs de la mer*), in 1866. Between writing these, he published several shorter works, two of which mocked Napoleon III and were subsequently banned in France: *Napoleon the Little* (*Napoleon le petit*) and *History of a Crime* (*Histoire d'un crime*). With the fall of Napoleon III in the aftermath of the Franco-Prussian War of 1870, Hugo finally returned to Paris. Parisian crowds gathered to mark his return and he was hailed in the press as a national hero.

However, just a year later Parisians were revolting again, in an event now known as the Paris Commune, which lasted between March and May, 1871. Fiercely patriotic and smarting under the humiliating reparations that Prussia had imposed on the nation—and which had been accepted by the newly elected leader of the French executive, Adolphe Thiers (1797–1877)—working-class members of the French National Guard, along with their allies in the socialist movement, rose up against Thiers's administration. Barricades were built around the city of Paris and the "Communards" formed their socialist government, founded on the principles set forth by Jean Pierre Proudhon (1809–65).[11]

The commune was crushed after just two months by the French army, but several thinkers in just as many countries such as Karl Marx (1818–83) turned their thoughts towards the question of revolution. Some fiction writers in succeeding decades likewise shone a light on the short-lived socialist revolution, a notable example being Herbert Hayens's *Paris at Bay: A Story of the Siege and Commune* (1895). Victor Hugo had conflicted feelings towards this revolution. Although Hugo was no stranger to revolutions, having participated in the French Revolution of 1848, he felt that the Commune was "idiotic", as he declared in his diary: "this Commune is as idiotic as the National Assembly is ferocious. From both sides, folly."[12]

Yet publicly Hugo defended the revolutionaries. It is his conflicting feelings towards the question of the morality of revolutions and counter-revolutions more generally that shine through in *Ninety-Three*.

---

[10] See for example the particularly critical piece "Les Miserables", *The Saturday Review*, May 10, 1862: 537–38 which lambasted Hugo for wanting to "revolutionize society" to redress a few isolated and individual wrongs.
[11] Mitchell Abidor, ed. and trans., *Voices of the Paris Commune* (Oakland, CA: PM Press, 2015), 1.
[12] Adam Begley, *The Great Nadar: The Man Behind the Camera* (New York: Crown, 2017), 164.

The Return of a King

Ninety-Three is set in France in the year 1793. The French Revolution has entered its bloodiest phase in Paris where the Committee of Public Safety, led by Maximillien Robespierre (1758–94), has initiated the Reign of Terror and supposed enemies of the revolution are being executed by guillotine. While Robespierre sees enemies all over Paris, the leaders of the revolution have a much bigger threat with which to contend: the War in the Vendée. The people of Brittany, Normandy, Caen, and Evreux have rejected the revolution and have taken up arms against the new French republic. In the novel, the scene of all the action is Brittany, and the war is a guerrilla war fought in the "nooks and corners" of the Breton forests.[13] To add some historical context: initially the peasantry in these areas revolted against the military conscription imposed on them by Paris.[14] Soon their revolt acquired an ideological dimension: the peasants became royalists, loyal to the king and his heirs—even though King Louis XVI had been executed—and they were staunchly Catholic. The revolutionary government in Paris decided that the rebellion needed to be crushed. Civil wars are always nasty, bloody affairs. But the war *had to* be fought, for as Hugo states reactionary sentiment in French society had to be stamped out because "it [was] the price of the regeneration of the people".[15] Brutal though it was, then, Hugo uses his anti-medievalism to justify the war in the Vendée: the lingering attachment to feudalism must be purged from society and the French people reborn.

This motif, that the feudal world represents backwardness, occurs throughout Hugo's novel. One of his arguments is that the "civil war" the Vendée was essentially a struggle between "Civilization" (the revolution) and backward-looking "barbarism" (royalism). For Hugo, the revolution, with its Declaration of the Rights of Man and Citizen and its destruction of royalty and nobility, represented "the vast regeneration of the human race" (66). The revolution was, as an extension of this regeneration, a "war against the past", for a nation can only be reborn if it throws off the dead weight of its traditions and heritage. As Hugo states in his description of Louis XVI's trial, the revolution represented

> [f]atal breaths which blew upon the old torch of monarchy, that had burned for eighteen centuries, and blew it out. The decisive trial of all kings in this

---

[13] Hugo, *Ninety-Three*, 14.
[14] James Maxwell Anderson, *Daily Life During the French Revolution* (Greenwood Publishing, 2007), 205.
[15] Hugo, *Ninety-Three*, 137.

one king, was like the point of departure in the great war against the Past
(107).

Of course, Hugo remarks that the revolution was not a *total* destruction of
the past. Hugo tells us that it was during the revolution that Duboe set out
cataloguing all the treasures held in French archives.[16] Other fruits of the
revolution include academies of music and museums. Alongside some older
things, new things could co-exist: new law codes, unity of weights and
measures, and calculation with the decimal system.[17] The feudal past still
needed to be swept away. But what the revolution does, or should do, in
Hugo's view is retain the best of the past but move forward with new ideas.
The revolution therefore was progress embodied.

The Vendéans want a king to lead them, and into this void steps
Lantenac, a Breton nobleman and one of the novel's most interesting
characters. Lantenac—whose ancestral estates are in Brittany—is funded by
the British Prime Minister, William Pitt (1759–1806), to serve as the
figurehead of the royalist movement in France which, it is hoped, will help
to put an end to the revolution while Britain and her allies carry on a war
against France on land and at sea. Hugo had qualified respect for Pitt. "The
greatest warrior of modern times is not Napoleon," declared Hugo in
Shakespeare (1864), "it is Pitt".[18] The reason for this is that "Napoleon
carried on warfare; Pitt created it. It is Pitt who willed all the wars of the
revolution and empire; they proceeded from him" (340). What Hugo meant
by this statement is that Pitt was the epitome of the coalition that sought to,
quite successfully we might say, repress France's revolution. Were it not for
Pitt, and his schemes—and his ability to marshal the entire financial might
of the British Empire against revolutionary France—there would have been
no war that lasted over twenty-five years. Lantenac is one such tool in Pitt's
war arsenal. Historically, despite the financial support from the British
government, the rustic Vendéans were poorly equipped to respond to the
might of a "modern" revolutionary army. The peasants in *Ninety-Three* may
be good at massacring a small regiment of revolutionaries and unarmed
farmers who decide to take no part in the Vendéans's counter revolution—
as they do later in the novel—but when they are forced to fight against an
organised army of Parisians they are ineffectual despite their large numbers,

---

[16] On French archival practices since the revolution see Édouard Vasseur, "French
archivists, the management of records and records management since the nineteenth
century: are French recordkeeping tradition and practice incompatible with records
management?" *Archives and Manuscripts*, 49 no. 1–2 (2021): 107–32.
[17] Hugo, *Ninety-Three*, 105, 107.
[18] Victor Hugo, *Shakespeare*, trans. A. Baillot (Boston: Estes and Lauriat, n.d.), 340.

and in one battle many of them simply run away (128, 144). By 1796 all the Vendéan rebels had been slaughtered. With a death toll of approximately 170,000 Vendéans, at least one French author has labelled the war a "genocide".[19] Lantenac's first object is to capture several ports in northern France which will allow British ships to dock. Lantenac's alliance with the English, however—against whom Revolutionary France was at war— makes him a traitor in Hugo's eyes, for "no one is a hero who fights against his country" (35).

Lantenac, as he is portrayed in the text, was described as "statuesque" by Robert Louis Stevenson.[20] The same is true in the illustrations, in which Lantenac certainly cuts a commanding figure. Our first glimpse of him as a royalist rebel leader comes in a full-page illustration by Fortuné Louis Méaulle (1844–1916) titled simply "I am the Marquis of Lantenac". See fig. 9.1. In this image we find him standing on top of a hill, quite literally "looking down" on the peasants who he will be leading into battle against the revolutionary army. His figure is almost statuesque yet his costume is peculiar. A seventeenth-century broad-brimmed hat and cloak adorn his upper body while on his lower body he wears hose—in fashion from the late medieval period to the seventeenth century—and knee-length leather boots.[21] Outfitted in a curious mixture of fifteenth- and seventeenth-century clothing, Lantenac is quite simply a man out of his time. The visual depiction of him is complemented by the textual description and Hugo's revelations of his character. In terms of his political philosophy, he praises the philosophy of Edmund Burke, who wrote the anti-revolutionary *Reflections on the Revolution in France* (1790), which praised Britain's supposed great constitution and its separation of powers into king, lords, and commons. Lantenac unsurprisingly pours scorn on those philosophers like Thomas Paine (1737–1809), Voltaire (1694–1778), and Rousseau (1712–78) whom he blames for having spread the seeds of revolution:

> To think that all this would not have happened if they had hanged Voltaire and sent Rousseau to the galleys. Oh! these writer fellows; they are a perfect nuisance … books are at the bottom of all mischief. "Rights of Man!" "Rights of People!" rubbish![22]

---

[19] See Reynald Secher, *A French Genocide: The Vendée* (Paris: University of Notre Dame Press, 2003).
[20] Robert Louis Stevenson, *Familiar Studies of Men and Books*, 4th edn, vol. 1 (1882; reis., London: William Heinemann, 1924), 21.
[21] See Janet Arnold, *Patterns of Fashion: the Cut and Construction of Clothes for Men and Women 1560–1620* (London: Macmillan 1985)
[22] Hugo, *Ninety-Three*, 229.

Most of the main characters in Hugo's novel are inflexible in their devotion to their own ideology. Lantenac's mission is to kill all who oppose a royalist restoration, and he has his sights on the Parisian politicians who ordered Louis XVI's execution: "The regicides have cut off the head of Louis XVI. We will tear off the limbs of the regicides" (17). And Lantenac will not hesitate to sacrifice the lives of the peasants who declare their allegiance to him; he remarks to one of his aides that he is quite willing "to draw up in line a hundred peasants to be mowed down by the artillery of Monsieur Carnot" (39). Indeed, the peasants are tools to him: a tool for winning the war. In "I am the Marquis of Lantenac", as we cast our eyes below the hill, therefore, there is a great multitude of peasants poised and willing to fight for this man who would be their king. See fig. 9.1. Yet to Lantenac, these people's lives mean nothing. They are nameless and faceless.

Humanity and Savagery

Of the Vendéan uprising, Thomas Carlyle in *The French Revolution* (1837) once remarked that the peasants had been "blown into flame and fury by theological and seigneurial bellows".[23] The "flame and fury", with its implication of mindless violence, was also represented by Hugo. With the War in the Vendée being a battle between the Revolution and Civilization on the one hand, and barbarism on the other, Lantenac's cruel behaviour towards the peasants is contrasted with the humanity of the revolutionary army. This comes through most clearly in one of the illustrations accompanying the early part of the book, when the revolutionary army takes under its wing a simple forest-dwelling peasant woman, Michelle, and her three children whom they find in the forest in a state of great distress. See fig. 9.2. No artist was credited in the illustration and it is unlikely to be Meaulle as all of his drawings were included in separate plates, while this particular one was included in the text itself. The revolutionary soldier, evident by his wearing of a Phrygian cap, extends his arm around Michelle who looks dotingly at the baby in her arms. The soldier, as if to further illustrate the humanity of the revolution, holds one of Michelle's other children by the hand and guides him. The message is clear: the revolution will help everyone, even the simple peasant; one's social class and background, and therefore birth—be one peasant or nobleman—does not matter. The guiding hand of the revolution will steer all peoples, on a footing

---

[23] Thomas Carlyle, *The French Revolution* (1837; reis., London: Chapman and Hall, 1889), 155.

of equality, towards a better future. The revolutionaries take care of Michelle in spite of the fact that Michelle's husband is a royalist. When the small flying column head to a farm and lodge there for an evening, Lantenac's royalist forces arrive and massacre the entire army. There is no quarter. The royalists also leave Michelle half-dead and kidnap her three children.

The massacre of the revolutionary army by the peasants quite simply appears like utter savagery. The peasants are in fact depicted as simple savages throughout. Seven thousand peasants flock to Lantenac's standard, despite his reputation as a cruel master. When Hugo explains *why* the peasants need a king, his contempt for the royalist peasants shines through: the peasants *need* a prince because they are not intelligent enough to think for themselves(14). They are barbarians, wedded to the past, and their savagery has medieval roots:

Figure 9.1. Fortuné Louis Méaulle "I am the Marquis of Lantenac" (1889). Image: Stephen Basdeo. Public domain.

Figure 9.2. Artist unknown. Michelle and the revolutionary soldier (1889). Image:
Stephen Basdeo. Public domain.

Opposite the French Revolution, which represents an immense inroad of all
the benefits—civilization in a fit of rage—an excess of maddened
progress—improvements exceeding measure and comprehension—you
must place these strange, grave savages, with clear eyes and flowing hair,
living on milk and chestnuts, their ideas bounded by their thatched roofs,
their hedges and their ditches […] speaking a dead language, which was like
forcing their thoughts to dwell in a tomb; driving their bullocks, sharpening
their scythes, winnowing their black grain, kneading their buckwheat dough,
venerating their plough first and then their grandmothers; believing in the

Blessed Virgin and the White Lady [...] loving their king, their lord, their priest, their very lice; pensive without thought (121).

Some peasants such as Michelle, it appears, are willing and capable of taking the help that the revolution offers them. Although she is a simple woman, her ideas are not "bounded by thatched roofs". This is not so with the peasant army who seem, in Hugo's opinion, to be truly lost in darkness. The anti-Catholic, and therefore anti-medieval, snipe against their veneration of the "Blessed Virgin" recurs throughout the novel. In other places Hugo declares that the Vendéan revolt is also a "revolt of the priests"; it is "darkness assisting darkness" and the peasants are in mental darkness and they are fighting with the forces of darkness (20). Indeed, at one point in the novel the priests beguile the simple-minded peasants into supporting the royalist cause—during a mass, several people appear with red marks around their necks and the priests tell the simple peasants that the men who appear before them are the spirits of the guillotined priests who have returned to urge them to fight against the revolution (137). Such sentiments were quite clearly a break with the earlier, fervent Catholicisim of Hugo's youth.[24] In an 1862 letter to M. Daelli, the Italian translator of *Les Misérables*, Hugo declared his regret that Italy, France, England, and indeed the whole of Europe, "have prejudices, superstitions, tyrannies, fanaticisms [...] you have [the figure of] a barbarian, the monk".[25]

Hugo seems baffled as to why any peasant would side with the royalists, and he never quite seems to be able to explain it to his readers either, other than to say that they were simple savages. He had earlier attempted to answer this question in more depth in *Les Misérables* when he said that "it sometimes happens that the rabble [...] offers battle to the people".[26] History provides a potential answer, however. By 1789, most French nobles were absentee landlords and were usually resident far away from their country estates which was the result of Louis XIV's absolutist rule and centralisation of government. Wanting to concentrate power in his own hands, Louis ruled from his newly built Palace of Versailles. The way for any nobleman to gain royal favour was to be close to Louis, which for the French nobility necessitated their residence either in or near Versailles. The exception to this, however, was the Breton nobles who often eschewed court

---

[24] John Andrew Frey, *A Victor Hugo Encyclopedia* (Westport, CT: Greenwood, 1999), 148.
[25] Victor Hugo, "Letter to M. Daelli, 18 October 1862," in *Les Miserables*, trans. Isabel Hapgood, vol. 2 (London: Walter Scott, n.d.), 281.
[26] Victor Hugo, *Les Misérables*, vol. 5 (Philadelphia: David MacKay, n.d.), 1.

life and, until 1789, usually lived on their estates alongside their peasants.[27] When the Bretons' typical "Gallic" resentment of all things Parisian is also considered—for Brittany, as Hugo remarked, had always had an "independent" spirit—then the Parisian revolutionaries' imposition of conscription and their attack on the Bretons' traditions provided a fertile ground for rebellion to grow.

Gauvain the Revolutionary Knight

One character complicates Hugo's anti-medievalism, however, for as if to exemplify the notion that the French Revolution was a battle between the past and the future, the man whom the Committee of Public Safety sends to hunt down Lantenac is none other than the latter's nephew and heir: Gauvain(159). He will lead a flying column of Parisians to put an end to the peasant revolt and either arrest or kill Lantenac. The War in the Vendée pitted the peasant against the patriot, the local against national, and townsman versus peasant (132,137). When Gauvain enters the fray, the revolution becomes an interfamilial battle.

Gauvain, however, represents the French Revolution at its best and is "anti-medievalism" embodied inasmuch as he exemplifies the fact that even the feudal world can give way to the forces of progress or, at the very least, represents what the feudal world might have been had it developed in a better manner not so opposed to individual liberty. Gauvain is a soldier and not a politician, a heroic and virtuous soldier at that. He is, recalling his namesake from medieval French chivalric romances, a true knight—pure of heart yet ever-ready for battle. He does not smoke, drink, or swear; he is hardy and tough and will sleep on the ground with his men when the campaign calls for it. He will show mercy to anyone deserving of it, even royalists, because he wishes to give the revolution friends and not enemies. Indeed, he has his own reservations about the revolution; he prophesies that Robespierre and the Reign of Terror will terrify not only the Europe of his own day, but people of the future as well (160). His own philosophy, therefore, is a more peaceful one: "Let us strike down the crowns but spare the heads. Amnesty is to me the most beautiful word" (161).

Despite his reservations about the revolution and the Terror, Gauvain is a firm idealist. Speaking in a tone that seems, at first glance, more marked by the "superstition" of medievalism—in that it sets forth a metanarrative

---

[27] Donald M. G. Sutherland, *The French Revolution and Empire: The Quest for a Civic Order* (Blackwell Publishing, 2003), 155.

of history which anticipates something glorious to come in the "hereafter"—
Gauvain argues that only progress will come out of the revolution:

> Grand events are coming. What the revolution enacts at this moment is
> mysterious. Behind the visible work stands the invisible. One hides the
> other. The visible work is ferocious, the invisible is sublime […] it is strange
> and beautiful […] Under the scaffolding of barbarism, a temple of
> civilization is building (240).

Hugo is on the side of the revolution and therefore on the side of rationalism
and Gauvain himself. Although this passage might seem to imply some
lingering fondness for Catholic mysticism applied to the revolution, in
actual fact it echoes more closely the philosophy of Georg W. F. Hegel
(1770–1831), whose thoughts have been found also in Hugo's *Les
Misérables*.[28] For Hegel, as the world, indeed the universe, operated
according to the function of natural and rational laws, so too did the
unfolding of history.[29] Hegel once argued that although some events may
seem irrational, the actions of major players in world history—in Hugo's
case, the revolutionaries' actions—are the means through which the world
spirit will realise its aim: the consciousness of human freedom.[30] Gauvain's
Hegelian view of the progress of the revolution, then, accords with Hugo's
own. When Hugo speaks directly to the reader, he argues that, although the
revolution, the Vendéan War, and the Reign of Terror are all chaotic and
seemingly "bad" events, out of this chaos will arise Justice, Tolerance,
Kindness, Reason, Truth, and Love (109). Gauvain is also a committed
socialist, although more in the mould of Proudhon than Marx, owing to his
ideas about making everyone a farmer, and thereby a tiller of the collective
social property.[31] Gauvain's system, therefore, would see "each man have a
piece of ground, and let each piece of ground have a man" (241). These
ideas were common among mid-nineteenth-century socialists and Red
Republicans (before Marx's "scientific" socialist ideas took hold on the
socialist movement after the 1880s). The British author George W. M.

---

[28] Stéphanie Haber, "Echoes of Kant and Hegel in Victor Hugo's Les Misérables,"
La Philosophoire, 55 no. 1 (2021), 69–99.
[29] Peter Singer, *Hegel: A Very Short Introduction* (Oxford University Press, 2001), 14.
[30] Georg W. F. Hegel, *Lectures on the Philosophy of History*, trans. Ruben Alvarado
(Aalten: Wordbridge, 2011), 35.
[31] Ian McKay, "Proudhon, Property and Possession," *The Anarchists' Library* July
12, 2014 theanarchistlibrary.org.

Reynolds, who was a great admirer and translator of Hugo,[32] and who likewise was a Proudhonian socialist, declared himself in favour of similar measures when he created his little fictional Italian republic of Castelcicala in *The Mysteries of London* (1844–48).[33] There is, in fact, in Gauvain's land-reform plan, some echoes of medieval economic and social structures. Under Gauvain's scheme each man can till the soil as they might have done in a feudal set up, but each would become self-sufficient and they would be toiling for themselves and not for their lord. In Gauvain's ideas, then, some inspiration from the feudal world has been taken and preserved—much like when the revolutionaries began cataloguing medieval texts—but such ideas would need a revolution founded on the Rights of Man to truly succeed.

Cimourdain and the Law of Absolutes

Gauvain may be, by blood, a scion of the aristocracy but he is intellectually a son of the revolution, and the man who accompanies Gauvain's flying column is none other than Gauvain's former tutor and priest, a man named Cimourdain, who is connected with the Committee of Public Safety. Gauvain and Cimourdain's relationship—the latter treats the former like a son—is symbolic of the fact that the revolution has turned the world upside down: the son of an aristocrat and a former priest go to war against the peasants, or "the people"—whom the revolution is supposed to serve— while the peasants, who *should* be in favour of the revolution, stick by their former feudal masters.

Cimourdain is mysterious, for no one knows his surname, and because he is inflexible in his devotion to the revolution, to the point of cruelty, Hugo describes him as a "dark soul". A former priest, he is probably based on the real-life priest-turned-revolutionary, or "Red Priest", Jacques Roux (1752– 94).[34] A flavour of Roux's ideology can be gleaned from remarks he made in 1793 when he said that "there is no destiny as glorious as that of crushing despotism, that of smashing, pulverizing, and annihilating those illustrious brigands, those decorated cowards who want to master us with so much

---

[32] Reynolds translated two of Victor Hugo's works: Victor Hugo, *Songs of Twilight*, trans. G. W. M. Reynolds (Paris: Librarie des Estrangers, 1836) and Victor Hugo, *The Last Day of a Condemned*, trans. G. W. M. Reynolds (London: George Henderson, 1840).
[33] Stephen Basdeo, "George W. M. Reynolds's Italian Chartist Republic," *Reynolds's News and Miscellany*, June 6, 2021 https://reynolds-news.com.
[34] Mike Rapport, *Rebel Cities: Paris, London, and New York in the Age of Revolution* (London: Abacus, 2017), 273.

pride and cruelty."[35] Cimourdain too has replaced his belief in god with a firm, staunch devotion to the revolution for which he believes people must be willing to die.

He is like an inquisitor, but a rational, secular, revolutionary inquisitor devoted to logic:

> No abstractions! [...] the republic is this: two and two are four [...] The abstract idea must become concrete. Right must assume the form of Law, and when Right has become Law it is Absolute. That is what I call the possible (241, 243).

He is a member of the Eveche club—a secret society who meet in the Eveche tavern in Paris. It is a club whose members are poor and violent, a hotbed of insane, would-be criminals turned revolutionaries who would show no mercy to anybody. The orchestrators of the Reign of Terror—Robespierre, Marat, and Danton—have all shown mercy before to supposed enemies of the revolution and let them live, but Cimourdain would never do this for he thinks that "Revolution is humanity's surgeon, it cuts out the tumour, it cuts off the gangrened limb" (160). He is the antithesis of Lantenac and a man like Cimourdain only emerges when, in his striving for Enlightenment rationality, a man forgets his humanity. Lantenac represents a complete refusal on the part of the old world to embrace the new.

Thus the stage is set for the final battle between the Revolution and its inflexible leader on the one hand, and the old royalist ways with its equally inflexible leader on the other. As Lantenac's forces dwindle he retreats with the peasant army to his medieval ancestral home of La Torgue. He lodges the kidnapped children in the tower; knowing the revolutionaries' fondness for the children, he plans on either ransoming them or allowing them to die in the fray. The soldiers of the modern republic come to crush this last outpost of the Vendéan War. As Gauvain draws up his cannon and 4,500 men against the royalists in the old tower, where his family's history is kept, the idea of destroying the past—the tower, the library, the books and manuscripts—to destroy the rebels in the name of modernity and the revolution sits uneasily with him. Hugo had earlier in the novel, of course, pointed out that one of the best things about the revolution was that it retained the best of the past while looking towards the future. Cimourdain, however, wants to destroy both Lantenac (the man) and the old tower as he knows the importance of symbolism: "He made up his mind that he should

---

[35] Jacques Roux, "Scripta et Acta," *Le Publiciste de la République Francaise par l'ombre de Marat*, 12 August 1793, trans. Mitchell Abidor, https://www.marxists.org.

be beheaded on the spot, as it were in his own house, that the feudal stronghold should see the head of the feudal lord fall" (192). This is why Cimourdain, in the midst of the siege, sends for a guillotine. Lantenac must be captured and sentenced in a revolutionary tribunal. He must not die as a hero in battle.

The illustration of the cannon drawn up in front of La Torgue is evocative of the battle between the feudal and modern worlds. See fig. 9.3. The defenders of the feudal order fight with largely medieval weaponry combined with a few guns. The modern revolutionaries have modern technology and, historically, it was evident even by the late medieval period that castle walls were a poor match for cannon, for in 1483 Sultan Mehmed II used the basilic to breach the walls of seemingly impregnable Constantinople.[36] By the seventeenth century some castles had survived and could mount a respectable defence against any siege using cannon, particularly if high earth mounds protected a fortress.[37] By the eighteenth century, however, they were all but pointless. In the novel, although the feudal domain is technically under siege, a siege will not be necessary to fell what is a rustic and not very imposing structure. The old world must fall to the new. A brutal battle ensues and a large portion of La Torgue burns to the ground. Lantenac does manage to escape via a secret passage and is initially content to leave Michelle's children to die in the conflagration. Suddenly, however, the old aristocratic spirit of self-sacrifice rises within Lantenac and "a hero [rose] out of a monster". The monster, who would previously not have flinched to sacrifice a thousand of his men, goes back into the castle to rescue the peasant children from La Torgue, which is now in flames. It seems the past, as represented by Lantenac, is not entirely without virtue after all. The accompanying image, titled "[t]hey are all saved", depicts the scene just after Lantenac has rescued the children from the fire and is descending the ladder, looking somewhat Jesus-like, where he will face arrest. See fig. 9.4. He is then told that he will face a revolutionary tribunal. The trial will be a show trial, of course, and the outcome is known from the outset: Lantenac will be guillotined.

---

[36] Edmondo de Amicis, *Constantinople* (Surrey: Alma Books, 2018), 271
[37] Barbara Donegan, *War in England 1642-1649* (Oxford University Press, 2010), 88.

Figure 9.3. Eduard Riou, Cannon in front of La Torgue. Image: Stephen Basdeo. Public domain.

Gauvain goes to see Lantenac in the castle dungeon and the latter explains why he is against the revolution:

> You know a gentleman is rather a curiosity nowadays; he believes in God; he believes in tradition; he believes in his family, in his ancestors, in the examples of his forefather; he believes in loyalty, in his duties towards his prince; in respect for the old laws, in virtue, in justice (241).

Lantenac's idea of justice was the reason why, although he initially did not seem to care about the children, he went back and sacrificed his own life to rescue them. This was to be expected of a feudal nobleman, as one manual on eighteenth-century pre-revolutionary noble etiquette reveals:

> Whenever the courtier chances to be engaged in a skirmish or an action or a battle in the field, or the like, he should discreetly withdraw from the crowd, and do the outstanding and daring things that he has to do in as small a

company as possible and in the sight of the noblest and most respected men in the army.[38]

Lantenac's act of self-sacrifice certainly wins the admiration and respect of all those in the French Revolutionary army and he appears almost godlike to them. The revolution, with its emphasis on the rights of the individual, was the antithesis of the "feudal" world represented by Lantenac, in whose world everyman owed a duty to someone else and in which everyone respected the traditions of their forefathers. Hugo's text overall is anti-feudal and anti-medieval, yet the "old world" will always lack that fellowship that was present between classes in the Middle Ages. Lantenac warns Gauvain that even though France wants to, it will never be able to fully erase its past with "modern" individualism and atheism. France will always be a product of its history and traditions:

> All this does not prevent religion from being religion; it does not prevent royalty from having filled fifteen hundred years of our history; it does not prevent the French nobility, even decapitated, from towering high above your heads (230).

Lantenac is correct to some extent; although the atheist revolutionaries in Paris attempted to do away with the Church, for instance, Napoleon soon had to reckon with the fact that Catholicism was the religion of the majority of French people.[39]

Yet Hugo makes an intervention into the text and argues against Lantenac. The new France is, indeed, a product of its past. But if that is the case, the revolution, then, is also a product of France's past. Hugo explains this when he describes the guillotine being constructed in front of the feudal castle:

> In La Torgue were condensed fifteen hundred years—the middle ages—of vassalage, serfdom, and feudality. In the guillotine, only one year: '93; and these twelve months counterpoised those fifteen centuries. La Torgue was Monarchy; the guillotine was Revolution. Tragic confrontation! … The fatal tree had grown out of this evil ground, watered by so many human tears, so

---

[38] Jay M. Smith, *The Culture of Merit: Nobility, Royal Service, and the Making of Absolute Monarchy in France, 1600-1789* (University of Michigan Press, 1996), 38.

[39] See William Roberts, "Napoleon, the Concordat of 1801, and its Consequences", in Frank J. Coppa, ed., *Controversial Concordats: The Vatican's Relations with Napoleon, Mussolini, and Hitler*, (Washington, DC: Catholic University Press of America, 1999), 34–80.

much blood … thus the guillotine had a right to say to the tower: "I am thy daughter."[40]

Figure 9.4. Fortuné Louis Méaulle, Lantenac descending the ladder. Image: Stephen Basdeo. Public domain.

---

[40] Hugo, *Ninety-Three*, 245–46.

There is a sense, however, if we look at Hugo's personal life and the friendships he made with other people that he did not have a *complete* disdain for monarchy at this late stage in his life. He had, after all, been a royalist in his youth and his *Odes et Poésies diverses* (1822) reflected the royalism and Catholicism of his early life.[41] In this collection, for example, there is a poem in honour of "King" Louis XVII, the boy and son of Louis XVI who died shortly after the revolution began in 1789.[42] In later life, Hugo struck up a friendship with the Dom Pedro II, Emperor of Brazil, who visited Hugo at his home in 1877.[43] Brazil, in particular, succumbed to what was known as *Hugolatria* (Hugo idolatry) during the nineteenth century,[44] when the country's greatest writer, Machado de Assis, was the first to translate Hugo's *Toilers of the Sea* into Portuguese (as *Os Trabalhadores do Mar*). When Hugo wrote his grand history of Shakespeare he declared that Elizabeth I was "on the whole, a remarkable queen".[45] Hugo's disdain for monarchy in later life, instead, was for *French* monarchy and its place in *French* history, and the whole novel can be interpreted as an expression of his own lifelong conflict between royalism and republicanism from youth onwards.[46]

Gauvain resolves to set his uncle free; he cannot allow a man who rescued the children from a blazing fire at the cost of his own life to be executed. He smuggles Lantenac out of the dungeon and switches places with him. Cimourdain's logical mind and fervent devotion to revolutionary principles will not allow him to spare Gauvain from the guillotine, for in his mind Gauvain has now betrayed the revolution by setting Lantenac free. Gauvain understands and, as a makeshift revolutionary tribunal—headed by Cimourdain—held in one of the castle's remaining apartments sentences Gauvain to death, he maintains a stoic attitude. Gauvain never abandons his faith in the revolution, however; even as he mounts the scaffold, ready to be executed in front of his ancestral home, he shouts "Vive la republique!" in front of the tricolour flag. As the blade descends and cuts through Gauvain's

---

[41] André Maurois, *Victor Hugo and his World*, trans. Oliver Bernard (London: Thames and Hudson, 1966), 24.

[42] Victor Hugo, "King Louis XVII", in Victor Hugo, *Poems*, trans. Isabel Hapgood, vol. 3 (Boston: Estes and Lauriat, n.d.), 21–24.

[43] Paulo Rezzutti, *D. Pedro II: A história não contada* (São Paulo: Leya, 2019), 345.

[44] Maria Cláudia Rodrigues Alves, 'Álvares de Azevedo e Victor Hugo: fontes estrangeiras dos poetas românticos e a crítica à imitação', *Lettres Françaises* 23, no. 1 (2022): 127–56.

[45] Hugo, *Shakespeare*, 310.

[46] Maurois, *Victor Hugo*, 114.

neck, a gunshot is also heard. Lantenac has ended his own life, unable to live with the guilt of sentencing his beloved "child", Gauvain, to death.

Conclusion

Hugo firmly believed that the French Revolution represented progress. The medievalism in his text was really anti-medievalism and marks Hugo's final shift away from the medievalism and Catholicism of his youth to secularism and socialism. His remarks about the Vendéan peasants, and the medieval past more generally, reveal little that is sympathetic to the era. The prevailing motif throughout the whole novel—one which is reinforced by the accompanying illustrations—is one of medieval barbarism and backwardness versus revolutionary civilization and progress. The revolution was a war against the past and the war needed to be fought so that France could be regenerated.

The idea of a just war against the past certainly recurs through the novel but underlying such sentiments was a highly nuanced discussion of the idea of progress. Certain things about the past were worthy of being preserved; the art, culture, and even the spirit of self-sacrifice. The Revolutionaries wanted to do away with the past but it is still important for them to have historical understanding. The values of Lantenac, on gentlemanliness and devotion to virtue, justice, and family will need to be kept. It was not the revolutionaries who managed to save the children from the burning tower but Lantenac, and as the illustration for that scene showed—when the soldiers looked to him as a godlike figure—it is possible to respect the old ways while embracing the new world. This is the only way in Hugo's view that any revolution based on anti-feudalism, or anti-medievalism, can truly progress.

Bibliography

Anon. "Les Miserables", *The Saturday Review*, May 10, 1862: 537–38.
—. *Maisons Victor Hugo* (n. d.), https://www.maisonsvictorhugo.paris.fr/.
Abidor, Micthell, trans. *Voices of the Paris Commune*. Oakland, CA: PM Press, 2015.
Alves, Maria Cláudia Rodrigues. "Álvares de Azevedo e Victor Hugo: fontes estrangeiras dos poetas românticos e a crítica à imitação." *Lettres Françaises* 23, no. 1 (2022): 127–56.
Anderson, James Maxwell. *Daily Life During the French Revolution*. Greenwood Publishing, 2007.

Arnold, Janet. *Patterns of Fashion: the cut and construction of clothes for men and women 1560–1620*. London: Macmillan 1985.

Basdeo, Stephen. Basdeo, Stephen. "George W. M. Reynolds's Italian Chartist Republic." *Reynolds's News and Miscellany*, June 6, 2021 https://reynolds-news.com.

—. "Victor Hugo's Ninety-Three (1874)." *Reynolds's News and Miscellany* September 27, 2021, https://reynolds-news.com.

Beecher, Jonathan. *Writers and Revolution: Intellectuals and the French Revolution of 1848*. Cambridge University Press, 2021.

Begley, Adam. *The Great Nadar: The Man Behind the Camera*. New York: Crown, 2017.

Brombert, Victor. *Victor Hugo and the Visionary Novel*. Harvard University Press, 1984.

Carlyle, Thomas. *The French Revolution*. London: Chapman and Hall, 1889. Originally published London: James Fraser, 1837.

Coppa, Frank J. ed. *Controversial Concordats: The Vatican's Relations with Napoleon, Mussolini, and Hitler*. Washington, DC: Catholic University Press of America, 1999.

de Amicis, Edmondo. *Constantinople*. Surrey: Alma Books, 2018.

Donegan, Barbara. *War in England 1642-1649*. Oxford University Press, 2010.

Frey, John A. *A Victor Hugo Encyclopedia*. Westport, CT: Greenwood, 1999.

Haber, Stéphanie. "Echoes of Kant and Hegel in Victor Hugo's Les Misérables." *La Philosophoire*, 55 no. 1 (2021): 69–99.

Hegel, Georg W.F. *Lectures on the Philosophy of History*. Translated by Ruben Alvarado. Aalten: Wordbridge, 2011. Originally published as *Vorlesungen über die Philosophie der Weltgeschichte*, Berlin: Duncker & Humblot, 1837.

Hugo, Victor. *The Hunchback of Notre Dame*. London: Milner, n.d.

—. "King Louis XVII." In *Poems*. Translated by Isabel Hapgood. 21–24. 3 vols. Boston: Estes and Lauriat, n.d.

—. *The Last Day of a Condemned*. Translated by G. W. M. Reynolds. London: George Henderson, 1840.

—. *Les Misérables*, 5 vols. Philadelphia: David MacKay, n.d.

—. "Letter to M. Daelli, 18 October 1862." In *Les Miserables*, Translated by Isabel Hapgood. 2 vols. London: Walter Scott, n.d.

—. *Ninety-Three*. London: Richard Edward King, n.d.

—. *Ninety-Three*. 2 vols. London: George Routledge, 1889.

—. *Shakespeare*. Translated by A. Baillot. Boston: Estes and Lauriat, n.d.

—. *Songs of Twilight*. Translated by George W. M. Reynolds. Paris: Librarie des Estrangers, 1836.

—. "Walter Scott." In *Things Seen (Choses Vue): Essays*. Boston, MA: Estes and Lauriat, n.d.

Maurois, André. *Victor Hugo and his World*. Translated by Oliver Bernard. London: Thames and Hudson, 1966.

McKay, Ian. "Proudhon, Property and Possession." *The Anarchists' Library*, July 12, 2014 theanarchistlibrary.org.

Rapport, Mike. *Rebel Cities: Paris, London, and New York in the Age of Revolution*. London: Abacus, 2017.

Rezzutti, Paulo. *D. Pedro II: A história não contada*. São Paulo: Leya, 2019.

Roberts, William. "Napoleon, the Concordat of 1801, and its Consequences." In Coppa, *Controversial Concordats*.

Roux, Jacques. "Scripta et Acta." *Le Publiciste de la République Francaise par l'ombre de Marat*, August 12, 1793, translated by Mitchell Abidor, https://www.marxists.org/.

Secher, Reynald. *A French Genocide: The Vendée*. Paris: University of Notre Dame Press, 2003.

Singer, Peter. *Hegel: A Very Short Introduction*. Oxford University Press, 2001.

Smith, Jay M. *The Culture of Merit: Nobility, Royal Service, and the Making of Absolute Monarchy in France, 1600-1789*. University of Michigan Press, 1996.

Stevenson, Robert Louis. *Familiar Studies of Men and Books*. 4th ed. 2 vols. London: William Heinemann, 1924. Originally published London: Chatto and Windus, 1882.

Sutherland, Donald M. G. *The French Revolution and Empire: The Quest for a Civic Order*. Oxford: Blackwell, 2003.

Vasseur, Édouard. "French archivists, the management of records and records management since the nineteenth century: are French recordkeeping tradition and practice incompatible with records management?" *Archives and Manuscripts*, 49 no.1–2 (2021): 107–32.

CHAPTER TEN

THE QUESTION OF AUTHORITY IN NINETEENTH-CENTURY BOOK ILLUSTRATION

FRANÇOISE BAILLET

In its very first number, in May 1842, *The Illustrated London News* declared that: "Art—as now fostered, and redundant in the peculiar and facile department of wood engraving—has, in fact, become the bride of literature"[1]. Prompted by significant advances in print technology and an increasing demand for reading matter, this union between "pen and pencil"—to borrow David Curtis's words[2]—appears as a key feature of Victorian culture. As Martin Meisel has suggested in *Realizations,* the nineteenth century saw the progressive coalescence of different art forms, pictures being "given to storytelling" and novels "unfold[ing] through and with pictures".[3]

From the late Regency, when writers were asked to create text to accompany pre-existing sketches—as in Pierce Egan's *Life in London* (1821-28), for instance—to the Edwardian age, when illustration was progressively excluded from adult fiction, pictorial literature thus provided a fit space in which text and image could meet, produce effect on one another, entering into a rich, complex and fruitful relationship. Given the large variety of graphic publications available in the mid-nineteenth century, the partnership between the textual and the visual was necessarily unstable, "renegotiated", to quote Julia Thomas in *Pictorial Victorians* "from one picture and historical moment to the next".[4] As it existed and progressively evolved, the pictorial novel therefore induced a confluence of

---

[1] "Our Address," *The Illustrated London News* 1, no. 1 (14 May 1842), 1.
[2] Gerard Curtis, *Visual Words Art and the Material Book in Victorian England* (Aldershot: Ashgate, 2002), 7.
[3] Martin Meisel, *Realizations: Narrative, Pictorial, and Theatrical Arts in Nineteenth-Century England* (Princeton: Princeton University Press, 1983), 3.
[4] Julia Thomas, *Pictorial Victorians* (Athens, Ohio: Ohio Press University, 2004), 15.

the "sister arts"—letterpress and drawings adopting common styles and subject matters—"in a way that cut across generic boundaries".[5] It is precisely the unstable and wavering border between text and image within the illustrated book that this paper purports to examine, through three distinct moments in the history of Victorian pictorial literature: the birth of the genre, when vignettes and sketches remained—sometimes literally—on the threshold of the book, the mid-century revival of wood-engraving which, under the influence of the Pre-Raphaelites and the artists of the Idyllic School, resulted in a shifting balance between the verbal and the visual, and the Arts and Crafts books—the Kelmscott publications in particular—whose elaborate blending of text and design went beyond a claim to beauty to suggest a new reading experience.

In one of his many letters to his illustrator Hablôt K. Browne ("Phiz"), Dickens wrote,

> "[...] the Major introduces Mr. Dombey to a certain lady, whom, as I wish to foreshadow, dimly, said Dombey will come to marry in due season. She is about thirty—not a day more—handsome, though haughty-looking— good figure—well dressed—showy—and desirable. Quite a lady in appearance, with something of a proud indifference about her, suggestive of a spark of the Devil within. [...] Wants a husband".[6]

The characters mentioned here are those of *Dombey and Son*, published between 1844 and 1846. On seeing Browne's design, entitled "Major Bagstock is delighted to have that opportunity", one is impressed by its delicacy, suggestiveness and fidelity to Dickens's instructions. See fig. 10.1. The group does appear exactly as he wanted. Placed on either side of an invisible parting diagonal, men and women greet the other pair, giving us an insight into their personal nature, ambitions and calculations. The daughter's flirtatious attitude is suggested by her posture and outfit— precisely those described by Dickens further down in his letter ("daughter has a parasol")—while Bagstock's coarse features and predatory smile unmistakably evoke his rapaciousness. Like many others in the series, this print could be defined as what Meisel calls a "realization" of the text: "the illuminating extension of one medium [or mode of discourse] by another".[7] Here, the impression is that the visualizing process behind the very

---

[5] Ibid., 15.
[6] Charles Dickens, Letter to Hablôt Knight Browne (« Phiz »), 10 March 1847 in G. Storey and K. J. Fielding, eds., *The Letters of Charles Dickens,* Vol. 5, (Oxford: Clarendon Press, 1981), 34.
[7] Meisel, *Realisations*, 36.

conception of the picture was shared between artist and novelist: the passage to be illustrated selected by Dickens, all the elements to be included—time, place, intentions, and relationships—thought out and specified by him. Closely monitored by the novelist's frequent and detailed instructions, "Phiz" seems to have lent his tool to the writer's imagination, to have provided his words with pictorial substance.

Of course, the illustrator's style played a great part in the type of relation it established with the text. Largely influenced by the tradition of Regency satirical prints—the kind Gillray, Rowlandson or Isaac Cruikshank produced only a few decades earlier—Browne's draughtsmanship is comic in feeling and sometimes verges on caricature. In depictions of large groupings, this pictorial mode implies a priority given to the theatrical, sometimes grotesque, aspect of the scene represented. In a manner not unlike Cruikshank's—in his *Inconveniences of a Crowded Drawing Room*, for example[8]—Browne focuses on the vitality and variety of the crowd, however scruffy it may appear, rather than on the psychological depth of the characters. In "Coming Home from Church", for instance, the artist is obviously more interested in his marriage tableau than in each of the individuals in the procession. See fig. 10.2. With the exception of Dombey, whose stand-offish look is quite telling, stereotyped facial expression—largely inherited from Lavater's *Essay on Physiognomy*—is here preferred to the depiction of character or emotion.[9] The overall effect produced on the reader is unmistakably humorous, but defines Browne's image as a light-hearted accompaniment to the story.

Thus, delicate, fine-lined and subtle though they are, Phiz's designs seem to remain in what Paul Goldman, in his 1996 book on *Victorian Illustration*, calls "an unspoken but clearly apparent subservience to the text"[10] with which they always interact but which they never "overpower", as Layard comments about Millais's illustrations to Trollope's novels.[11] This does not mean, of course, that these images are simply "the text

---

[8] *Inconveniences of a Crowded Drawing Room*, hand-coloured etching. Inscription: 'G Cruikshank fect […] Pubd. May 6th 1818 by G. Humphrey 27 St James's St'. British Museum, no. 1859,0316.138

[9] John Caspar Lavater, *Essays on Physiognomy*. 3 vols. (London: John Murray, 1789).

[10] Paul Goldman, *Victorian Illustration. The Pre-Raphaelites, the Idyllic School and the High Victorians* (Aldershot: Scolar Press, 1996), 1.

[11] George Somes Layard, *Tennyson and his Pre-Raphaelite Illustrators* (London: Elliot Stock, 1894), 19.

pictured".[12] The "reciprocal, interactive, and often compellingly persuasive dialogue" which Robert L. Patten convincingly mentions in *The Victorian Illustrated Book* (about another of Dickens's pictorial novels, *David Copperfield)*, is obviously at work here, with Browne's vignettes sometimes anticipating the text, explaining it or even subverting it, creating tensions and complexities.[13] But despite this essential interplay between pen and pencil, Phiz's plates and those of his contemporaries remain—sometimes literally, since a few publications only included a frontispiece—on the margin of the text. "Clearly" Patten continues "the widespread assumption is that [they] are separable from the text, not an integral, complexly dialogic, and essential feature".[14]

Figure 10.2 Hablôt K. Browne ("Phiz"), "Coming home from Church", in Dickens, *Dombey and Son.* Project Gutenberg. Public domain.

---

[12] Robert L Patten, "Serial Illustration and Storytelling in *David Copperfield*" in Richard Maxwell, ed., *The Victorian Illustrated Book,* (Charlottesville and London: University Press of Virginia, 2002), 92.

[13] Ibid., 92.

[14] Ibid., 122.

One of the technical reasons for this may be the choice of the then quite popular intaglio technique, which meant that the drawings had to be incised into a separate metal plate and therefore could not be used in a print press and printed together with the text. It is true, moreover, that at a time when the recent launch of the parts-issue serial had not yet challenged artistic hierarchies, the status of illustrators was very different from what it was to become a few decades later. As with Cruikshank or Seymour before him, Browne had been trained not as a book-illustrator but as a caricaturist.[15] Little acknowledged by the art Establishment (they did not access the Royal Academy before 1870), illustrators were also, most of the time, largely underpaid. Lastly, the prevalent view at the time was that the text was "ideologically, if not chronologically, prior to the illustrations", Rosemary Mitchell explains in *Picturing the Past* (2000).[16] Pictures, therefore, should not alter the letterpress, but reproduce it, providing a mirror-image or transcription of the words.

As John Hall and John Harvey have argued, the Victorian illustrated text therefore appears as a highly controlled space, words and pictures each being allotted a definite slot not to be trespassed—hence, perhaps, Dickens's famous insistence on keeping the upper hand on Browne's work, selecting the scenes to be to be illustrated and describing the characters' precise outfits.[17] This attempt at retaining some form of authority—which a significant number of writers shared at the time—is of course to be replaced within the larger frame of nineteenth-century cultural discourses, which insisted on preserving all sorts of boundaries, particularly those concerning class, race and gender, at a time when the divisions between them were consistently eroded.

The advent of the Pre-Raphaelite Brotherhood, in the late 1840s, however had a major impact on Victorian graphic art, allowing a series of borders to be crossed: those, of course, between text and image within the illustrated book, but also those between fine art and decorative art or between poetry and its visual representation: an "instance of translation".[18]

---

[15] John Robert Harvey, *Victorian Novelists and their Illustrators* (London: Sidwick & Jackson, 1970), 30.

[16] Rosemary Mitchell, *Picturing the Past* (Oxford: Clarendon, 2000), 22.

[17] Kathleen Tillotson, ed., *The Letters of Charles Dickens,* vol. 4 (Oxford: Clarendon Press, 1977), 653, 677-78.

[18] Elizabeth K. Helsinger, *Poetry and the Pre-Raphaelite Arts* (New Haven and London: Yale University Press, 2008), 184.

"Allegorizing one's own hook"[19]

Because they were painters as well as illustrators—which had not been true of their predecessors—the Pre-Raphaelites certainly played a major part in the transformation of the Victorian illustrated book. With their insistence on a return to nature, their overcrowded compositions, and their close attention to detail, the illustrators of the Moxon edition of Tennyson's poems (1857)—Hunt, Rossetti or Millais, to mention only a few—were largely responsible for the changes which affected black-and-white art in the eighteen-sixties.[20] For these artists, who all used text in their paintings, notably on the frames, image and word were "significant others"[21] mutually enriched by their constant interaction. Moreover, they brought to illustration the "high seriousness" which all commentators, Victorian or contemporary, define as the hallmark of their graphic productions. In a letter to his mother, the young George du Maurier—who was not a Pre-Raphaelite, but worked for the same illustrated magazines as them, such as *Good Words* or *Once a Week*—expressed this guiding principle: "I want to reach the utmost perfection that my talent is susceptible of, and get to that point that everything I attempt should turn out a complete and perfect work of art".[22] This earnest approach, coupled with a marked tendency to idealise their subjects resulted in the production of stronger, deeper and more powerful illustrations which, by their strength, Goldman says, "were [now] on an equal footing with the text"[23] and thus shifted the balance between word and image within the pictorial book.

---

[19] Rossetti to Allingham, quoted by Forrest Reid, *Illustrators of the Eighteen Sixties, An Illustrated Survey of the Work of 58 British Artists* (Dover Publication Inc.: New-York, 1975), 31.

[20] Alfred Tennyson, *Poems* (London: Edward Moxon), 1857.

[21] Lorraine Janzen Kooistra, *The Artist as Critic Bitextuality in Fin-de-Siècle Illustrated Books* (Aldershot: Scolar Press, 1995), 4.

[22] Daphne Du Maurier, ed., *The Young George du Maurier A Selection of his Letters 1860-1867* (London: Peter Davies, 1951), 163.

[23] Goldman, *Victorian Illustration*, 1.

Figure 10.3. Dante Gabriel Rossetti, "Saint Cecilia" (1857), Moxon Tennyson. Rossetti Archive. Public domain.

In what came to be called the "Moxon Tennyson", the text, precisely, originated from one of the most widely acclaimed poets, who had succeeded Wordsworth as Poet Laureate since 1850. Tennyson, who is said never to have shown any real interest for the visual arts,[24] left his illustrators to their own interpretation of the poems. Rossetti made five designs for the Moxon Tennyson, among which "Saint Cecilia" is certainly the one which aroused the most discussions and conflicting opinions.[25] See fig. 10.3. Inspired by a single stanza of "The Palace of Art"—

Or in a clear-wall'd city on the sea,
    Near gilded organ-pipes, her hair
Wound with white roses, slept St Cicely
    An angel look'd at her (lines 97-100)[26]

---

[24] George Somes Layard, *Tennyson and his Pre-Raphaelite Illustrators* (London: Elliot Stock, 1894), 7.
[25] Reid, *Illustrators*, 31, and Layard, *Tennyson*, 56-64.
[26] Alfred Tennyson, *Poems*. 2 vols. (London: Edward Moxon, 1842).

—it depicts the saint playing the organ and leaning back to accept a kiss from an angel, while an indifferent guard, in the foreground, seems to be walking away from the scene. In the background, beyond the circular walls of the fortified city, the sea is visible, crowded with embarkations. On this powerful picture whose composition and strong contrasts are clearly influenced by the German Nazarenes—notably Peter Cornelius and Fiedrich Overbeck—Saint Cecilia is not asleep, as in the poem, but, to borrow William Vaughan's terms, "swoon[ing] in erotic, submissive extasy".[27] Besides Tennyson who, according to Forrest Reid "gave up all attempt to discover what it had to do with his poem",[28] many commentators were puzzled by this design, and more particularly by the angel whose strange wings actually prompted George Layard to suppose that he was no divine being but "great, voluptuous human being [...] *masquerading as an angel*" to become Cecilia's lover.[29] Beyond the intensity of the picture, with its two dominant figures in the centre ground, what strikes the viewer here is certainly the sensuality of the whole scene in which Cecilia, with her long flowing hair and closed eyes, abandons herself in the arms of the angel ready to kiss her and wrapping his invisible arms around her shoulders. With its four long-haired queens whose features are highly reminiscent of those of Elizabeth Siddal, the second illustration to "The Palace of Art", "King Arthur and the Weeping Queens" provides the same impression that—to quote Layard again—Rossetti "gave freest rein to his imagination" (55). See fig.10.4. Personal and imaginative, Rossetti's designs for the Moxon Tennyson thus appear more as a critical interpretation of the text than as a "realization" of it, as Browne's plates for Dickens had been. In this sense, one could agree with Kooistra who says that "illustrated texts are composed of two texts, a verbal/creative text and a visual/critical text",[30] a viewpoint which also applies to Leighton's illustrations to George Eliot's *Romola*, according to Mark Turner.[31] Departing from his conventional role as a draughtsman—one who would express the writer's ideas with his own medium—Rossetti is offering here a personal reading of Tennyson's poems or, to quote the painter's own words in a letter to William Allingham (whose *Music Master* he had illustrated two years before), "allegorizing [his] own

---

[27] William Vaughan, *German Romanticism and English Art* (New Haven and London: Yale University Press, 1979), 58.
[28] Reid, *Illustrators*, 39.
[29] Layard, *Tennyson*, 56-58.
[30] Kooistra, *Artist as Critic*, 4.
[31] Mark W. Turner, "Drawing Domestic Decline: Leighton's Version of *Romola*" in *Frederic Leighton : Antiquity, Renaissance, Modernity*, eds. Tim Barringer and Elizabeth Prettejohn (New Haven and London: Yale University Press, 1999), 174.

hook".[32] It is true, remarks Elizabeth Helsinger in her article devoted to "Rossetti and the Art of the Book", that in those days when illustration was still little acknowledged—many book reviewers did not even mention the plates, when commenting on a pictorial novel—Rossetti may have been "anxious to defend his status as a creative artist".[33] The result was of course that stunning series of plates whose emotional power suggested a different reading/viewing experience.

As part of a newly established artistic policy, many periodicals indeed now hired men whose association with "high culture" provided book illustration with increased dignity and respectability. For these artists who were now much better paid for their drawings (Leighton was paid £480 for his illustrations to *Romola* and Millais offered £500 a year for his contribution to *The Cornhill*), adding up regular magazine work to their pictorial activity became more acceptable. One of the consequences of such a policy was that many black-and-white artists now treated their wood-engravings exactly as they would a major painting, sometimes actually repeating their oil portraits on wood. This is true for example of *Romola*'s plates, many of which echo or anticipate Leighton's major works, as Hugh Witemeyer has shown. The result, unanimously acknowledged, was that the border between decorative and fine art had been crossed, to the benefit of readers, engravers and publishers alike. In his "Academy Notes 1875", John Ruskin proudly remarked that "our press illustration, in its highest ranks, far surpasses—in indeed, in that department finds no rivalship in—the schools of classical art".[34]

For the essentially middle-class readers of such publications, many of whom were also familiar with the oil paintings of these artists, the interaction between word, image and their own cultural assumptions—assumptions they necessarily projected onto the text—the reading/viewing experience was significantly altered, making the illustrated book of the eighteen-sixties the place of multiple junctions. From title pages to binding and, of course, illustrations, the contents of the pictorial book were now thought out as a whole, making it—to quote Samuel D. Albert—"the product of several identities working towards a common aesthetic goal".[35]

But it was only through the work of William Morris that this approach to the book as a total work of art found its full expression, providing the

---

[32] Reid, *Illustrators*, 31.

[33] Elizabeth K. Helsinger, "Rossetti and the Art of the Book" in Catherine J. Golden, ed., *Book Illustrated: Text, Image, and Culture 1770-1930* (New Castle, Del.: Oak Knoll Press, 2000), 155.

[34] Curtis, *Visual Words*, 17.

[35] Ibid., 225.

late-Victorian art public with a new reading experience. In his introduction to *The Ideal Book*, William Peterson traces back Morris's interest for the arts of the book to a lecture given by Emery Walker at the first Arts and Crafts Exhibition in London, in 1888. "The essential thing with regard to illustration," Walker had said, "is to have harmony between the type and the decoration".[36] As opposed to academic art, perceived as static, "organic art"—art that was meant to be "genuinely growing"[37]—was to provide harmony between storytelling and adornment, between text and image. At the Kelmscott Press (1891-98), where he produced fifty-two titles, Morris strove towards the creation of "a visible work of art".[38]

Figure 10.4. Dante Gabriel Rossetti, "King Arthur and the weeping queens" (1857), Moxon Tennyson. Rossetti Archive. Public domain.

---

[36] William S. Peterson, ed., *The Ideal Book* (Berkeley and Los Angeles: University of California Press, 1982), xvii.
[37] Ibid., 26.
[38] Curtis, *Visual Words*, 225.

Figure 10.5. First page of Morris, *The Glittering Plain* (1894). Internet Archive, University of Carolina at Chapel Hill and the Victorian Web. Public Domain.

"A kind of derangement of the senses"[39]

On admiring some of these Kelmscott publications—like, for instance, the frontispiece of *The Story of the Glittering Plain* (1894)—one is struck by the unity of the whole design.[40] See fig. 10.5. On these two pages, which obviously mirror each other, text and image fully intermingle, resulting in what Lorraine Kooistra calls an "imagetext".[41] On the left, the full title— *The Story of the Glittering Plain, or the Land of Living Men*—appears in an outlined box, its large black and white Gothic letters standing out against a background densely filled with leaves and flowers while outside the box, surrounding it, a large ribbon of white arabesques on a dark background seems to frame the whole design. The same flowery motif appears on the

---

[39] Jeffrey Skoblow, "Beyond Reading Kelmscott and the Modern" in Richard Maxwell, ed., *The Victorian Illustrated Book* (Charlottesville and London: University Press of Virginia, 2002), 247.

[40] William Morris, *The Story of the Glittering Plain*, illustr. Walter Crane (London: Kelmscott Press, 1894. Originally published in *English Illustrated Magazine*, Vol. VII, 1890; and in book form without illustrations at the Kelmscott Press in 1891.

[41] Kooistra, *Artist as Critic*, 4.

right page, where a heavily decorated initial marks (bottom left) the beginning of the text as such, itself interspersed with leafy designs. In the very centre of the page, the carefully delineated picture of Hallblithe and the three horse riders illustrates the first lines of the story. For Jeffrey Skoblow, whose article offers an interesting insight into Morris's aesthetics, this insistence on margins should be seen as "a gesture towards materiality","a kind of metaphor of the book's separation", as if one had to "cross and cross to get inside".[42] With its rich and varied ornaments—one is actually tempted to observe the various flowers, vines and leaves represented, maybe to identify some of them—this page offers its viewer a distinctive—and indeed more complex—reading experience. The traditional forward motion of reading is here impeded by the variety of alternative impressions or sensations provided by the decorations. "The work", to borrow Jerome McGann's phrase, "forces us to attend to its immediate and iconic condition"; "[i]t declares its radical self-identity".[43]

In the highly industrialised context of late-Victorian England, this idea of the book as the source of a sensual experience is of course meaningful. At a time when Aestheticism rejects the commodification of art, which it means to free from its social and political mores, what the arts-and-crafts book suggests is not only a "redemption of the senses" but also a redemption of the arts, thought to have been stifled by modern civilisation. Books, Morris implies, should be more than mere vehicles for information. "I claim that illustrated books should always be beautiful", Morris says, "unless, perhaps, where the illustrations are present rather for the purpose of giving information than for that of giving pleasure to the intellect through the eye".[44] Hence, of course, Morris's marked interest in the Middle-Ages—an interest he shared with the Pre-Raphaelites—and which underlies the whole of the Kelmscott production.

With its decorated borders and initials, the *Kelmscott Chaucer* (1896)[45] has often been described as "the culmination of the amalgamation of the sister arts", "not so much a book to be read as a book to be looked at", to borrow Curtis's words.[46] See fig.10.6. Lavishly illustrated by Edward Burne-Jones, it suggests the same insistence on the book as a material

---

[42] Skoblow, "Beyond Reading," 248.
[43] Jerome McGann, "Rossetti's Iconic Page" in George Bornstein and Theresa Tinkle, eds., *The Iconic Page in Manuscript, Print, and Digital Culture* (Ann Arbor: University of Michigan Press, 1998), 75, 74.
[44] Peterson, *Ideal Book*, 37.
[45] Geoffrey Chaucer, *The Works of Geoffrey Chaucer,* ed. F.S. Ellis, illustr. Edward Burne-Jones, engraver W.H. Hooper (London : Kelmscott, 1896).
[46] Curtis, *Visual Words*, 225.

object. With its ornamented borders and elaborate woodcuts—Burne-Jones's pencil designs were painted over in Chinese white, transferred on the woodblock and engraved by William H. Hooper—it provides that sensory experience all commentators describe. Text, adornment and woodcuts are here meant to blend for "the pleasure of the eye, the pleasure of the hand, the pleasure of the body, reading".[47] "Kelmscott", Skoblow concludes, "[is] fundamentally committed to a programme of synesthesia, a kind of derangement of the senses".[48]

Then again, these aesthetic concerns need of course to be replaced in the wider cultural context in which they were expressed. For Morris, a social reformer, opposing the reduction of books to mere thought was also a form of resistance to the commercial imperatives which, as the century drew to a close, became more and more pressing. "The arts-and-crafts book," Kooistra explains, "[...] is the material embodiment of political struggle. Its cooperative mode of production results in a mixed-art form which recognizes the value of each craftsperson's contribution to the overall design".[49] As a committed socialist, William Morris therefore not only insisted on harmony between text and image, but also between craftsmen and artists who produce the book. "This," Morris said, "is the only possible way in which you can get beautiful books".[50]

---

[47] Skoblow, "Beyond Reading," 239.
[48] Ibid., 247.
[49] Kooistra, *Artist as Critic*, 30.
[50] Peterson, *Ideal Book*, 40.

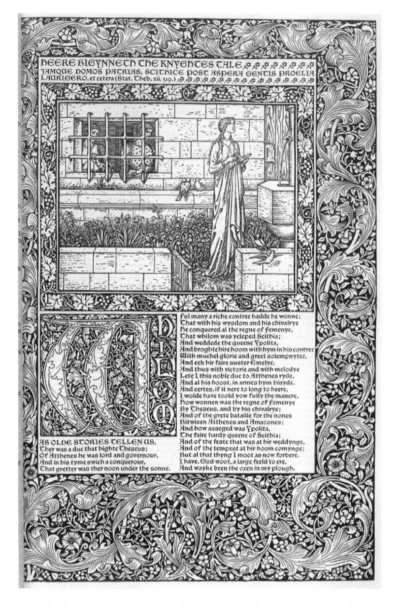

Figure 10.6 Page from Chaucer, *The Works*. British Library. Public Domain.

Conclusion

When du Maurier's *Trilby* was published, in 1894, Henry James remarked,

> In going over *Trilby* in the first English edition, the three volumes from which the illustrations were excluded, I have found it a positive comfort to be left alone with the text; and quite in spite of my fully recognizing all that, in the particular conditions, was done for it by the pictures and all that it did in turn for these.[51]

Despite the harmony between text and pictures in *Trilby*—whose author was also its illustrator—James clearly resented the irruption of non-verbal representation in the book. A conflict, he felt, existed between these two competitive systems of communication, as if the Horatian Ut pictura poesis—the ability of fiction to suggest pictures, "word-painting" to borrow George Eliot's term—and ekphrasis—image as a source of literary inspiration—could not be reconciled. By the close of the century, changes in the nature of book illustration (which became more realistic), developments in literature and the influence and competition of other media—like photojournalism or, of course, the cinematograph—led to the gradual disappearance of pictures from adult fiction.

Simultaneously, the emergence of the Aesthetic Movement with its rejection of narrative painting and insistence on the autonomy of art meant that the "open borders" along which the textual and visual had met were now closing. As painting ceased to serve, mirror or even educate bourgeois society, and as narrative painting gradually gave way to Impressionism and later to Abstraction, the novel shifted from Victorian Realism to Modernism, rendering illustration superfluous and indeed more difficult.

New boundaries emerged, protecting the newly acquired independence of art.

Word and image would only be reunited a few decades later, through Cubist and Dadaist, and Surrealist written and pictorial experiments, not "so much of a modernist discovery," says Curtis, as "a search for, or a harkening back to, a unity that had already existed in the nineteenth century".[52]

---

[51] Henry James, *Harper's Magazine,* vols. XCV-XCVI (1897), 605.
[52] Curtis, *Visual Words*, 47.

Bibliography

Anon. "Our Address," *The Illustrated London News* 1, no. 1 (14 May 1842), 1.

Barringer, Tim and Prettejohn, Elizabeth, eds. *Frederic Leighton : Antiquity, Renaissance, Modernity.* New Haven and London: Yale University Press, 1999.

Boris, Eileen. *Art and Lebor.* Philadelphia: Temple University Press, 1986.

Bornstein, George and Tinkle, Theresa, eds. *The Iconic Page in Manuscript, Print, and Digital Culture.* Ann Arbor: University of Michigan Press, 1998.

Camille, Michael. "Sensations of the Page: Imaging Technologies and Medieval Illuminated Manuscripts" in Bornstein and Tinkle, *The Iconic Page.*

Chaucer, Geoffrey. *The Works of Geoffrey Chaucer,* ed. F.S. Ellis, illustr. Edward Burne-Jones, engraver W.H. Hooper. London : Kelmscott, 1896.

Coupe, Robert L. M. *Illustrated Editions of the Works of William Morris in English.* British Library: Oak Knoll Press, 2002.

Curtis, Gerard, *Visual Words Art and the Material Book in Victorian England,* Aldershot: Ashgate, 2002.

Dickens, Charles. *Dombey and Son.* London: Bradbury and Evans, 1848.

Du Maurier, Daphne, ed. *The Young George du Maurier A Selection of his Letters 1860-1867,* London: Peter Davies, 1951.

Faulkner, Peter. *Against the Age.* London : George Allen and Unwin, 1980.

Golden, Catherine J., ed., *Book Illustrated: Text, Image, and Culture 1770-1930,* New Castle, Del.: Oak Knoll Press, 2000.

Goldman, Paul. *Victorian Illustration. The Pre-Raphaelites, the Idyllic School and the High Victorians.* Aldershot: Scolar Press, 1996.

Graham Storey and K. J. Fielding, ed. *The Letters of Charles Dickens,* Vol. 5, Oxford: Clarendon Press, 1981.

Hall, John, *Trollope and his Illustrators.* London and Basingstoke: The Macmillan Press Ltd, 1980.

Harvey, John Robert, *Victorian Novelists and their Illustrators,* London: Sidwick & Jackson, 1970.

Helsinger, Elizabeth K. *Poetry and the Pre-Raphaelite Arts.* New Haven and London: Yale University Press, 2008.

—. "Rossetti and the Art of the Book" in Golden, *Book Illustrated.*

James, Henry. *Harper's Magazine* Vols XCV-XCVI (1897).

Kooistra, Lorraine Janzen. *The Artist as Critic Bitextuality in Fin-de-Siècle Illustrated Books.* Aldershot: Scolar Press, 1995.

Latham, David and Latham, Sheila. *An Annotated Bibliography of William Morris*. London: Harvester Wheatsheaf, New-York: St. Martin's Press, 1991.

Lavater, John Caspar. *Essays on Physiognomy*. (in 3 vols.) London: John Murray, 1789.

Layard, George Somes. *Tennyson and his Pre-Raphaelite Illustrators*. London: Elliot Stock, 1894.

Maxwell, Richard, ed. *The Victorian Illustrated Book,* Charlottesville and London: University Press of Virginia, 2002.

McGann, Jerome. *Black Riders*: *The Visible Language of Modernism*. Princeton University Press: Princeton, 1993.

McGann, Jerome. "Rossetti's Iconic Page" in Bornstein and Tinkle, *The Iconic Page*.

Meisel, Martin. *Realizations: Narrative, Pictorial, and Theatrical Arts in Nineteenth-Century England* Princeton: Princeton University Press, 1983.

Mitchell, Rosemary. *Picturing the Past*. Oxford: Clarendon, 2000.

Mitchell, W. J. T. *Iconology: Image, Text, Ideology*. Chicago: University of Chicago Press, 1986.

Morris, William, *The Story of the Glittering Plain*, illustrated by Walter Crane (London: Kelmscott Press, 1894. Originally published in *English Illustrated Magazine*, Vol. VII, 1890; and in book form without illustrations at the Kelmscott Press in 1891.

Muir, Percy. *Victorian Illustrated Books*. London: B. T. Basford Ltd, 1971.

Patten, Robert L. "Serial Illustration and Storytelling in *David Copperfield*" in Maxwell, Richard, ed. *The Victorian Illustrated Book,* Charlottesville and London *:* University Press of Virginia, 2002, pp 91-128.

Parry, Linda, ed. *William Morris*. London: Philip Wilson Publishers, 1996.

Peterson, William S., ed. *The Ideal Book*. Berkeley and Los Angeles: University of California Press, 1982.

Quarterly Review (The), Vol. LXXIV, London : John Murray, Albemarle Street, 1844.

Reid, Forrest. *Illustrators of the Eighteen Sixties, An Illustrated Survey of the Work of 58 British Artists,* Dover Publication Inc.: New-York, 1975.

Skoblow, Jeffrey. "Beyond Reading Kelmscott and the Modern" in Maxwell, *The Victorian Illustrated Book.*

Stansky, Peter. *Redesigning the World*. Princeton: Princeton University Press, 1895.

Stetz, Margaret D. And Lasner, Mark Samuels. *England in the 1890s*. Washington, D. C.: Georgetown University Press, 1990.

Storey, G., and K. J. Fielding, eds. *The Letters of Charles Dickens*, vol. 5. Oxford: Clarendon Press, 1981.

Tennyson, Alfred. *Poems*. London: Edward Moxon, 1842. In 2 volumes.

—. *Poems*. London: Edward Moxon, 1857.

Thomas, Julia. *Pictorial Victorians*. Athens, Ohio: Ohio Press University, 2004.

Tillotson, Kathleen, ed. *The Letters of Charles Dickens*, Vol. 4, Oxford: Clarendon Press, 1977.

Turner, Mark W. "Drawing Domestic Decline: Leighton's Version of *Romola*" in Barringer and Prettejohn, *Frederic Leighton.*

Vaughan, William. *German Romanticism and English Art*. New Haven and London: Yale University Press, 1979.

Witemeyer, Hugh. *George Eliot and the Visual Arts* London : Yale University Press, 1979.

BIOGRAPHICAL NOTES

AMINA ALYAL has published co-edited academic collections including *Victorian Cultures of Liminality* (Cambridge Scholars, 2018), *Classical and Contemporary Mythic Identities* (Edwin Mellen, 2009), and creative writing collections including *Words from a Distance* (Stairwell Books, 2021). She has published scholarly articles on Renaissance and Victorian topics and two collections of poetry (Stairwell, Indigo Dreams). Senior Lecturer in English and Creative Writing at Leeds Trinity University, she often works with cross-overs, sometimes synaesthetic, between text and the visual image, or music and the spoken word. She has written ekphrastic poems, and written text for musical performances with Oz Hardwick and Karl Baxter, with the Japanese drumming group Kaminari UK, and for Leeds Lieder. Email and Twitter: a.alyal@leedstrinity.ac.uk, @DrAlyal

CASSANDRA ATHERTON is an award-winning prose poet and international expert on prose poetry. She was a Visiting Scholar in English at Harvard University, a Visiting Fellow at Sophia University, Japan, and is currently Professor of Writing and Literature at Deakin University. Cassandra co-authored *Prose Poetry: An Introduction* (Princeton University Press, 2020) and co-edited the *Anthology of Australian Prose Poetry* (Melbourne University Press, 2020) with Paul Hetherington. Her most recent book of prose poetry is *Leftovers*. She is a commissioning editor for *Westerly* magazine and associate editor at MadHat Press (USA). Email: cassandra.atherton@deakin.edu.au

FRANÇOISE BAILLET is Professor of British History and Culture at Caen Normandie University, France. Her research generally addresses the role of the periodical press in the shaping of class, gender and national identities in nineteenth-century Britain. She has widely published in areas related to Victorian cultural history and print culture, taking a particular interest in aestheticized renderings of working-class life in *The Illustrated London News* and *The Graphic*. She is also the author of *Visions et divisions. Discours culturels de Punch et ordre social victorien, 1850-1880* (Presses Universitaires de Rennes, 2022) which examines *Punch* as a discursive and ideological construct, the site of a pictorial (re)configuration of the mid-

Victorian social scene. Current projects include work on print workplaces such as the Bradbury & Evans publishing firm in London.
Email: francoise.baillet@unicaen.fr

STEPHEN BASDEO completed his PhD at Leeds Trinity University where he wrote a thesis on eighteenth- and nineteenth-century portrayals of Robin Hood. Having taught at several universities, Stephen is now a lecturer at Global Banking School on the University of Suffolk partnership. He has, since his PhD, published widely of nineteenth-century social and cultural history topics with a particular focus on England, France, and Brazil. This has led to a further focus on the lives of four authors in particular: G. W. M. Reynolds, Eugene Sue, Victor Hugo, and Álvares de Azevedo. Recent books include *Victorian England's Best-Selling Author: The Revolutionary Life of G. W. M. Reynolds* (2022) and Basdeo's current project involves translating the letters and poems of the aforementioned Àlvares de Azevedo with Luiz F.A. Guerra and Leandro Machado Pinheiro.
Email: stephen.basdeo@outlook.com

HANNAH-FREYA BLAKE is a Gothic scholar and creative writer based in Leeds. Her PhD, "Horror and Humour in the Male Gothic", was awarded research excellence by the University of Leeds in 2022. Publications include "Penny Pinching: Reassessing the Gothic Canon through Penny Blood Reprints" for the edited collection *Penny Dreadfuls and the Gothic* (2023), co-authored with Marie Léger-St-Jean; and, as co-editor with Dr Edwin Stockdale, *Sleeping in Frozen Quiet*, a collection of poetry inspired by the Brontë family in association with the Leeds Centre for Victorian Studies at Leeds Trinity University. Her debut novel, *Cake Craft*, published by Nyx Publishing, is characteristically Gothic and comic.
Email: freya_cw@hotmail.co.uk

ZOE COPEMAN is an art historian specializing in eighteenth-century European print culture. Her research primarily concerns the history of medical visual resources and its foundation in early psychology, natural history and folklore. She holds a BA in Psychology and Art History from the University of Maryland and an MA in the History of Art from University College London. Currently studying at the University of Maryland College Park, her doctoral dissertation investigates the history of mastectomies and their visualization in European and American print and pop culture. Zoe has presented her research at various conferences, including those sponsored by the Barnes Foundation, SECAC and the Real Colegio Complutense at Harvard." Email: zcopeman@umd.edu

PAUL (OZ) HARDWICK is Professor of Creative Writing at Leeds Trinity University. He has published extensively on medieval art and literature, and on modern medievalisms, and is author of the monograph *English Medieval Misericords: The Margins of Meaning* (Woodbridge: Boydell Press, 2011). As Oz Hardwick, his poems have been widely published in international journals and anthologies. He has published "about a dozen" full collections and chapbooks, including *Learning to Have Lost* (Canberra: IPSI, 2018) which won the 2019 Rubery International Book Award for poetry, and most recently *A Census of Preconceptions* (Dublin & Reggio di Calabria: SurVision Books, 2022).
Email: p.hardwick@leedstrinity.ac.uk

PAUL HETHERINGTON is a distinguished scholar and poet who has published 17 full-length poetry and prose poetry collections and has won or been nominated for more than 30 national and international awards and competitions. He has written numerous articles and co-authored *Prose Poetry: An Introduction* (Princeton University Press, 2020). He has also edited nine further volumes. He is Professor of Writing in the Faculty of Arts and Design at the University of Canberra, head of the International Poetry Studies Institute (IPSI) and joint founding editor of the international online journal *Axon: Creative Explorations*. He founded the International Prose Poetry Group in 2014.
Email: paul.hetherington@canberra.edu.au

ERKIN KIRYAMAN completed his B.A. at Ege University, English Language and Literature Department in 2011. He earned his first M.A. at Yaşar University with the thesis "Psychoanalysis, Trauma and War: A Comparative Study of Virginia Woolf's *Mrs Dalloway* and Pat Barker's *Regeneration*" in 2015. His second M.A. is completed with the thesis entitled "Images of the 'New Woman' in the Works of Late Victorian Male Novelists" at Ege University in 2016. He gained his PhD with the dissertation entitled "Beyond Words: Art and the Artist in the Twentieth-Century British Novel" at Ege University in 2022. He is currently a research assistant at Hatay Mustafa Kemal University, English Language and Literature Department. His fields of interests include literature and the arts, trauma theory and memory studies, feminism and gender theories, late Victorian novel, and twentieth century British novel.
Email: erkin.kiryaman@gmail.com

COURTNEY KROLCZYK is a PhD candidate at Rutgers, The State University of New Jersey. Her dissertation focuses on Victorian illustration and looks at the changing relationship between text and image across the middle decades of the nineteenth century in order to theorize the limits and affordances of adaptation across different media and generic forms.

RICHARD LEAHY is a senior lecturer at the University of Chester. His research interests include the intersections of science, technology and literature, and visual culture - particularly of the nineteenth century. In 2018 he published his first criticism book, *Literary Illumination,* which examined the relationship between artificial light and modes of literary expression during the nineteenth century. As well as this, Richard is an avid creative writer and has a number of fiction projects in the works. He lives in Chester with his partner and their cat, Bella.
Email: r.leahy@chester.ac.uk

NATHAN UGLOW has degrees in Classics, Renaissance Art History and eighteenth-century historical culture. He was a post-doctoral student with the British Academy, focusing on the historical writings of Thomas Carlyle. His academic career has included teaching in History, English Literature, Film and Media. He has served as Head of the Department of Communication and the Director of the Leeds Centre for Victorian Studies. Pre-millennium he also presented memorable TV segments on "How to Send an Email" and "How to Send an Email Attachment" for the BBC's Webwise series.
Email: n.uglow@leedstrinity.ac.uk

INDEX